MW01037949

Pike's Plaque

A Novel

Stephen J. McInerny

Silver Bay Press

Minneapolis

ISBN 978-0-9915600-0-4 (paperback)
ISBN 978-0-9915600-1-1 (epub)
ISBN 978-0-9915600-2-8 (mobi)
ISBN 978-0-9915600-3-5 (pdf)

Published by
Silver Bay Press, Minneapolis, Minnesota, USA
www.silverbaypress.com

For Bob Armstrong and muni golfers everywhere

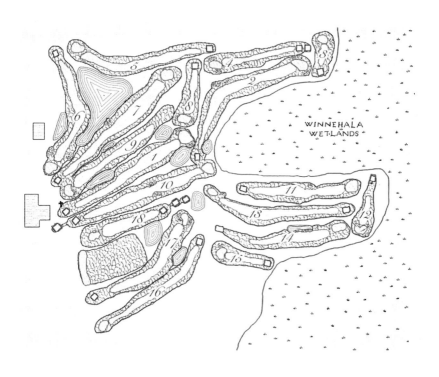

The Zebulon Pike Golf Course

The Zebulon Pike Clubhouse

PROLOGUE

Lewis and Clark are firmly fixed in the pantheon of American heroes. Their contemporary Zebulon Pike, on the other hand, the man who searched for but failed to find the source of the Mississippi, climbed but never reached the summit of the peak that bears his name, and died in a failed attempt to conquer Canada, is a forgotten footnote in the annals of American history. So it is a mystery why the first municipal golf course opened in this fair city and the subject of this story was named after him. Were the city fathers just celebrating the career of a man who gave it his best and never succeeded? Was it how his name rolled off the tongue? Or did they just pick it out of a hat? No one really knows. One thing is certain: Zebulon Pike never visited our city and he never played golf.

However it came by the name, the course seemed from its inception to be saddled with the same fate as its namesake. Like Pike, it was doomed to strive for great things and achieve none of them. In 1931, the city approached Donald Ross to design the course. He politely declined. In the five years following its opening, the PGA Tour, then in its infancy and struggling to survive, couldn't be lured to play an event at the Zebulon Pike Golf Course—or the ZPGC, as it is commonly referred to—and neither the USGA nor the state golf association ever selected it as a tournament site; nor, for that matter, has anyone who ever played its uneven fairways gone on to do great things in golf or any other human endeavor. Nothing, in fact, of any note ever happened here, aside from that inauspicious summer day in 1944 when a B-24 Liberator with engine trouble made an emergency landing on the seventh fairway and accidently decapitated the then club professional, Ambrose Keegan. Seemingly aloof but actually just hard of hearing, Keegan was attempting a slippery downhill four-footer just as the bomber cleared the tree line behind the green. He might have survived if he could have heard the engines and hadn't straightened up abruptly when his putt lipped the cup. According to his playing partners his last words were "Son of a..." Cut off in midsentence and just above the shoulder, Keegan fell, a victim of shoddy engine maintenance and the fickleness of the game. A tournament has been played at the ZPGC in memory of Keegan's death ever since: The Keegan Cap. The classic soft cloth golf cap he wore that summer morning—the style associated with Hogan in his prime—was bronzed and set upon a white dimpled orb, which was affixed to a block of wood hewn from the oak tree the B-24 took down right after it did Keegan. On that block are affixed small brass plates, each with the name of a winner of the Keegan Cap. The trophy holds a place of honor behind the counter of the ZPGC right over the cash register. Keegan's putter hangs above the fireplace; no plaque describes its significance; it is part of the oral tradition of the course that is passed down, embellished upon, lied about, and argued over by each succeeding generation. The rest of Keegan's clubs they'll tell you (even if you don't ask) were buried with him.

Keegan had no family, so his friends petitioned the city for the right to inter him on the course. There was a war on at the time and with the world hanging in the balance, the city fathers saw no harm in it. Back then the neighborhood around the Zebulon Pike Golf Course was still sparsely populated and some on the city council feared one grave on the property could set a precedent, allowing a future council to turn the whole place into a cemetery; but those concerns were set aside and the burial site approved unanimously. The Army Air Corps, already on the hook for repairs to the golf course and eager to mend any further damage to its image, agreed to do a flyover the morning of Keegan's funeral. He had, after all, served honorably albeit locally during the Spanish-American War. They even sent a be-medaled ace in town on a War Bonds tour to attend the funeral. They laid Keegan to rest near the starter's shack where he had wiled away the hours when he wasn't playing or teaching the game. The ground over his grave was built up to resemble a tee box and his marker was cut from the same stone and to the same size as the squat little obelisks on each of the actual tee boxes. His epitaph is brief and poignant: "Ambrose Keegan. 1880–1944. PGA Professional. Fallen But Not Forgotten."

In the 1980s the first tee was moved closer to the clubhouse and a squeamish soul on the Parks Commission suggested Keegan's body be moved to a cemetery. Since that would cost money and only the regulars at the golf course even knew Keegan was there, the motion was tabled. The starter's shack naturally migrated with the first tee, leaving the grave more exposed to view. That lead to it being mistaken at times for the forward tee, so a tasteful sign was posted to notify the unwitting: "Grave. Keep off." Newcomers usually assumed it to be ancient Indian burial mound.

And so the years and decades passed at the ZPGC; from the day the course awoke from its long winter's nap sometime in still chilly April to the last bitter round of November, patrons flowed over its verdant surface littering its tee boxes with splintered pegs, gouging its fairways with dollar-bill-size divots, and riddling its greens with pitch marks in their futile, unrelenting effort to conquer the unconquerable game. In short, putting aside the fact that a man was buried there, the ZPGC was just another unexceptional, absolutely ordinary, run-of-the-mill municipal golf course.

SPRING

Ralph Milbank looked up and removed his reading glasses, tapping them three times on the piece of paper in front of him to set the tempo for what he was about to say. The frown on Milbank's face masked inner satisfaction. As he tapped, Karl Ketterman, sitting across the desk from him, leaned slightly forward.

"These numbers are not good, Karl. Play is down. Income is down. And let's face facts; interest in the game is down. I fail to see a silver lining here."

Ketterman shifted in his chair. He was just beginning his first year as manager at the ZPGC and this was his first meeting with Milbank. The outgoing manager and the Parks Commission's personnel director had interviewed Karl, but it was Milbank, the chair of the subcommittee on employee relations, who made the decision to hire him, as he made clear to Karl at their first meeting. Now Milbank was grilling him over what he was going to do to improve the course's bottom line. A more experienced manager would have bridled at the unfairness of doing this just two weeks into the job, but Ketterman, twenty-three and with a freshly minted Bachelor of Arts degree in golf course management from a small Southern California college, could only steel his soul and do his best to defend his new golf course.

To focus his mind he studied the triangular granite nameplate on the desk before speaking. Ralph Milbank, Parks Commissioner. He decided to take a casual, collegial approach to their conversation. "Ralph, there—"

"Long 'a,' silent 'l.'"

Ketterman could only counter this non sequitur with a blank stare.

"Like the composer *Ralph* Vaughan Williams or the actor *Ralph* Fiennes. That's how my name is pronounced. Sorry to interrupt, Karl. You were saying?"

Ketterman heard him roll the "r" as well as extend the "a" and mute the "l." He wondered if Milbank was aware of how pretentious he sounded. "'Rafe' as in 'safe:' I get it," he thought to himself. The mnemonic fixed it in his brain. The next time the name would come tripping off his tongue. He made a tactical adjustment to formal address in deference to Milbank's position.

"I was saying, Mr. Milbank, I think things are about to take a very positive turn at the course, lots of things. For example, I'm starting a program to get the kids in the neighborhood into the game. The women's club has a new director. The men's club is doing outreach for new members. I've got a plan to get more nine-hole leagues started, part of which is to lure the city employees' league back to ZPGC."

Milbank raised his brows and glanced heavenward, as if to say fat chance of that happening. Ketterman licked his lips before continuing.

"And I have some ideas to generate more interest in both the Keegan Cap and the other events that are held at the course; you know, get the media to do stories on them, make people aware of how they're a rich part of the city's history. There's a ton of potential in those events; I know it. The ZPGC can come back to life, Mr. Milbank, and in a few years I'm confident we're going to be a more reliable source of income for the city. I'm excited, sir." He smiled wanly, hoping Milbank would smile back. He didn't. Ketterman held his until the corners of his mouth began to twitch.

Milbank sat back and formed a triumphal arch with his fingertips. Not as excited as I will be when a new gated community of fifty to sixty luxury homes inside the city limits and just minutes from downtown starts generating property taxes, he thought to himself. Once that was an accomplished fact, attributable largely to his foresight and initiative, Milbank's path to the mayor's office was all but assured. The planning of the development had already begun, there were discussions underway, and the hour fast approaching—fast in the world of city politics, anyway—when the only thing going down the fairways of the ZPGC would be bulldozers.

"I wish you all the best, Karl. But you have to realize that in these times it is vitally important that facilities like the Zebulon Pike not be a drain on Parks Commission resources."

Milbank's subtle glance toward the door signaled to Karl their meeting was over.

*

Even though it is now smack dab in the middle of town, it is entirely possible to drive past the Zebulon Pike Golf Course without noticing it. It is at the end of a long drive, the old sign is small and weathered, and there is no inviting glimpse of fairway or green from the street in front of it. This is partly by design, partly due to how the city has changed since the course opened. At that time there were no homes around the ZPGC and little traffic on the dusty road that ran past it so it didn't matter if they set the course far off the street and left the small forest that blocked it from view undisturbed.

The clubhouse, a stout one-story structure reminiscent of a snug English country home, is built of local stone and has deep-set windows with prism-edged panes that color the floor with rainbow pastels, and a steep-sloping slate roof that glistens like onyx after a rain. The front faces due west and the potholed parking lot. A low screened-in porch was added to the back of the building right after the Second World War. The interior consists of a grillroom with twelve stools and eight tables, two bathrooms, a small locker room (men's only), the counter where green fees, balls, tees, and tokens for the driving range are purchased, and a recently added, rather sad-looking display of logoed apparel next to it.

The most distinctive feature of the interior is the large brass plaque in the middle of the floor featuring a bust of Zebulon Pike in his high-collared uniform above crossed golf clubs. Above his bust is a scroll banner reading "Zebulon Pike Golf Course," below it another with the course motto, *"Vita est ludus et ludus est vita,"* which roughly translated means, "Life is the game and the game is life." High on the east wall of the clubhouse is a small round window. The light through that window falls directly on the plaque the June morning on which the Keegan Cap Tournament is annually contested—though no one noticed until years after the event began. Superstitious regulars now see it as a portent, a sign that both the course and the event's namesake shower their blessings on the tournament.

The clubhouse's understated elegance and solid dignity, even after years of neglect, are testaments to the expectations the city had for ZPGC in 1934. The course itself, unfortunately, never lived up to them. Location was its biggest challenge. The city had ceded some of its poorest land to the project, approximately two-hundred acres abutting the Winnehala Swamp—a name changed in a more ecologically sensitive time to the Winnehala Wetlands—a huge reedy expanse that stretches along the east and much of the south side of the course, an area that remained boggy even after tons of dirt and fill had been brought onto the site during construction; to this day the frost heave after every winter leaves the fairways as rumpled and uneven as an unmade bed.

Who exactly designed the course is unclear. At one time a story circulated that Donald Ross, after turning down the project, had been approached by a leading citizen of our city who pleaded with him to reconsider. Moved by the man's passion, Ross took the map of the property and quickly sketched out the course design. It was just a rough outline and Ross refused any compensation for it; still, some say the look of the holes and the way they flow into a unified whole reflect the genius of his touch. In the 1960s a regular at the ZPGC set out to find the truth but to no avail. There were no plans in the City Engineer's Office, no correspondence in the Records Department, and nothing on file at the Parks Commission to say who did or didn't design the course, so the story lost credibility and faded away.

The Zebulon Pike Golf Course officially opened on Saturday, June 9, 1934. Ambrose Keegan, its newly appointed head pro-fessional, is supposed to have hit the ceremonial first drive. The mayor gave a short speech and play began and it has continued ever since regardless of wars, droughts, financial downturns, or the not-infrequent summer thunderstorms that leave the course waterlogged for days.

As the years passed, the city grew to the edges of both the course and the wetlands, but today the once tidy middle-class neighborhood around the ZPGC looks seedy and tired. The population of the city is older, less affluent, and less interested in golf; if you were to stop and ask the average citizen on the street where the Zebulon Pike Golf Course is, odds are they'd say they never heard of it.

The majority of the course's clientele is older, white, and male, but it becomes a slimmer majority every season. There are a few younger players yet not enough to overcome the course's reputation as a haven for aging hacks, a motley assortment of eccentrics, recluses, and deadbeats held together by their devotion to the game and loyalty to the ZPGC.

Charley Lumley turned his cart off the path at the far end of the driving range, facing it directly into the rising sun. This was his time of the day, just a few ancient early birds on the course and no one at all down here. He was alone, out of sight of the clubhouse, and he was content.

Charley's face mapped a life spent on and around golf courses. After decades in the sun and wind it had the texture of a crumpled brown paper bag. Of medium height and slight build, Charley Lumley still possessed a powerful game, although like every golfer his age he bemoaned the distance the years had stolen from him and mused how magnificent his game would have been in his salad days if he'd had the benefit of modern technology. He set his weathered straw fedora on the seat and ran a hand through his closely cropped white hair.

"A balata ball, forged irons, persimmon woods, and steel shafts; that's what we played with. If you drove that ball two-forty you were putting it out there. Hell, I hit these new balls farther than that now and I'm seventy goddamn years old," he would say, usually to himself and frequently out loud.

Charley had a peculiar habit of speaking what was on his mind whenever he was inspired to, whether alone or when others were around. He did it without any of the standard modes of prefacing remarks to another person: a greeting, a tap on the shoulder, a slight clearing of the throat. No, Charley just started talking; this often startled people, especially when they turned to see he was not even looking in their direction. When Charley stopped speaking, some might offer an opinion or pose a question and be baffled when he either continued as if he had not heard them or just drove away. What they failed to understand was that Charley was a monologist, not a conversationalist. He was not speaking to garner a response or a reaction; he was speaking, as it were, *ex cathedra*, to enlighten the wider world; he was delivering an oracular pronouncement that, no matter how cryptic, had gems of wisdom for those willing to sift them out. Be that as it may, most people were put off by it; they considered Charley a cantankerous old prick and gave him a wide berth.

I say Charley drove away because he was seldom seen afoot. If he bemoaned many things about the modern game, the motorized cart was not among them. To be fair, Charley sat in his cart more than he drove it, spending the greater part of the day down at the range. Watching. Waiting. Ruminating.

In recent years, Charley's days were spent almost entirely at the ZPGC driving range. He began every morning by changing the hitting positions, moving the markers that spaced the golfers and formed the line they were to hit behind and filling in the divots from the previous day's clients with soil and seed mix. He did that without leaving his cart, ladling the mix from the five-gallon bucket on the floor next to him with a scoop he'd made from an old plastic bleach bottle, pouring it liberally wherever he saw a gouge in the grass, then leveling it off with an old bunker rake. He had sawn off the handle so he could wield it from a sitting position. His dexterity at this task amazed any who beheld it. The moving of the markers, which required he get out of the cart, took much longer, of course, but the process in its entirety had a certain rhythm and grace. Once the markers were set, Charley went to the ball shack and refilled the two machines with the balls he retrieved at the end of every day.

This had not always been Charley's life. For three decades he had been the teaching professional at ZPGC, and it's safe to say more than half the regulars had taken lessons from him over the years. Charley taught the game as he had learned it from the stern taskmasters of the Old School, men who didn't mollycoddle and suffered fools not at all. Yet for all his foibles and eccentricities,

Charley Lumley was a brilliant instructor. His methodology was to go through the fundamentals—grip, posture, alignment—without allowing the student to hit a ball. First they had to see and absorb how these essential things looked and felt, how they linked the club and the body and the earth, to contemplate their meaning in the larger scope of the game and the game to the cosmos. Only when Charley felt they were gripping the club properly and could comfortably set up to the ball like a golfer would he allow them to swing the club; and that is when the inexplicable would happen. Somehow, through some celestial dispensation, this embittered, soured, and largely unlikeable man was able to make the complexities of the golf swing clear as a mountain dawn. Somehow, Charley Lumley's students not only learned to swing the golf club without the encumbrances of self-analysis or muscle tension, they became enamored with the game, which, like chess, looks simple yet demands incredible focus and constant adaptation. They became obsessed with its history, lore, and traditions, its great controversies and scandals, its beauty. They abjured mulligans, do-overs, and winter rules and always played the ball where it laid. They favored blades, limited themselves to fourteen clubs, frowned on long putters, and waved *The Rules of Golf* about like a Maoist his *Little Red Book*. They might be liberal and opened-minded, even progressive, off the course but on it they were dogmatic, an immoveable obstruction to the less-than-serious player. And Lumley was their god.

Like all gods, Lumley shrouded himself from man. He might acknowledge a former student with a nod or a touch of his cap and even speak at them on occasion, but he never fraternized. Not in his heyday, not now when forced retirement had put him out to pasture on the far end of the driving range. Yes, Lumley, like all city employees, had retired at sixty-five—more accurately, been retired—but, like a prisoner released after a thirty-year sentence, he found life on the outside confusing and incomprehensible so he came back to ZPGC, assuming his duties on the range without saying a word to Art Castle. He just stood in front of him, gave a nod in the direction of the range, and they had an understanding. Cybil had coffee ready for him every morning and the paid employees stayed out of his way. It was as Lumley liked it. When Art retired, the new kid didn't even know Charley had something to do with the course, assuming he was just another one of the ZPGC regulars who haunted the driving range. And why wouldn't he? Aside from picking up his morning coffee and coming back for a refill or two during the day, Charley wasn't often seen in the clubhouse.

Charley's old students found solace in knowing he was on the range when they were hitting balls. They knew he was taking everything in. They looked his way and if he liked their swing he nodded. If he didn't he drove closer and watched a second swing, then corrected their mistake with a single pithy phrase: turn more; keep your spine angle; rotate your right hand. Lumley scoffed at professionals that used video; it was a crutch, a cover for poor observational skills. The golf swing wasn't a series of separate positions, it was a continuous motion; why befuddle people with frozen images of themselves coming over the top or too far from the inside? They didn't need to understand the problem; that was his job. All they should concentrate on is what he told them to do. His students heard and obeyed his words and, now that he was retired, would subtly tuck a dollar or two in the cup holder on his cart before he drove away. Charley took their offerings without comment, although he might leave them with a thought to ponder, often something about the only golfer he considered worthy of adoration.

"Hogan's Cadillac hit that bus in February 1949. He had to have major surgery to prevent a blood clot in his leg from killing him; even after that the doctor said he might never walk again. He was in the hospital for fifty-nine days. The circulation in his legs was so bad that for the rest of his life he had to wrap them in ACE bandages before he played. In 1953 he won the Masters, U.S. Open, and British Open. The only reason he didn't win the PGA Championship too was because it overlapped the British Open. That's the greatest feat by the greatest player in the entire history of the game; any son of a bitch who says different is full of shit."

Charley had just completed his self-appointed tasks to his satisfaction when he turned his cart sunward. He lit a cigarette and raised his thermos cup, wincing slightly as the steaming brew hit his lips. The shock of the combined pleasures of nicotine and caffeine brought forth a brief but vigorous phlegm-gurgling cough followed by a throaty rasp. He launched a gob of spit into the air, took a second pull from his Camel and plucked a fleck of tobacco from the tip of his tongue. He looked at it pensively, remembering wistfully the days when a pack was fifty cents and as available as God's grace to the repentant. Pretty soon, Lumley mused, marijuana was going to be cheaper and easier to get. But something else preyed on his mind. Something Cybil had said to him yesterday as she twisted the cap on his cup.

"Bright boy was asking about you," she said. She paused, forgetting for a moment to whom she was speaking and expecting a response. Lumley's blue unblinking eyes fixed on her. They held her for a moment, bringing back a time, a quarter century ago now, when her heart had belonged to Lumley alone. Holding her emotions in check, she went on. "He just found out you're working here. I guess someone told him." She didn't bother to mention it was she who'd done the telling. "He didn't seem to mind until he found out you're a retired employee, then he started going on about liability and civil service regulations and a load of crap like that. I wasn't really listening. The upshot is I think he means to talk to you."

Charley's reaction was limited to a slight elevation of his eyebrows as he put the top on his thermos cup and walked out.

3

"Afternoon, guys."

Karl's salutation drew a few nods from the golfers scattered among the tables in the grillroom and a stony stare from Cybil as she set the sandwich Dan Doherty had ordered in front of him.

"What's this?" Dan asked, genuinely confused, as always. Whether it was the onset of dementia or the effects of catching a shanked 3-iron on the back of the head while caddying in the 1955 Keegan Cap—those who had known him before that incident would say that was the cause—Dan lived in a world of pleasant surprises and curious turns of events.

"Tuna on whole wheat, toasted, with lettuce and tomato; pickle on the side," Cybil said, her eyes following Karl into his office.

"Sounds great. I'll have one."

"There you go."

Dan's face shone like a child's on Christmas morning. Cybil sighed and marked it down on the tab next to the register that Dan's brother settled at the end of each month. As she cleared plates from the counter Cybil pondered the wisdom of stirring the pot, not the literal one of chili on the stove but the metaphoric one of Lumley at the range. Now that the kid knew about it he'd have to deal with Lumley and that could be entertaining.

*

Karl plopped down in his chair and put his feet on the desk. He felt the meeting with Milbank had gone well, all things considered. Milbank hadn't been exactly friendly and had grilled Karl closely on his projections for the year, but he had been professional; besides, Karl liked people that were blunt and dealt with things out in the open. He felt Milbank was someone he could deal with. The important thing now was for ZPGC to make progress, to generate more revenue for the city and secure its future and Karl's career. Karl looked up at the photos of his predecessors above the filing cabinets on the other side of the office: Wilbur Odegaard, 1934–1947; Adolphus Smythe, 1947–1957; Clarence McAdoo, 1957–1957; Michael St. Mane, 1957–1981; Art Castle, 1981–2009. Whether that line of photographs would continue to expand or soon be on its way to a landfill was on Karl's shoulders and he felt the weight of it. But would this servant be worthy of his hire?

Karl knew he had some things going for him the boys on the wall didn't; first of all, he actually had an education in the golf business. They had all been Parks Commission employees assigned to ZPGC according to the arcane rules of the civil service, and most had been ill-suited for the job. The halcyon days, if there had been any at ZPGC, were during Odegaard's watch. A scratch golfer and an enthusiastic promoter of the game, Wilbur Odegaard worked hard, albeit unsuccessfully, to bring professional and amateur events to the course and to make it a centerpiece of civic pride. He was responsible for both the Keegan Cap (legend has it Odegaard was the one who found Keegan's head laying under a bush near the green) and the Ebon Invitational, a controversial and forward-thinking decision at the time. Odegaard's commitment to the course was unquestionable; he even died in harness, succumbing to a heart attack during the 1947 Keegan Cap.

His replacement, Adolphus Smythe, a twenty handicap and an official with the local Civil Defense, spent his tenure trying to convince the city fathers to build a network of underground bunkers deep beneath the clubhouse. A Cold War pessimist, Smythe reckoned that after the post-Armageddon radioactive dust settled and the Russians invaded, they would be set upon and overwhelmed by a cadre of hard-charging patriots hidden in the last place a Red would look for them, *under* a golf course. His grand plan never came to fruition. He had to settle for a now long-forgotten twelve-by-twelve-foot space under the clubhouse accessed through a trap door in the kitchen.

Clarence McAdoo's tenure was the shortest and most poignant. A sensitive soul and amateur violinist, McAdoo had been responsible for scheduling musical programs in the city parks when he was suddenly wrenched from his sinecure and sent off to the Zebulon Pike. He knew nothing of golf and could not understand why, after decades dedicated to promoting music and culture, he was relegated to this green purgatory. Needless to say, it was a shock, one he never fully recovered from. It seems a member of the city council with a musical relative in need of a job had masterminded McAdoo's transfer; it could be argued it was a case of manslaughter. McAdoo was the most ill-suited man on earth for the ZPGC job. He came in every morning without saying a word and never left his office; the staff knew he was in only when they heard the muffled sounds of his violin coming from behind the locked door. Then one warm summer evening, just after the last golfers had left the course, Clarence McAdoo walked down to the pond that ran along the left side of the ninth green, tied a gunnysack filled with old golf balls around his neck, and walked into murky oblivion. He was discovered two days later when his corpse rose, feet first, the soles of his wingtips heavenward. It's been considered good course etiquette ever since for a golfer whose ball flies into that pond to shout, "That one's for you, McAdoo!"

Michael St. Mane, twelve handicap and chronic alcoholic, succeeded McAdoo. He liked to hang around the maintenance buildings and drink beer with the grounds crew; on weekends he drank gin and played high stakes matches, which, as the years went on, he lost more and more frequently as the forward motion of his putting stroke looked as if it were initiated by a cattle prod. He died shortly after retiring; a broken man with a twenty-four handicap averaging forty-seven putts a round.

Art Castle, Karl's immediate predecessor, never played golf, made waves, or assumed the mantle of authority on the job. An affable, chubby man with a crew cut and perpetual protective smile, Art filled his working days avoiding responsibility and confrontation. Never once did he tell an employee what to do; instead he made suggestions ("Say, I'm hearing the rough is really long; could you take a look at that?), statements of simple fact ("No soap in the ball washers this morning"), or general requests in the presence of a specific offender ("Guys and gals, it would be great if you could all be here on time in the morning") that he never followed up on.

Now, after more than sixty years of varying degrees of mismanagement, incompetence, and neglect, it was up to Karl Ketterman to right the ship and give the ZPGC some semblance of credibility in the community, for it didn't take a genius to see that if things didn't improve, if the course continued to fail to pull its weight and make money, the Parks Commission could turn it into a gigantic dog run. Yet in his heart of hearts Karl knew he was the man to save the day. He not only understood the ins and outs of managing a golf course, he understood and loved the game, his own handicap fluctuating between a four and an eight. He hadn't gotten out this year yet, what with moving to town, finding a place to live, and getting oriented at ZPGC. Right now he was far more interested in the business aspects of the game. When he looked around the ZPGC his mind raced with the possibilities. The club could use a major renovation, sure, but Karl wasn't naïve enough to think for a moment the Parks Commission would give him a dime for that. A deep cleaning, however, was something he could manage, and it was obvious the clubhouse had gone years without one. The floors, walls, and windows were caked with dirt and grime and dust dimmed every picture and shrouded every trophy, knick-knack and display. The grill was the one shining exception.

The grill was under the command of the food and beverage manager, Cybil Stumpher, a clean- and control-freak who ran her fiefdom according to rigid and rigorous standards. She started at the ZPGC as a part-time employee when she was in high school and never left. In her thirty years, she had transformed the grill into one of the favorite lunch stops for cops, city maintenance workers, and people in the neighborhood around the course. The food was simple, good, and plentiful. Thanks to her, the grill and the beverage cart that wandered the course actually made money.

Karl turned his attention from his predecessors on the wall to the task at hand. He took up pen and legal pad and set to work; today he would draft his list of action items. Tomorrow a new era at the Zebulon Pike Golf Course would begin, starting with resolving the issue of the retiree working on the range.

*

Karl arrived at ZPGC bright and early the next morning. A soft mist covered the course. Peering into it, Karl saw Dunn moving the pin on the eighteenth green. He heard the thud of the cutter slamming into the turf and watched the quick back-and-forth movement of Dunn's shoulders as he twisted it into the earth. You had to get up early to catch sight of Dunn, for he stayed as far away from people as he could; it was hinted that he had reasons to do so, that there were things in his past that plagued him. According to some, Dunn was wanted for a string of gas station robberies in the west; others said he was the prodigal son of an aristocratic English family who still maintained a tireless search around the globe for his whereabouts; others, with less romantic imaginations, suggested he simply owed a lot of alimony and child support payments in another state. In truth, the tall, gaunt, brooding Dunn was none of those things; his story was far more tragic. A gifted child, if not a prodigy, Dunn had graduated from high school at fifteen and college at seventeen, double majoring in biology and English, with an emphasis on Elizabethan poetry and drama. In 1990, at the age of twenty, he was a graduate student at Harvard University preparing to defend his doctoral thesis in agronomy. It dealt, I've been told, with new uses of plants for fuel and food, ideas years ahead of their time and of such sheer brilliance the committee hardly felt qualified to question a single sentence in his dissertation. The outcome of his exam was foreordained. Dunn was to be awarded a doctorate and a teaching position at the university on the tenure track. Dunn knew all this was before him, but it was ashes in his mouth. Sometime in the days just before his dissertation defense something had caused him to simply lose interest in it all. A woman, a crisis of faith, an improperly prepared seafood dinner; whatever it was, it changed him irrevocably. He stood before the professors. They awaited his opening remarks. Dunn scanned the room with a wistful, distant look in his eyes, spread his arms in a theatrical pose and intoned,

Cut is the branch that might have grown full straight
And burnéd is Apollo's laurel bough,
That sometime grew within this learnéd man.

Thus, with a quote from Marlowe's *Doctor Faustus*, Dunn ended his academic career. The professors, unfamiliar with Elizabethan drama and struggling to make biologic or agronomic sense of his references to "branch" and "bough," watched in utter confusion as he turned and left the room. That was the last Harvard University ever saw of Dunn. Where he went next is unclear—the CIA, a Cistercian monastery, Skid Row, a Wal-Mart loading dock—maybe one, maybe all of them had been part of his journey. Some years later, Gabriel Dunn showed up at the Zebulon Pike Golf Course and joined the grounds crew. He mowed greens, picked up trash, moved tee markers, and kept to himself, but while he could hide his past he could not disguise his talent for making the things of the earth grow and be fruitful. The few people at the course who had any contact with Dunn at that time considered him to be what the French call an *idiot savant*, a mentally challenged person with a single, sharp, narrow lane of intellectual capacity so powerful it's astounding. A more apt description might be a loner with sociopathic tendencies and a knack for golf course maintenance.

Dunn looked his way so Karl waved. Dunn turned and walked into the mist. He would probably always remain an elusive character to Karl since the esoteric civil service rules stated the greenskeeper, like the manager of the grill, reported directly to the Parks Commission, not the golf course manager.

*

As Dunn set the flag on the eighteenth green, Merril Stokes prepared to tee off on one. His almost daily eighteen holes were Merril's Stations of the Cross, a repeated reenactment of heart-wrenching suffering; each hole a scourge upon his psyche, every shot leaving a taste as bitter as gall. At times Stokes questioned why he even played. He seldom broke ninety and the random shank ceased to surprise him anymore; he thinned shots over the green, he skulled them out of the bunker, he chunked them in the fairway, yet he still spent hours watching the Golf Channel and reading golf magazines, hoping to discover the one key to a consistent game. Stokes didn't ask for much, he would be happy to be a legitimate twelve, but the game remained an unrequited quest. That's why he preferred to go out early, keeping his frustration and his score to himself.

Stokes pegged his ball and stepped back, rehearsing his swing, visualizing the ball's flight—like all the great instructors advised— seeing it rising high and straight then bounding down the fairway for an additional fifteen yards. The first at the ZPGC is an ideal starting hole, a straightaway par four, measuring three-hundred-eighty-eight yards from the middle tees. Stokes felt good. His mind was centered, his spirit at peace. This could be his day.

"Mind if I play along, Merril?"

The sound was enough to buckle Stokes' knees. It was the voice of his nemesis, Tom Crupshaw, twelve-time club champion, two-time state amateur champion, and at seventy still a formidable competitor. Stokes' antagonism was unreciprocated for Crupshaw was a gentleman on and off the course. His game was effortless, controlled, consistent, almost lyrical. He still drove the ball over two-fifty off the tee, carved his iron shots whichever way his lie dictated, and was as steady and smooth over a putt as an eighteen-year-old; in other words, everything that Stokes lusted for Crupshaw possessed purely and naturally as a gift from the gods, for he was never seen on the range. A putt or two on the practice green and Crupshaw was off, carding a smooth seventy-seven or better regardless of weather conditions. He did it on brisk spring mornings, stifling summer afternoons, and in the low cold light of raw autumnal days. Every so often (but never at the ZPGC), he would even shoot under par; and always with aplomb and grace. While Stokes practiced and studied, Crupshaw played and enjoyed; while Stokes cursed and spat, Crupshaw cruised and scored, while Stokes watched his diet and stretched his muscles, Crupshaw smoked his cigar and sipped his beer, and for all of that Stokes quietly, secretly hated him.

"Of course," Stokes said with a smile, "It's always good to play with you, Tom."

"Fire away," said Crupshaw, and the game began.

Stokes was tense and tentative and kept his weight back on the downswing, slicing his tee shot into the tree line on the left. Crupshaw followed with a drive down the middle, thirty yards ahead of Stokes.

"What's your handicap, Merril?" Crupshaw said as he folded the scorecard and clipped it to the steering wheel.

Stokes didn't want to admit he'd let his membership in the Men's Club lapse this year and had no intention of keeping an official USGA handicap anymore. Why bother?

"It's a miracle if I break ninety, Tom," he replied as he put his bag on Crupshaw's cart. As the only golfer to win the club championship more than five times, and probably to assure he kept ZPGC his home course, Crupshaw's cart was always gratis.

"Okay, I'll give you a stroke a hole and we'll play a quarter a hole; what do you say?"

"Sure," said Stokes, too proud to back away from a bet he felt sure to lose. He quickly calculated the damage: $4.50. So be it.

Stokes punched out from the trees, hit his third on the green, and sunk a challenging par putt. Crupshaw's birdie putt grazed the cup and he tapped in for par. Stokes breathed a sigh of relief. He had withstood the juggernaut for one hole and his losses were down to $4.25. Crupshaw congratulated him as the cart carried them down the winding path to two.

Stokes continued to play well and after three holes they were still even. Maybe this really was his day, he mused as he teed his ball on the fourth hole. Then, sensing this was the moment to strike, he tried to hit his drive a little harder. The second he took the club away from the back of the ball, he knew he was lost. His swing felt like a semi with brake failure heading down a six-percent grade road in an ice storm. Nothing was connected. For a moment he wondered if he was suffering a seizure. His right heel carved a semicircle in the grass and he watched his ball rocket to the right over the tree line and out of bounds. He could hear the golf ball bouncing down the street. He breathed a sigh of relief when he didn't hear a car alarm go off, but from that point Merril Stokes went to pieces and Tom Crupshaw went on to victory. On the eighteenth green they removed their hats and shook hands. As Stokes got out of the cart at the clubhouse he handed Crupshaw $3.75 and slumped his way to his car.

Raised a Catholic, Stokes reverted to the lessons of his childhood and paused to examine his conscience as he sat on the tailgate of his SUV taking off his golf shoes. Why did he continue to err? He had been instructed in the fundamentals of the game, he knew right from wrong when it came to swing mechanics, yet he continued to swing too fast, go past parallel, and come over the top, returning to these evils again and again like a dog to its vomit. As he went into the clubhouse to book a tee time for tomorrow he wondered why he couldn't just relax and enjoy the game and whether he should just quit playing it. He stood for a moment in front of the counter, looking around the clubhouse at its dirty windows and shabby furnishings.

"What a dump."

It struck him that maybe all he needed was to play a different course. Sure, the Zebulon Pike was handy, but maybe if he went somewhere else he'd shoot a better score. Maybe he should even consider joining a private club.

"Help you?"

The guy behind the counter brought Merril back to reality and he booked a tee time for the next morning.

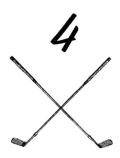

4

"His name is Lumley, Charley Lumley. He was the teaching pro here for years. When he retired, Art gave him the okay to work the range in the morning, fill the ball machines, move the markers, that sort of thing. He doesn't get paid for it. It just gives him something to do, a reason to get up in the morning."

Mo Mittenthal took a sip of coffee, giving Karl a little time to digest what he'd just said. The kid was deliberate and sincere, and Mo liked him. Karl was standing at the white board in his office, setting the schedule for the part-timers for the following week. Mo's name was written in the Monday morning spot and a blue line ran from it straight through to Sunday. No one else wanted to be here at five-thirty, especially the younger employees.

"It was a mitzvah."

"A what?"

"A mitzvah; a good deed, a charitable act. Charley's got no wife, no kids, no family, no friends, no hobbies; hell, he doesn't even have any vices, except smoking and being cantankerous. All he's got is golf and this course. So Art let him do a job that no one else would do as well if you paid them. He's here every morning before me; before Dunn, for all I know. The range looks great, the ball machines are filled and ready, and no one's complaining, so what's the harm?" Mo was a widower and knew what it was like to be old and alone, and he felt sorry for Lumley.

Karl went to his computer and brought up his email. "Ah, but I *am* getting complaints, Mo. This morning, in fact, I got an email from a guy. It seems he was hitting balls a step or two in front of the markers the other day and an older gentleman in a golf cart drove up and said, "Stay behind the marker or get the hell off my range." He's wondering if my employee could have softened that a little, seeing it was a first warning."

"He couldn't have been a regular or he wouldn't have done something that stupid with Lumley around."

"Mo, we need more golfers on the course and using the range. That's how we make money. We've got to widen the net and increase the number of regulars. That means we've got to make guys like that feel welcome and encourage them to come back. If we don't expand our customer base, we're in trouble. You've run a business; you know if it's not growing it's dying. The Zebulon Pike is dying, Mo. It's on life support; we've got to bring it back."

Karl was up and pacing the room. Ah, youth, thought Mo as he watched Karl become more animated with each sentence.

"This place is amazing, Mo. There's not a muni in the world with a clubhouse like this. And the history! This town should be proud of this place, but most don't even know it's here. We can't change that if we insult people on the range for some minor infraction of a rule they don't even know about."

"I'll talk to him."

Karl shook his head. "Thanks, Mo, but that's my job. I'm responsible for the management of this course and Mr. Lumley and I have to come to an understanding if he's going to work here, even if it's for nothing."

Mittenthal shrugged and took his leave. Back in the starter's shack he tried to see the ZPGC as Karl did, as an asset to the community, rich in tradition, and still, after decades of half-hearted management and underfunding, filled with potential. He couldn't do it.

*

The email wasn't the only reason Karl had for seeing Lumley this morning. Cybil had met him as soon as he came in the door and brought up the issue with a hypothetical question; she wondered if the city would be liable if Lumley hurt himself loading the ball machines, broke his ankle stepping into a duffer's divot or maybe said something offensive to someone on the range. The last one hit home, yet Karl sensed her real purpose was not the greater good of the golf course but to stir something up. Why? Was it to test the new guy or just plain mischievousness?

Cybil's reason was far more primordial and complex than mundane envy or malice; the old cliché "a woman scorned" sums it up best. Cybil Stumpher had not always been an overweight middle-aged woman with her hair in a tight bun fronted with greasy bangs, her breasts untethered and resting on the protruding arc of her belly, brow knit in a perpetual scowl and chin shaded with downy hairs. No, once she had been slender and lithe and lovely, the beaming sprite behind the counter that the older guys liked to flirt with and the younger ones yearned to caress.

There is a photo hanging in a corner of the clubhouse that proves Cybil at twenty had, in fact, been the apotheosis of female beauty. It is a photo of a Keegan Cap winner accepting the trophy, but Cybil can be seen in the background. She is delivering an order to a table, captured in full stride. She looks like Diana in pursuit of a stag, and the stag she pursued back then was Lumley. He was in his thirties, a tall, lean, striking figure, sort of a composite image of Clint Eastwood and Gregory Peck, and Cybil was smitten with him. Lumley, being a man with all the concomitant failings and desires of his sex could not help but notice Cybil and be stirred. She knew he was drawn to her but it took all her charms to pierce his taciturnity; a smile directed at him alone, the brief touch of his hand as she refilled his coffee cup, her breasts straining her blouse as she pulled her raven-black hair back into a ponytail in front of him. Eventually, Lumley gathered up the nerve to speak to her.

It may seem strange that a desirable, beautiful girl would take a fancy to the reclusive and monosyllabic Lumley, yet he was everything Cybil dreamed of; a mature, sober, dependable man, nothing like the boys who pawed at her in parked cars or in her parent's family room. What appealed to her even more was finding a man with those attributes here at the Zebulon Pike Golf Course, the place where she had found refuge from a tiresome home life, a boring education, and an ambiguous future. Here she had found stability. Here things moved in synchrony with the seasons. Here her life could follow in the predictable sequence of civil service employment: a secure job, good benefits, and a generous pension.

Lumley was then not as antisocial as he would become in later years, still it was a surprise to many to see him suddenly in the clubhouse more often. Almost every morning, in fact, he was at the counter for breakfast, striking up conversations that soon included Cybil, conversations that, of course, were always about golf. One day as they were chatting, Cybil matter-of-factly mentioned that she had never played golf, had never even picked up a club. An eerie silence followed, a silence that lasted long enough to allow Lumley's reply to be heard throughout the grillroom.

"Come down to the range when you get off and I'll give you a free lesson."

Cybil felt a blush color her cheeks.

"Sure."

"I'll be waiting for you."

With those few words two lives were changed forever.

*

Golf lessons combine the cerebral and the physical, the abstract and the tactile, the hands and the loins, but you can't learn the game unless you've been seduced by it first. That's why lessons are often the winnowing process that separates the dilettante from the truly devoted. There is no compromise; you either love the game or you don't.

Cybil arrived on the range for her first lesson promptly at four, after first changing into a sleeveless sundress that fell just above her knees and hid none of her physical attributes. She strode confidently out to Lumley, her body swaying like the giant cottonwoods behind her. Even Lumley's focus on the game blurred for a moment. The lesson began with Charley handing Cybil a book.

"Is that you?" Cybil said, pointing to the cover.

Lumley paused to recover his poise.

"That's Hogan, the man with the greatest golf swing in the game. This is his book, *Five Lessons: The Modern Fundamentals of Golf.*"

"Doesn't look very modern to me," Cybil giggled. He attempted a grin but she knew she was taking the wrong approach and became serious.

"The object of golf is to get the ball from the tee to the cup. The art of golf is to do that in the fewest strokes possible. The secret to that art is controlling the flight of the ball. Our goal is to learn how to do that here on the range; once you can hit the ball at your target, you can play the game."

"All right, give me a club!"

Lumley, ignoring Cybil, took a 7-iron out of his bag and moved her to the side. He drew a range ball from the overturned bucket into position, gripped the club, waggled, and swung, hitting a crisp shot that sailed high over the hundred-fifty-yard marker.

"Wow, you're really good!" Cybil, like most women of that era, praised men as instinctively as she petted puppies and gushed over babies.

"How did I do that?" Cybil knew this was an important question. She pondered before she answered.

"You wound up and hit the ball." She was relieved when Lumley seemed to like her answer.

"True, but what is the first thing I did?"

"You took the club out of your bag."

Cybil was beginning to feel confused and uncomfortable even though Lumley attempted to smile.

"The first thing I did was grip the club."

After an hour of demonstrating the intricacies of the Vardon grip and how it allowed his wrists to hinge at the top of the swing, put the clubface squarely behind the ball at impact, then hinge his wrists again in the follow-through, Lumley concluded lesson one.

Cybil thought he'd take her out to dinner or at least walk her to the clubhouse, but he just told her to come back tomorrow at the same time and waved up his next lesson. While the other men on the range stared at Cybil as she walked away, Lumley's attention was on his next student.

The lessons progressed, but the relationship did not; as least not at the pace she expected. Cybil was in a quandary. Lumley, attentive in the clubhouse, seemed impervious to her on the range even when she wore tight tops that forced the eye to her ample bosom and shorts that stretched like a second skin across her firm buttocks. When she set up over the ball, knees apart, rump pushed out, and spine tilted, the eyes of every man on the range were riveted on her. Though the siren call of Cybil's sensuality might have been enough to rouse Lazarus three days in the tomb, Lumley remained focused, fixated even, on the task at hand. If he thought of positions at all, they had to do with Cybil's golf swing. He was like a blind man in front of a neon light; he might have felt some warmth but he was missing the message. Cybil was flummoxed.

If Cybil felt frustration, it was nothing to Lumley's. He took pride in his ability to teach the game yet he was beginning to feel he was failing with Cybil. Her swing was quick and vicious, almost angry, and he just couldn't get her to let go of the tension in her body. He had never had a student this difficult.

After two weeks of this, Cybil decided it was time for her to instruct. She postponed their lesson until late in the day with the excuse that she had errands to run after her shift. She went home, showered, and prepared for conquest; then, shiny, scented, and at her loveliest, Cybil went down to the range. It was a gorgeous late June evening. Lumley's last lesson was long over and only a few old diehards remained on the range. She walked up to Charley. When he tried to start the lesson she placed a finger softly on his lips. She could feel the sharp inhalation of his breath and it moved her. She took his hand.

"Let's go for a walk, Charley."

They walked off the range and onto the golf course, continuing until they reached the stand of trees behind the fourth green where Cybil had left a basket of food, a bottle of wine, and a blanket. Even though they walked but a short distance, Lumley and Cybil had taken the journey of a lifetime. Later, as she held the thrice sated and slumbering Lumley in her arms, Cybil, thinking she had finally made Lumley her own, gazed up to the emerging stars and thanked whoever put them there for this moment.

But Cybil's victory was short-lived, for even though Lumley

loved her and told her so, there was a canker gnawing at his heart. For all her physical beauty and the earthly pleasures she showered upon him could not disguise the fact that she had no interest in golf. Try as she might, Cybil couldn't hide it; she thought golf was a silly game.

The demise of their relationship was foreordained. Cybil captivated Lumley, but she couldn't win his heart without sharing his passion for the game. She was no fool; she saw the irony: they had been drawn together on a golf course but the game of golf was about to tear them apart.

The night before Lumley told her it was over Cybil had a terrible dream. She and Charley were facing each other across a fairway that seemed to extend forever in both directions. He smiled at her and she ached to be in his arms. She started to run toward him when the sprinkler system went on. Cybil stopped, knowing the water would be icy cold. She thought of running around the rotating arc of water but saw the sprinklers overlapped each other as far as the eye could see. Water splashed her face and drove her back. She tried calling to Charley but he didn't answer. Then, as suddenly as they had started, the sprinklers stopped. Lumley was no longer there in front of her. Cybil awoke weeping.

Lumley didn't say farewell in person. He left a letter on the counter. The blurred words on the page told her Lumley had wept writing it. It hardly mattered. The message, brief and clumsily composed, was clear. It was over between them. At that moment Cybil's grip on life did what her grip on the golf club never could; it unhinged. She changed. At first she was just quieter, more reserved. But soon it was clear to everyone she was no longer the same person. She became more and more remote, keeping life at bay by staying behind her counter, a modern-day Ophelia drowning in a cold numbing pool of depression, eventually evolving into a slovenly, obese and bitter harridan. Lumley fared no better, marooning himself on the range and burying himself in his career. The years passed; their souls remained unhealed.

*

Karl approached Lumley by walking the full length of the range. Somehow he felt it best if he didn't come up on him suddenly from behind.

"Charley? Hello, I'm Karl Ketterman, the new manager here."

Lumley flicked his cigarette away and touched the brim of his hat. An auspicious start, Karl thought.

"Look, I know you had an arrangement with Art and I guess I'm fine with that. I checked with the Parks Commission lawyer and he sees no liability issues, but if you're going to work here you've got to be a little nicer to the people here. You cussed out a guy the other day for hitting ahead of the markers and I heard about it. That's got to stop."

Lumley's cold blue eyes locked on Karl's. This kid can't be more than twenty-three, he thought. Karl didn't flinch under Lumley's glare and didn't look away. Lumley liked that.

"Got it," Charley said.

Karl saw the weathered hand reach out to him. He understood the significance of the gesture and took a step to grasp it. He was surprised by the strength in the old man's hand.

"If there's anything I can do for you, you know where to find me."

Lumley pursed his lips slightly and nodded. Karl was almost to the cart path when he heard that raspy voice again.

"Thanks."

5

A foursome of regulars—Sundbaum, Rankel, Armstead, and Hood—reported the first sighting to Karl.

"Hey, chief, you got a homeless guy on the premises," said Armstead.

"I knew this place was going to shit, but bums camped on the course? Gawd almighty!" said Rankel. Hood nodded, mutely agreeing that this surely was a sign of the End Times.

Another day, another dilemma, Karl thought, turning from his computer to the four men crowded into his doorway. He asked for details and they delivered, overlapping and contradicting one another, arguing minutiae and glossing over the facts. The upshot was this: as they were bouncing down the heaving peat bog euphemistically called the eleventh fairway, they saw a figure in a hooded sweatshirt and jeans come loping out of the bushes on their left. They were at least a hundred yards away so he didn't see them at first. When he did, he froze for a moment like a deer in headlights, then sprinted into the ravine that runs along the west side of the fairway.

"What makes you think he was homeless and living out there? Couldn't it have been a kid just cutting across the course?"

The looks he got ranged from stunned to dyspeptic.

"On the left side of eleven is the Winnehala Wetlands, to the right run the thirteenth and fourteenth holes," Sundbaum said, speaking slowly and deliberately, as if to an infant or someone new to the language. "Beyond the out-of-bounds fence on fourteen is the

Winnehala Wetlands, and beyond the eleventh green is the par-three twelfth and the Winnehala Wetlands; in other words, we were on a finger of land surrounded on three sides by swamp, so unless he was a muskrat I can't think of where he was coming from or where he was going."

Karl reddened. Okay, he didn't have the layout of the course fixed in his head yet but he still didn't buy their explanation.

"Thank you, gentlemen, I'll look into it."

Sundbaum rolled his eyes at the others and they left. Karl heard an inaudible voice then an abrupt burst of laughter. He had, he assumed, just been made the butt of someone's joke. He grabbed the two-way radio from its cradle and headed toward the door.

"Burchell, meet me at the clubhouse." The radio crackled and hissed when he released the button.

"Roger that."

*

The rangers at the Zebulon Pike Golf Course were volunteers. Some of them were "lifers," guys who had been hanging around the place since they were kids. Most were retired city employees—policemen, firemen, a few schoolteachers. They were zealous in enforcing rules they personally never observed, like driving carts slowly around the clubhouse. The greatest among these sinners was Conrad "Rambo" Burchell, retired street maintenance foreman and, in his youth, a Marine, a fact borne out by the snarling bulldog wearing a World War One helmet festooned with the eagle, globe, and anchor emblem of the United States Marine Corps tattooed on his forearm. Burchell had several tattoos, all of them blurred by age and muscle atrophy; this particular one he'd gotten on Okinawa at the tail end of a two-day tear in a cesspool of iniquity called Kim Village. Too drunk to oversee the artist's work, Burchell later discovered to his chagrin the banner under the bulldog, which should have read "Devil Dogs," had been indelibly misspelled "Divel Dags." The following morning, he was off to Vietnam where correcting this typographic error failed to make his priority list for the next thirteen months.

There are some who would say Burchell never came back from Vietnam, or maybe never wanted to come back. It was the high point of his youth, the transformational event that nothing else in his life ever lived up to. He got a Purple Heart—a small fragment from a mortar round pierced his deltoid muscle as he slept on the roof of a sandbag bunker, leaving a scar the size of a smallpox vaccination—and a Navy Achievement Medal with "V" for valor. His company commander had recommended him for that, ostensibly for his participation in four major combat operations, but really because he thought Burchell was going to make a career of the Corps and believed a personal decoration would help solidify his decision. At the time Burchell put little value in either, knowing the former was for an insignificant scratch it took six stitches to close and the latter a glorified good conduct medal; but as the years passed, their significance—and the deeds behind them—increased and multiplied in his mind. That hadn't always been the case. For decades Burchell had hardly mentioned his war experiences, but that changed when he saw the reception Iraq and Afghanistan veterans got on their return home. He felt cheated and wanted everyone to know that he too had served his country. Suddenly, his minor military achievements became, to him at least, the stuff of legend. He bought license plates that told the world he was a Vietnam Vet and had earned a Purple Heart. He plastered Marine Corps, First Marine Division, and Vietnam service medal decals on his car windows. And from the depths of the old sea bag in the corner of his attic he resurrected the sweat-stained, threadbare camouflaged cover he wore through most of his tour, its crown festooned with grenade rings and the three-inch nail-like missiles from an M-79 beehive round; one for each combat operation he fought in. He wore it every day as he patrolled the rambling acres of the Zebulon Pike Golf Course, an aging warrior on guard and on the ready. This quirky, faded remnant of youth long gone is what earned Burchell the sobriquet "Rambo." He didn't mind it at all.

*

"Burchell, could you slow it down?"

Karl winced as his rump slammed down on the cart seat. Moments earlier Burchell had hit the cart brakes hard in front of the clubhouse porch, stopping just long enough for Karl to hop in. Now they were rocketing down the tree line on the right side of the first fairway about to make a hard right toward the back nine. Burchell let up on the accelerator a bit, but just a bit. A few bone-jarring yards later they came to a stop by the eleventh tee. One player had yet to hit and the other three turned to give them a dirty look. Burchell and Karl waited for the foursome to head down the fairway before going up on the tee box to survey the terrain. Karl realized he had to get out on the course more, understand the lay of the land and commit it to memory; he still felt sheepish about his "kid cutting across the golf course" comment earlier. It remained a possibility that the mysterious stranger was just someone wandering around the course and not a homeless person taking up residence, but if he were just someone out for a walk, why would he feel the need to run away? They rode down the fairway near the place where the man had been seen coming out of the Winnehala.

"I guess he must have come up here, then dee-dee-mau'ed over there."

"Dee-dee what?"

"Dee-dee-mau'ed. Ran. High-tailed it. It's Vietnamese." Burchell gave the horizon a hard look.

Karl got out of the cart, pushed his way into the bushes, and found the ground quickly descended down to the fetid-smelling water. He saw footprints but no sign of a camp or that someone had spent the night. Coming back to the fairway, he crossed over to the ravine where he found more footprints. Karl knew the homeless, especially those with mental health issues, usually chose to hunker down as far away from others as possible, but why here? The ZPGC had been built in an age when wetlands were called swamps and not worth preserving, so no one had given a second thought to the idea of filling in enough of the Winnehala Wetlands to form this peninsula, but try as they might they couldn't alter the miasmic atmosphere of this part of the course; it was a boggy and cold and damp place even on midsummer nights, the worst possible campsite.

If the man Sundbaum's group had seen had spent the night out here, Karl mused, he must have been lost or drunk or both.

"You're out on the course bright and early, Burchell; you ever see anyone wandering around out here?"

Burchell shook his head. "Once in a blue moon I'll catch some numbnuts walking his dog, but that's pretty rare and never on this part of the course. These holes are the farthest point from the clubhouse and the street, so if he's not playing golf I can't figure out why anyone would be here."

"Well, it's probably nothing, but keep an eye out for him."

*

Sundbaum, Rankel, Armstead, and Hood weren't the only ones who had come across the mysterious stranger that morning. Dunn too had seen him. He was out on the fourteenth fairway marking a leak in the irrigation system for his crew to repair when he noticed a man in a hooded sweatshirt watching him from behind a tree between the thirteenth and fourteenth holes. Hardly one to be judgmental of eccentric behavior, Dunn paid no attention to him until the man's need to hide himself began to puzzle him. He certainly didn't mind if someone not intent on gouging up his turf with a golf club was on the course. This was, after all, the best time to appreciate its beauty, before the course was defiled by golfers and while the fairways and greens were still pristine. Who couldn't appreciate the beauty of a golf course, acres of verdant fields, each linked to the next, the whole sculpted, shaped, and mown into a living piece of art? If it wasn't for the idiots in the golf carts, Dunn thought, it could be mistaken for paradise.

Society is all but rude
To this delicious Solitude.

The few lines from Andrew Marvell failed to draw the man out so Dunn turned his attention back to the damp ground around the irrigation leak. When Dunn looked up again, he was gone.

*

Karl had Burchell drop him off near the first hole, saying he wanted to walk the course for a bit; the real reason was just to get out of the cart. Karl stopped to introduce himself to a foursome on the second tee and chatted with them about course conditions and the pace of play. Karl was pleased to learn this was their first round at ZPGC and, so far, they were enjoying the experience. Karl watched them rumble down the fairway in their carts and hit their second shots before he set off, keeping to the path on the right side of the fairway. It was turning into a fine day. The trees were bringing forth their leaves and spring was finally taking hold of the land. The greens had weathered the winter well and were already in mid-season shape. Karl made a mental note to run down to the maintenance building and compliment Dunn on his work. All he needed to do, Karl reflected, was to bring all of this to the attention of the golfing public and the Zebulon Pike had a very good chance of gaining market share and improving its prestige in the community.

Karl pondered these things as he cut across the second fairway to watch the play of the group going down four. He noticed one person didn't get out of the cart while the others hit. Karl followed them down the fairway. When they got to the green the same guy stayed in the cart; as he got closer, Karl recognized him.

"Ralph," said Karl, remembering to rhyme it with "safe." "It's good to see you here!"

"Ah, Ketterman, how do you do? Yes, I'm just tagging along with some friends, taking the opportunity to get a closer look at your realm."

Karl shook Milbank's hand, expecting to hear him say some nice things about the course, but he just smiled serenely. Karl waited for Milbank to introduce his friends, but he didn't do that either, so after a few more awkward words Karl walked off toward the clubhouse. As he passed the other cart he noticed both bags had membership tags from Lochenberry, the most exclusive and prestigious club in the state. That's the kind of people he liked to see out on his golf course.

*

Not everyone at the Zebulon Pike Golf Course was old, eccentric, or antisocial. There was a coterie of sane, healthy young people about the place, both among the staff and the clientele. All shared the foibles of youth in bloom—smoking pot, drinking to excess, farting in enclosed spaces, sexting—but these venialities were mitigated by their passion for the game. They admired Lumley's diagnostic eye, stood in awe of Crupshaw's achievements, hailed Franzen—Lumley's replacement as teaching professional— as their swing guru, and genuinely loved the anomalies of the ZPGC's layout, the often spongy, uneven fairways, diabolically undulating greens, cantankerous rough, and less-than-level tee boxes. Among the promising younger generation of golfers were Billy Lupus and Tony Hallenback, talented athletes to be sure, but the greatest of them all was Gretchen Schumacher, a nineteen-year-old scratch golfer who also worked part-time at ZPGC driving the beverage cart.

*

Karl saw Gretchen for the first time as he walked back to the clubhouse. It was her first day back at ZPGC as a seasonal employee. She was standing next to her cart digging out sports drinks for two pudgy fifty-somethings. The juxtaposition of her beauty and poise and their repulsive leering took him aback momentarily. He'd never seen a woman quite like her. She seemed almost a hallucination, a vision. Even this early in the season Gretchen was already lightly browned and, at six-feet tall, half a head taller than her customers—yet it was obvious she was completely comfortable with her height and physicality. To Karl, she looked like a Nordic fertility goddess with her golden plait of hair hanging almost to the middle of her back and her legs spaced in an athletic stance, ready and alert. As he watched her patiently waiting for one of the men to get his wallet from his bag, Karl thought Pygmalion must have imagined something very much like her when he sculpted his perfect woman: sensual, vibrant, virtuous, alluring and unattainable. Karl, rousing himself from his reverie, decided this was the perfect time for management to meet labor.

"Hello."

She looked at him a little askance then surrendered a slight smile. "Hello."

"I'm Karl Ketterman, the new course manager. I've only been here a couple weeks and haven't had time to meet everyone yet. I thought I would take the opportunity to introduce myself."

"Nice to meet you, Mr. Ketterman." Her hand was warm and soft and he realized he was holding on to it too long.

"Karl. And you are?"

Her laugh revealed her perfect snow-white teeth. Her eyes twinkled. He could see the pulse pump in her neck, sense the pure animal life in her. Karl felt himself stagger slightly.

"Wow! Where are my manners? Gretchen. Gretchen Schumacher. I work here too. I'm the cart girl."

Karl never knew stating the obvious could sound so charming, and her ingenuousness and sincerity really did make it charming.

"Really? Hey, that's great. Well I don't want to keep you from your job, Gretchen, but feel free to drop by my office any time."

She finished serving her customers, mounted her cart, and roared away, her breasts syncopating to the rhythm of the overloaded springs as she drove by Karl. He felt a stirring in his loins. His heart was full; Karl Ketterman had met the woman of his dreams.

Karl learned two things very quickly about Gretchen Schumacher. The first was that most of her male contemporaries found her unappealing; the truth was she intimidated them. She never deferred to men as other girls often did, never fawned over, petted, or made the slightest effort to build up a man's ego. But Gretchen was no daughter of Sappho; she liked boys. She was simply constitutionally incapable of being either coy or cute and physically beyond the bounds of cuddly. She was what most men liked least, a self-assured woman completely confident in her talents and her physical presence. She never viewed herself through the eyes of others, never judged her appearance wanting, and never weighed her worth on a scale balanced by contemporary ideals of femininity. Behind her back, girls called her "bitch" and boys whispered "dyke," but if Gretchen ever heard them she didn't let on. She was a bit of a loner, which was why she loved golf. The only people her age Gretchen hung around with were golfers, and in that sport she was far superior to most of them. Just watching her warm up on the range was cause for performance anxiety so the young golfing males at the ZPGC mostly stayed away from her. That pleased Karl. The second thing he learned about Gretchen did not, for it seems Gretchen was being drawn into the clutches of Phil "Fabio" Franzen, the PGA teaching professional at the Zebulon Pike Golf Course.

*

Franzen filled the void left by Lumley's retirement but not, at first, as a Parks Commission employee. He spent his first two years at the Zebulon Pike as an independent contractor. This arrangement, masterminded by Milbank, meant the city provided him no benefits, just an exclusive venue from which to ply his trade, but that came to an end when the civil service union got wind of it. Franzen taught the game very differently from Lumley; his teaching method was as far afield from Hogan's *Fundamentals of Modern Golf* as the space shuttle was from Lindbergh's *Spirit of St. Louis*. Franzen never just looked at a person's swing. He watched it on video, overlaying the images on a laptop with graphics and freezing the frame to analyze a particular point in the swing. It was a precise, analytical, detailed, and literal process. There was no poetry in either the method or the man.

In his second year at the ZPGC Franzen began to develop a following: his methods caught on, and not just those that dealt with golf. It wasn't surprising; Franzen was a striking figure, tall, powerfully built, and tan, but his hair was his real vanity. It was long and blond and he never covered it with a hat; every two weeks he had the highlights in it touched up. Franzen's conceit was so obvious everyone at the course was soon calling him Fabio, for like the Italian model famous for his handsome face and flowing locks, Franzen was a favorite with the ladies. It was said if a woman took lessons from him at least one of them was sure to be between the sheets.

*

Lumley watched Franzen work through the thin veil of smoke that drifted in front of his eyes. He kept his distance, of course, so he wasn't a distraction. It was hardly his fault if Franzen chose to conduct his lessons at the same end of the range where Charley parked. Lumley had to admit he was fascinated by Franzen at first, watching him set up his digital cameras, one down the line, the other to the side. The kid had introduced himself and invited Charley to take a closer look at the technology, to see the split-screen images, the way he could click and select the graphics to show alignment and swing plane and then juxtapose any of his students' swings with Tiger Woods' or Phil Michelson's, or even Hogan's. Franzen could see Lumley was impressed, but it wasn't in the way he thought. Lumley was impressed not by the technology, but by the need for it. Why would you want to fragment the swing, he thought, to see it in stages when it was a continuous motion? Lumley had learned to create a golf swing like the Pope creates bishops, by the laying on of hands. He formed their grip, set their posture, guided their takeaway and, with a touch of his finger, turned their shoulders that extra millimeter to get them to the perfect position at the top.

Of course, Lumley knew there was nothing really new in what Franzen was doing: Bobby Jones had used slow-motion photography in the instructional films he made in the 1930s. Armour, Sarazen, Hogan, and a hundred others had done essentially the same thing with a series of drawings or photos in their books and it all served a purpose, but not here, not on the driving range. Once a person took a golf club in hand, as Lumley saw it, he entered a kinetic, instinctive world. Lumley wanted his students to think of the swing as unity, not sequence. A musician learns scales and masters technique but when he plays a piece he has to get beyond mere mechanical execution to create a transcendent, sensual, emotional experience. The golf swing, in Lumley's mind, was no different. "Pick a target and hit the ball at it," Lumley would say. He didn't need to watch a video to know whether the swing was good or not. He watched the ball. It could only go where the swing sent it; his job was to teach the golfer to watch his ball flight and learn from it. That was what the game was all about, to flight the ball left or right, high or low, with however slender a sense of confidence one could muster. In the end, that's what it got down to: believing you could propel that little white ball at your target. There are no video monitors on the course, just you, the ball, your clubs, and eighteen holes to conquer. If a golfer starts to break down his swing on the course, he is sure to hit the shoals of self-doubt. The great saints warned of the dangers of over-scrupulousness, of how nitpicking your peccadilloes can lead to spiritual aridity and loss of faith; Lumley's sentiments exactly.

Lumley took it all in and marveled at the human inventiveness that created this amazing technology. He wished Franzen success and stepped away to watch from a distance, occasionally sharing a thought with no one in particular.

*

After being embarrassed by his unfamiliarity with the course, Karl decided to spend time boning up on both its topography and history. He knew the general outline of that history but with the season underway and the Ebon Invitational and the Keegan Cap coming, Ketterman began to delve into the dust-covered albums, work journals, maps, and account books that filled his office.

While his predecessors may have had their foibles, Karl soon discovered they had all followed the precedent established by Odegaard and kept detailed records of the yearly events at the course. On the bookcase behind his desk Karl found the records of every event held at the ZPGC over the years—the Juniors Tournament (Boys), the Juniors Tournament (Girls), the Women's Club Championship, the Men's Club Championship, the Ebon Invitational for Negro Golfers, the Keegan Cap, and the Autumnal Open. Each volume covered a decade; the ones up to 1980 were perfect-bound and had leather covers. After 1968 the title on the volumes for the Ebon Invitational for Negro Golfers was shortened to the Ebon Invitational. He knew the Keegan Cap was the ZPGC's cornerstone event, but Karl decided to start with the one he was least familiar with and most curious about: the Ebon Invitational.

*

Hindsight usually gets things ass-backwards and to say from our vantage point that Wilbur Odegaard—the man responsible for the existence of the Ebon Invitational— believed in racial equality and the brotherhood of man would be to serve both the truth and the man badly. He was, in fact, no different from most white men of his time or this time: uneasy around blacks, unsure how to converse with them, and confused by why they seemed to speak louder the closer they got to one another. While he may have had no special love for blacks, Odegaard hated snobs and overt bigotry, racism, and exclusion, attitudes he had faced growing up as a Swede right off the boat with illiterate parents and a funny accent. He worked hard to lose the accent and to fit in and he succeeded. He captained his high school football team and left college to fight in the First World War. When he returned he won a seat on the Parks Commission, which he resigned to become the first manager of the Zebulon Pike Golf Course, where his sense of fair play received its greatest test.

Odegaard never intended to create a controversy or to start a tournament that would become a minor national sensation. It began innocently enough when one of the grounds crew, a fellow named Obadiah Sumter, approached him one afternoon as he was walking to his car and asked if he and three other blacks on the staff could play Monday mornings if they promised to tee off before five-thirty a.m. and only play the holes farthest from the clubhouse. Odegaard was taken aback; first, because it had never crossed his mind that blacks played golf, and second, because Sumter had felt it necessary to ask his permission. In fairness to Sumter, it should be noted he was from rural Louisiana and had only come north the year before; to him this was the prudent path for a black man to travel. To Odegaard, who had been schooled under the benevolent gaze of Abraham Lincoln, it smacked of the plantation and the antebellum South, and he bristled. Odegaard was no naïf; he knew the PGA specifically excluded blacks, as did virtually every golf course from Massachusetts to California, but they also excluded Jews and Catholics, neither of which group Odegaard particularly liked either, but that had nothing to do with the matter at hand. You didn't have to like someone, he reasoned, to believe they had a right to life, liberty, and the pursuit of happiness, and in Odegaard's reckoning those three truisms were what golf was all about; more to the point, the Zebulon Pike Golf Course had no written ban prohibiting anyone from the premises, and from the day it opened it had reserved Monday mornings before eleven a.m. for employee play.

Odegaard opened his truck, took out his driver, and with a crooked finger beckoned Sumter to the first tee. Asking the group on the tee for their forbearance, he teed a ball and invited

Sumter to hit it. At first Sumter demurred, but Odegaard insisted it was absolutely necessary if he was to make a decision on his request. Sumter took the driver, set up to the ball, and hit a slight draw down the middle of the fairway, not particularly long, but considering the circumstances an admirable shot.

"I look forward to greeting you and your group next Monday, Mr. Sumter, anytime before eleven a.m. I am afraid, however, I cannot accommodate any special requests. You will begin play on the first tee and play the course in the same order as all other players. I assume you will observe the etiquette of the game at all times," Odegaard said as he took his driver from Sumter's hand, which he shook, then he walked back to his car.

This historic moment in the history of race relations in our city was recorded on three handwritten sheets of paper, written and signed by Obadiah Sumter on the day after Wilbur Odegaard died in 1947. Karl then found tucked in the back of the record book for *The Ebon Invitational for Negro Golfers.*

7

Sumter's group played the following Monday and, as expected, Odegaard got complaints. He bore the invective from all who offered it then countered by asking by what authority, according to which rule, bylaw, or regulation either of the course, the USGA, the city, or state was he to ban Negroes from playing the course? That was usually all it took to send intolerant blusterers on their way. Even in those long-ago days, most citizens of this fair city considered themselves progressive and forward-thinking, so after the shock wore off—and a little posturing by the more bigoted patrons of the course about legal action—the controversy lost its edge. And no one, regardless of race, creed, national origin, economic status, or any of the other categories we love to parse ourselves into in our great nation, has been turned away from the ZPGC since—as long as they wore the requisite collared shirt and footwear, played from their own bag, and paid their greens fees.

Sumter's initiative gained him some prestige among his friends, and a few years after his first meeting with the manager, he was delegated to approach him again with the idea of a tournament for Negro golfers at the Zebulon Pike. Odegaard hadn't seen this coming so he demurred, saying he had to take it up with the Parks Commission as, he quickly added, he would with any request to hold a tournament at the course. The Parks Commission was thrown into turmoil, fearing their vision of operating a municipal course with the dignity and tone of a country club hung in the balance. But it was 1936, play was down and some felt the age of the country club, if not golf itself, had reached its nadir and a new proletarian state was on the horizon, so what did it matter if some Negroes took over the course one day a year? Others weren't so sure. A compromise was reached when someone suggested they not be allowed to use "Negro" in the tournament's title, thus keeping the whole thing out of the public's attention. The commissioners then fobbed the duty of announcing this cavil to Sumter onto Odegaard. On the drive back to the course Odegaard devised a brilliant stratagem for doing it.

"Sumter, the Parks Commission says okay. You boys can have your tournament. All you have to do now is propose a couple of dates and we'll see which one fits into next year's events calendar."

"Why, thank you, Mr. Odegaard, I'm very pleased to hear that and I appreciate you going to bat for us."

Odegaard squirmed a bit at the compliment. "So, what are you thinking of calling it?"

"Sir?"

"Your tournament. It's going to need a name."

Sumter thought for a moment. "I don't know. How about the City-Wide Negro Golf Tournament?"

Odegaard frowned. "That's okay, but I'd consider a name that would really class it up a little; say, the Ebon Invitational. If it's an invitational not just any Negro can show up and play; you've got to *invite* him."

Now it was Sumter's turn to frown. "I get that, Mr. Odegaard, but I don't get the Ebon part."

"It's just a fancy word for Negro; kind of gives it a little pizzazz."

Sumter's frown softened. "Tell me exactly how this invitational thing works."

"Well, the committee, which right now is you, has to extend a personal invitation to each participant. That's the only way they can play in the event."

Odegaard could see Sumter was warming to the idea and he was pleased. He felt he had found the way to keep things under control. An open event would mean a big tournament; an invitational assured it would most likely be limited to Sumter's immediate friends. An open event could take on a life of its own; an invitational might die in its infancy. His gambit played, Odegaard awaited Sumter's response.

Sumter was not an educated man, but he was not a stupid one, either. As he sat there, thoughts began to swirl in his brain and as they did they cleared away all his doubts and fears about running a golf tournament. Obadiah Sumter was about to become somebody to reckon with.

*

The 1937 Ebon Invitational was indeed a modest affair, three foursomes in all participated. A tent was erected near the maintenance building where the wives of the players laid out a sumptuous meal. Mr. Odegaard made an appearance but excused himself shortly after presenting the trophy to the winner. He left feeling very good, however, for it appeared to him the Ebon Invitational, even if it continued, would be a small and relatively obscure event.

Obadiah Sumter had a very different take on the day. As small as it was, the Ebon Invitational had changed his life. He was beginning to be seen by other blacks as a man who could get things done, who could open doors and expand opportunities for them in this city. And that had an effect on how Sumter saw himself. He was no longer just a worker on the golf course, he was a leader in his community, and while it pleased him to be seen as someone who opened doors and expanded opportunities, he began to think about how this tournament might benefit him financially as well.

The next year the Ebon Invitational had six foursomes. In its fourth year, to Odegaard's chagrin, Sumter changed the name to the Ebon Invitational for Negro Golfers. Ten years later there were fourteen foursomes. After Wilbur Odegaard died during the 1947 Keegan Cap, Obadiah reserved four spots for white golfers from the ZPGC as a tribute to him. By 1955 the Ebon Invitational was one of the biggest events in the United States for black golfers, drawing players from as far away as Saint Louis, Kansas City, and Chicago, facts the Parks Commissioners were loathe to admit and careful not to advertise.

49

As it grew, the tournament remained firmly in the hands of Sumter. He set the entry fee, he collected the money, he ran the Calcutta, he distributed the prizes, and he prospered mightily as the Ebon Invitational went from a single afternoon round to a three-day event—Friday practice round, Saturday qualifying round, Sunday final—that gathered a fairly significant gallery. No one questioned his authority; after all, wasn't Sumter the man who had demanded (so the story went) the right of Negroes to play the course in the first place? Wasn't he the one who had single-handedly brought one of the biggest golf events for Negroes in the country into being?

Even though non-golfers in this city knew nothing about the Ebon Invitational, enthusiasts of the game of all races were soon coming to see the high caliber of play exhibited at the Ebon Invitational. Excluded from the PGA and marginalized by the USGA, some of the greatest black golfers in America flocked to the ZPGC to compete, gamble among themselves, and take part in the festivities on and off the course. And all this pageantry and splendor remained exclusively under the benevolent, dignified, sober, and unquestioned guidance of Obadiah Sumter until the day he died in 1966.

The world outside ZPGC changed quickly in that decade and the Ebon Invitational soon began to wane. War, social upheaval, and assassinations created a demand for equality and events like the Ebon Invitational for Negro Golfers, once the pride of the Negro community, now seemed to smack of second-class citizenship to them. By the early seventies, the Ebon Invitational stopped drawing out-of-town players. By the turn of the century, it was a vapor trail of its former self, down to four foursomes and ineptly and unprofitably run by Sumter's son Tyreal. But like his father before him, Tyreal still saw potential, albeit dormant, in the Ebon Invitational.

*

At six-foot-five and three-hundred-seventy pounds, Tyreal "Fort" Sumter commanded attention. He carried himself with the military bearing drummed into him during his Army career. Even though he'd spent most of it stationed in Kentucky and Georgia, when he retired as a Master Sergeant he came back home to the Midwest. Drawn by family, childhood friends, and a desire to resuscitate the Ebon Invitational and restore it to its former grandeur, Tyreal returned to his hometown and the course he had grown up on, spending every fair weather day in the intervening twenty years at the ZPGC.

In many ways, Tyreal was exactly where his father was in 1937. He too had complete control of an event that every objective observer felt had no future, yet Tyreal waded into the challenge with absolute confidence and, even after years of futility, he continued to charge forward with a bigger, more grandiose agenda every season. Year after year, he made outrageous promises he failed to deliver on: first he said Charley Sifford would be the honorary starter; then Tiger Woods would play in the Ebon; then Calvin Peete would be his co-chair; then Jim Dent would come to receive a lifetime achievement award. The general consensus around the clubhouse among players of all races, genders, and handicaps was that Tyreal was long on talk, short on delivery, and the Ebon sank even lower in their estimation.

The only true believer left was Cyrus "Scrumpy" Scroggins, Tyreal's boyhood pal. Tyreal was Scrumpy's hero; too timid to follow his pal into the Army, Scrumpy lived vicariously through Tyreal's stories of military life, never mind the fact that Tyreal spent most of his career operating EM clubs; it was still an adventurous life compared with Scrumpy's as a school janitor. When Tyreal went to see Karl Ketterman to discuss his plans for this year's Ebon Invitational, Scrumpy Scroggins followed him into the office like a pilot fish trailing a shark.

Karl, gazing across the room and daydreaming about Gretchen, didn't notice Tyreal in his doorway until his booming voice shattered his concentration.

"I'd like to talk to you, Hoss." Tyreal called people he didn't know or didn't particularly like "Hoss;" the jury was still out on whether Ketterman fell into the latter category. Even the sixty pounds Tyreal had put on since mustering out couldn't obliterate the posture of a soldier or the cadence and intonation of a senior NCO. He had Ketterman's attention.

"Take a seat." Karl gestured to one of the ancient oak office chairs in front of his desk. Scrumpy stayed in the doorway.

Before taking a seat Tyreal reached across the desk. "I'm Tyreal Sumter, chairman of the Ebon Invitational tournament, the senior event here at the ZPGC and one of the most prestigious events in the black community nationwide."

Karl felt his hand being consumed by Tyreal's. He tried not to wince.

"Very glad to meet you, Tyreal. As a matter of fact, I've been reading up on it and how your dad got it started. You must be very proud."

Tyreal eyed Karl. He'd been smooth-talked before and could tell when it was coming his way again, but the kid seemed to mean what he was saying.

"Yes I am. That's why I've worked so hard to keep up the tradition he began. This year, in fact, I believe it will be bigger than it has been in years."

"Well, Mr. Sumter, I certainly will do anything in my power to help. The more successful the Ebon Invitational is, the better for the Zebulon Pike. I'd love to hear what you've got planned."

Karl sat back; Tyreal spun a tale. And so the morning passed.

8

As Ketterman lent his ear to Tyreal's delusions, Gabriel Dunn, barely distinguishable from the shrubbery in his ubiquitous green jumpsuit, passed the clubhouse like a specter. It was a rare occasion when he ventured this far from the maintenance building, so the few people who did notice him, even most regulars of the ZPGC, had no idea who he was.

Gabriel was in a meditative mood, thinking about the odd fellow he kept seeing on the golf course, someone who didn't belong out there. Sundbaum, Rankel, Armstead, and Hood called him the "homeless guy," but Dunn wasn't so sure. In his experience with homeless people—he'd been one himself for a while some years back—they could be in a world of their own, sullen, unresponsive, even angry, but not as skittish and elusive as this guy. True, they did tend to keep their lairs secret, but this fellow made a considerable effort not to be seen at all, and the only time he'd been seen was early in the morning.

Dunn had seen him again this morning, moving through the mist toward the Winnehala Wetlands, which seemed the least likely location for anyone to camp out. There were better places around the golf course or in the neighboring parks far less miasmic and mosquito-ridden and more conducive to a comfortable night's sleep. No, Dunn was convinced this guy was up to something.

*

Karl, in a bit of a haze after an hour listening to Tyreal, sat at the counter waiting to get a cup of coffee from Cybil when Mo Mittenthal tapped him on the shoulder.

"Dunn wants to talk to you."

It took a second for the name to register. "The greenskeeper?"

"Yep, he's outside."

Ketterman hadn't seen Dunn since his first week on the job when he'd introduced himself to the crew down at the maintenance building. All he'd gotten out of Dunn was a handshake and a nod of the head; now Dunn wanted to chat. Karl was intrigued. Dunn was standing out near the golf carts, his tall, lank body floating somewhere inside the oversized coveralls; Ketterman thought he looked like an inmate in a third-world prison. When Karl was within a few yards of him, Dunn made eye contact, turned and walked toward the maintenance building. Karl followed. Dunn lead him to a rickety old picnic table at the back end of the building where the crew congregated for lunch and after-work beers. Dunn sat and gestured to Karl to join him. Dunn surveyed the sky, then scrutinized Karl for a moment.

"There was a guy out on the course in the morning; I've seen him a couple times now on the back nine."

"The homeless guy. Yeah, I've heard about him. Some players were complaining about him. I suppose I should call the cops or social services."

"He's not a homeless guy."

"I guess all the more reason to call the cops."

Dunn stared over his head so intently Karl was tempted to turn around, but then Dunn directed his eyes at him again, tapping his finger on the table.

"I'd wait on that. Let me look into this more first."

Karl shrugged. "Fine by me. I mean he's not hurting anything, right? And other than you and a few early birds, nobody else has seen him, so I'd just as soon leave him alone; maybe he'll just go away on his own."

Dunn shrugged, got up, and disappeared into the depths of the maintenance building.

"Nice chatting with you," Karl mumbled as he walked back to the clubhouse.

*

Ralph Milbank caught a faint whiff of bacon in the air.

"A Ms. Stumpher here to see you, Mr. Milbank."

He looked up to see his secretary and a rather formidable female. "Thank you, Grace. Please have a seat, Ms. Stumpher."

The chair gave a submissive creak as Cybil's voluminous buttocks settled down on it. "Big demand for BLTs today?"

The comment confused Cybil. She stared blankly at him. Milbank could see beads of sweat forming on her upper lip. He smiled a secret smile, knowing the effect his position and this office had on Parks employees. He allowed himself to be magnanimous.

"I know you must feel a little uncomfortable coming to me like this, but I want to assure you our conversation will be held in the strictest confidence. Whenever I get an email or a phone call from any Parks employee with a concern, I want to address them in person. I was more than willing to meet anywhere convenient to you, so I appreciate you dropping by after work like this. Now, if I recall correctly, you work at the Zebulon Pike Golf Course?" Milbank in his youth had thought his future lay in the law and fancied himself a natural at questioning people, of conducting a methodical interrogation that slowly turned the facts to his advantage. He studied Cybil's personnel file as he asked a series of inane questions, transferring the sheets of paper from one side of the manila folder to the other, nodding sagely at her answers. When he felt the moment was ripe he moved onto the main topic.

"It's obvious," he said, giving the sheet below his hovering hand a slight tap with his index finger, "you've been an exemplary employee of the Parks Commission for a number of years, Ms. Stumpher, so when someone like you feels they have to come directly to me with an issue, I know it has to be important; tell me what's on your mind."

Cybil swallowed. She simultaneously wanted a drink of water and a bathroom break. By putting so much importance on what she had to say, Milbank was making her question whether it really was. Cybil was terrified. She pushed her tongue between her teeth and lips, trying to break the dry seal forming between them. Why had she come here?

"I'm not...I feel, maybe, Mr. Ketterman is in over his head," Cybil blurted out. She looked at the floor waiting for Milbank's response.

Milbank discreetly texted his secretary and in a moment she came in with a bottle of water and offered it to Cybil. She twisted off the cap and drank deeply. Milbank looked at her benignly, saying nothing. He counted to ten and then took a deep breath.

"Change is difficult for us all, Ms. Stumpher, and the Zebulon Pike is going through a lot of it right now, so I understand how you must feel. At the same time, I must allow Mr. Ketterman to do his job as he sees fit." He could see her wilting under this mild reprimand; it was time to build her back up. "At the same time, it would hardly be fair to ignore your concerns. Coming here was not easy for you, I can see that, but I know you did it out of a sense of duty and I commend you for it; however, before I can address any shortcomings in Mr. Ketterman's job performance I need to give him time to prove his worth. And I need specific examples of where he's not measuring up." Milbank rose and came around his desk. The smell of bacon began to commingle with a hint of Lysol. He looked down on Cybil but she kept looking straight ahead.

"My duties make it difficult to get out of this office very often, so I'm going to ask a favor of you, Cybil." She looked up, softened by the sound of her name. "I want you to keep notes, a journal of anything that concerns you about the management of the golf course. Be specific, note the date and time of each incident and give details. At the end of the season, before I do Mr. Ketterman's performance appraisal, I'll ask for your notes. I know I'm asking a lot of you, Cybil, but I'm confident you're up to the task. I want to thank you again for coming down."

He went to the door and opened it. It took Cybil a moment to understand their meeting was over. Rising and turning to leave, she saw his extended hand and beaming face. He covered her hand with both of his, patting it as he turned her gently out, like a tug guiding an ocean liner out to sea.

*

While Karl Ketterman held the title of general manager of the Zebulon Pike Golf Course, the city's byzantine civil service rules actually put control of it under a triumvirate. As general manager, he was responsible for overseeing the staff that worked in and around the clubhouse and the revenue generated by the course, driving range, and pro shop, but the food and beverage manager and the greenskeeper ran separate fiefdoms. If Dunn needed a new mower, he sent in a requisition to Supervisor of Lands and Buildings, if Cybil needed a new grill, she dealt with the Supervisor of Food Services. The general manager did participate in their performance appraisals but they were autonomous in their daily duties. This arcane arrangement lead to much confusion; for example, Karl was responsible for Gretchen's salary, but the income she generated selling soda, beer, candy bars, and sandwiches on the course were accounted as food and beverage income. And when Dunn got the mower he requisitioned through Lands and Buildings it appeared in Karl's budget as an expense. These anomalies were not explained to Karl before he took the position; they were among the many little surprises that seemed to greet him every day.

T.S. Eliot said April is the cruelest month. Gabriel Dunn and Karl Ketterman would, no doubt, concur. Even though golf in our climate is best played from late May until early October, public golf courses, if they're going to make a profit, are forced to open as soon as the frost leaves the ground, and to stay open until the first snow falls. At a private course the greenskeeper usually determines when it opens and closes; Dunn had that prerogative when it came to closing for the year, but the Parks Commission, frustrated with the ZPGC's falling income, had in recent years mandated it open as soon as the snow was off the ground, regardless of how it affected the fairways and greens. Dunn's deft touch with all growing things was the only reason the ZPGC looked as good as it did. And while Ketterman studied the daily receipts and Dunn husbanded the vegetation, Rambo Burchell herded the mammals.

*

Stokes despised the third hole. He hated its simplicity, its obviousness. There was no challenge to it, just an unobstructed hundred-and-thirty yards to a generous and level green. True, there was a small bunker on the right but it was set far enough from the green that a push or slight slice would land safely above it. There was nothing intimidating in front or to the left side, but ten yards behind the green there loomed a thicket of trees. When he didn't chuck his tee shot and leave it fifty yards short, Stokes usually thinned it into those trees; either led to a five more often than not.

Stokes marveled at how he could stand on the range and hit ball after ball right between the one hundred and one-hundred-and-fifty-yard signs yet still fail so consistently on this hole. His hatred of it was further exacerbated this day by playing not only with Crupshaw, but also with Franzen and the Lupus kid. Franzen was playing rounds with all the junior golfers he thought had the potential to qualify for the State Amateur this year; he invited Crupshaw along to share his experience in it with Lupus. Stokes had had the choice of playing with them or waiting an hour for the next open spot on the tee sheet; he reluctantly filled out the foursome. Such was the fate of a man with no regular golf buddies.

Their tee shots were all on the green and they stood to the side of the tee box politely awaiting Stokes' shot. He pegged his ball and stepped back, taking several deep breaths, trying mightily to force positive thoughts into his head. He shrugged his shoulders to release the tension, took two practice swings and addressed the ball. He picked the club up, turned his shoulders, and made his move back to the ball. Somewhere in that split second he came up just enough to put the leading edge of his 9-iron on the equator of the ball. He watched as it flew low over the green and rattled off several trees before coming to rest somewhere among them.

"Caught that one a little thin," Lupus observed casually.

"Are you sure? Really? Cause it felt pure to me," Stokes said as he slammed his club into his bag and got in the cart. Crupshaw, his cart partner, said nothing.

The undergrowth wasn't fully leafed out so it should have been easy to find his ball had it not rolled behind a root. All four of them were searching for it when Rambo came rolling up. A stiff plastic flag with "Ranger" stenciled on it quivered over the cart's roof. Merril despised many things and most men, but very few more than he did Rambo.

"Slow play is killing the game, gentlemen," Rambo barked.

Crupshaw looked at Rambo and jabbed a thumb in Stokes' direction. Franzen and Lupus walked on the green and marked their balls. Merril tried to pretend Rambo wasn't there.

"You're falling off the pace, guys." With that parting shot Rambo hit the accelerator and drove down the cart path. Stokes was livid.

"Who does that little tin god think he is? There's no one behind us. I've been looking for my ball for thirty seconds, for chrissakes!" He pulled a ball from his pocket, threw it on the ground, and went to the cart to get a club. The next shot didn't go so well, nor the next, and he walked off with a six. Sitting in the cart looking back toward the green put him in the perfect position to notice his first ball behind the tree root. He retrieved it as his blood pressure approached one-forty over ninety.

Stokes hated playing with better players. When he did he was always the shortest and the most wayward off the tee, the one who took the most putts, the one the others had to help to find his ball, yet time and time again he put himself in this position. All he had to do was say no and wait for another opening in the tee sheet. What did it matter to him? He was retired. He had all the time in the world. Why did everyone say if you played with good golfers it would rub off on you? Nothing rubbed off on Stokes, but many things chafed. And it only took the third hole and Rambo to sour this round and ruin the day for him.

*

Psychological studies have shown how heartlessly human beings can behave, how ordinary people will gladly inflict physical or psychological pain on others if they believe they are duly authorized to do it. Rambo Burchell validated those studies the second he sat behind the wheel of the ranger's cart. The ZPGC scorecard states golfers should finish eighteen holes in approximately four hours. It was an ideal, something to be striven for, not a mandate. But Burchell saw it as an absolute and felt it his duty to keep every foursome on pace for a four-hour round whether they were playing on a weekday morning or weekend afternoon. Everyone, without exception, should be in position to complete the round in four hours as far as Burchell was concerned; "approximately" be damned. Being a ranger is a thankless job. The pay is low, no one is glad to see you, and if you suffer from piles like Burchell, spending eight hours bouncing down boggy fairways makes for a long and uncomfortable day. But Burchell was a man consumed with a sense of duty. He rode on through the pain, constantly in motion, racing about the course, zigzagging from front to back nine, doubling back suddenly to make sure a group was heeding his warning, never keeping to a predictable pattern, and always, always on the alert for laggards. His motto was simple, "Slow play is killing the game," and he meant to keep it alive.

Stokes followed his triple on three with a double bogey on four; his brow darkened. Crupshaw had played enough with him to read his mood and after getting several monosyllabic responses, he stopped trying to talk with Stokes and let him stew in silence. Franzen and Lupus were in a world of their own, discussing how Lupus should play each hole, the best way to recover from an errant shot, and how best to attack every pin. Crupshaw, although shorter than both of them off the tee, still hit most greens in regulation; when he didn't, his short game made up the difference and he remained one shot off the pace set by a kid fifty years younger than him. All of this was gall and wormwood to Merril Stokes.

*

By the time they reached the ninth tee Stokes had descended into his own personal hell. He was twelve over par and needed no worse than a bogey to finish the front with a score under fifty. He watched Lupus, Franzen, and Crupshaw drive straight down the fairway, Lupus' ball finishing well over three hundred yards. The spirit drained from Stokes. He teed his ball up and hit without attempting anything resembling a pre-shot routine. He swung without thought, without commitment, without hope; he was a man going through the motions. The ball cracked off the clubface and flew off down the fairway.

"Nice ball."

It was the first time he'd heard that all day and Stokes' heart was full. He could see the ball coming to rest in the middle of the fairway, almost up with Crupshaw's. He wanted to talk about his drive but knew the group would ridicule him if he suddenly switched moods so he kept silent. Yet in that silence he heard a voice saying, "Par this hole and you'll have a forty-eight on the front; shoot forty-one on the back and you've broken ninety." He'd shot forty-one on the back before, why shouldn't he do it again?

The ninth hole is the number one handicap at the Zebulon Pike Golf Course, a long par four with an elevated green and a large water hazard running down the left side of the fairway from about the two-hundred-yard mark to just short of the green. Franzen gave Stokes his distance with his rangefinder; one-hundred-seventy-two-yards, a distance Stokes felt he could carry comfortably with his 5-iron. He was walking the few steps back to the cart when he heard the rumble of another one coming across the fairway. It was Burchell. Stokes was determined to ignore him.

"You gentlemen should be on your way to the tenth tee by now. Please pick up your pace."

Franzen saluted Rambo. Lupus bowed. Crupshaw gave him the finger. Stokes fumed. Burchell held his ground. He was out of Stokes' peripheral vision so it was fair to assume he was staying put so Stokes wouldn't hear the sound of his cart driving off as he swung; or maybe he just wanted to see the shot. Stokes interpreted it differently. He saw it as a provocation, a subtle act of intimidation, a hex. He was tense and angry; he came over the top of the ball and hooked it into the water hazard. Through a haze of hatred he heard their voices chanting in unison like the chorus in a Greek tragedy.

"That one's for you, McAdoo!"

A very thin line separates the rational human being from the purely reactive primate, and the sight of his ball skipping twice then disappearing in those waters, and the sound of that chant erased it in Stokes' mind. His breath came fast and shallow and the sound of his heartbeat filled his ears. His mouth went dry and when he tried to speak it was unintelligible aside from a few random words—"you...goddamned...smash...your...!"

Lupus and Franzen turned away, unable to keep from laughing. Crupshaw thought Stokes was having a stroke. Burchell wasn't really paying attention and that was unfortunate because it left him open to Stokes' initial salvo, a 5-iron flung like a lumberjack's axe right at his cart. The Plexiglas windshield took the full impact of Stokes' rage, booming like a gunshot when the club hit it. The stunned Burchell got out of the cart, ducking an incoming 9-iron. He remembered on old axiom he had learned in the Marines: when unarmed, rush a man with a gun, run from a man with a knife; deducing a golf club was more like a knife than a gun, Burchell turned heels and started running just as Stokes' wedge helicoptered over his head. He could hear Crupshaw yelling at Stokes to calm down. He didn't look back.

*

Ketterman, head in hands, stared at the desktop. He hoped when he looked up again it would have all gone away; it hadn't. Merril Stokes, disheveled and more or less back to his senses, sat handcuffed to a chair, bracketed by two Parks policepersons: Officer Clack, gigantic, male, and placid; Officer Spurgeon petite, female, and stern. Burchell stood against the wall on Officer Clack's right. The proceedings awaited the arrival of the three witnesses to the incident who had gone to their cars to put away their clubs. When everyone was in place Karl asked Officer Spurgeon to close the door. He could see a crowd of gawkers gathering outside his office; some had been on the course when Stokes erupted, others were drawn by the police car turning into the ZPGC, lights on and siren screaming. Karl wished they hadn't done that.

Karl asked Merril if he was calm enough to discuss the situation. Stokes nodded his head, keeping his eyes to the ground. Karl asked the officers to remove the handcuffs. Clack was willing but Spurgeon balked. Clack reminded her that Stokes had shown no resistance when they arrested him; in fact, he seemed remorseful and embarrassed. Spurgeon frowned when Clack took the cuffs off, keeping her hand on the butt of her pistol.

"Mr. Stokes, what happened out there?" Karl asked.

Merril had a hundred things he wanted to say but knew not one of them justified what he had done. The good news was he hadn't hit Burchell either with the clubs or when he tried to run him down with the ranger cart. He was still sitting in that cart, gripping the steering wheel and staring off into space when Clack and Spurgeon arrested him.

Stokes looked up at Karl and shrugged.

Karl turned to Franzen, Crupshaw, and Lupus. The big lumpish youngster described the situation pithily: "Stokes went ape shit." Franzen phrased it more delicately: "I guess we were playing with a dangerous psychotic." Crupshaw alone offered some defense for Stokes' actions by stating what everyone knew: sometimes Rambo rubbed people the wrong way; Crupshaw realized he had a job to do, but there was no doubt he could be a bit too zealous.

"So I deserve a 5-iron in my forehead?" Burchell said, pushing his camouflaged cover back on his balding head.

"I didn't say that, Burchell; but I think it would be best for everyone if you two guys just shook hands and we all forgot about this," Crupshaw replied.

Karl gave Burchell a pleading look. Burchell scowled. Franzen piped in. "Maybe Stokes should be taken in for a psychological evaluation; for all we know he could have homicidal tendencies. He might go off again and kill a whole bunch of us."

Stokes groaned. Now it was his turn to bury his face in his hands. If there was anyone on the verge of murder, now it was Karl; he glared at Franzen.

"It's the game," Crupshaw said. He left it at that until he noticed everyone was waiting for more. "Anyone who plays golf knows how it gets to you. Didn't Bobby Jones say something about golf revealing character? Well, character varies. Some people are laid back, others are high strung; some are happy-go-lucky, others pretty much pissed off all the time, like Merril. It doesn't really matter who you are, sooner or later golf is going to bring something out you're not particularly proud of."

He paused and gestured at Lupus and Franzen. "The kid there stuck his sand wedge in the ground after he left his ball in the bunker on five; some would call that going ape shit." Lupus offered a weak smile. "And half the course must have heard the F-bomb Franzen dropped when he three-putted two. To someone who didn't play golf I bet that would have seemed kind of psychotic." Franzen rolled his eyes. "I think Burchell and Stokes should"—Crupshaw checked himself before "bury the hatchet" came out of his mouth— "make peace. Turning this into a big deal isn't going to do anyone any good and it certainly isn't going to help the golf course any."

The room was silent. Karl gave Burchell a pleading look. Burchell stepped forward, tapped Stokes on the shoulder and extended his hand. Officer Spurgeon's grip tightened on her automatic as Stokes stood, took Burchell's hand, and shook it. The look on Merril's face showed how truly sorry and deeply contrite he was. Karl felt a wave of relief wash over him when he heard Stokes apologize and Rambo accept it with a smile. All was right at the Zebulon Pike. At least for now.

Ralph Milbank abhorred nature, preferring to live in environments he could control, so even though it was a lovely spring afternoon, his car windows were up, the inside air conditioned to a perfect sixty-five degrees Fahrenheit, and the sounds of birds and happy children smothered by the local Golden Oldies station. Milbank turned off a suburban street to the sounds of the Mamas and Papas and entered the wrought iron gates of Lochenberry, our state's most prestigious private golf club and the playground of the leading scions of business, media, and politics in this most Midwestern of cities. He parked in the back of the lot to avoid tipping the attendant and walked up the curved drive to the front door of the clubhouse.

A young woman waiting in the entryway led Ralph to the boardroom where Robert Midge and Frank Chartreuse awaited him. The width of a long mahogany table separated them; Robert and Frank reached across to take Ralph's hand. He looked down to see an aerial map of the Zebulon Pike Golf Course, the lots of the new housing development superimposed over the fairways. Then he noticed a fourth person seated at the far end of the table. Ralph gave him a nod and took a seat.

"That's Dan Casserly," Midge said with a dismissive wave of his hand in the man's direction, "He's just leaving." Casserly got up and left. Midge waited a moment after the door closed before he continued. He was a loud, loutish, imperious man of thirty-five, raised in affluence and suckled on arrogance, one of the blessed for whom everything is provided; Midge had never wanted, never struggled, never lacked, yet he never tired of pontificating on things he knew nothing of, like want, struggle, and lack. Midge was providing the funding—actually, it was his father's money—for the proposed development that would establish his independence as a man of business (so his father prayed) and elevate Milbank's political power. Frank Chartreuse built luxury homes, the "McMansions" that littered the two-acre lots at the far-flung edges of the metropolitan area, glittering dreamlands of marble, high ceilings, glass, and wasted space. It was his aesthetic that would transform the ZPGC into the most desired home sites in the area.

"Casserly's a hydrologist; I've got him snooping and pooping around the ZPGC." Midge saw concern on Milbank's face. "Don't worry. He's being very discreet. He's been there a couple times early in the morning. Look, we've got to make sure our ducks are in a row before we go forward with this thing, Milbank. We don't want any issues with the environmentalists or the state. For this deal to work we've got to have all these home sites sell fast. We can't have someone telling us we're too close to the Winnehala Wetlands and have to leave valuable land unused; to be profitable we've got to build all these homes." Midge jabbed a pudgy forefinger at the table.

Milbank studied the map, looking through the topography and lot lines and into the future, his political future as mayor, maybe even governor someday.

"We know they moved some dirt down there in the thirties to build the golf course," Chartreuse said, "but we won't be able to do that now; too many environmental rules against it."

"Goddamn socialists."

Chartreuse waited to see if Midge had anything else to add before he continued. "Drainage is what concerns me at this point, Ralph. The round we played there gave me a better sense of what I've got to work with. You could feel where the frost heaves the ground when you drive down the fairways. That tells you there's a lot of moisture in it and that's not a good thing. No one's going to buy a luxury home with a wet basement. Casserly's job is to figure out if there's a way to move that moisture away from the home sites without costing us too much money."

"And without getting every tree-hugging hippie on our ass," added Midge.

"I know people at the county and state level who can help us with those kinds of issues. If we're creating jobs and taxable real estate within the city limits, they're going to want to help us. Sure, there are rules we have to be concerned about but every rule is open to interpretation, and if you know the guy doing the interpreting you've got less to worry about," said Milbank.

Midge checked his watch, announced he had a tee time in fifteen minutes and abruptly left the room. Chartreuse rolled up the map and walked out with Milbank. "If everything goes to plan, we should be able to start developing the site next summer."

"Oh, it will," said Milbank, giving him an awkward slap on the back.

*

The unphilosophic Cybil Stumpher faced a moral dilemma, an existential moment. She was tasked by Milbank to document the failings of Karl Ketterman yet she was unsure of its purpose. True, she didn't care much for the kid; he was an outsider with too many new ideas. Life had been easier with Art Castle around, but it slowly dawned on her that once Ketterman was gone someone else would follow. There was no guarantee the next general manager would be any more to her liking, and she certainly couldn't go back to Milbank again and claim that Ketterman's successor was also an incompetent boob. And she couldn't help wondering why Milbank seemed so keen on getting rid of Ketterman. Cybil pondered these things as she cleaned the grill, pushing the wire brush back and forth in a steady rhythm. Scouring away the residue of the day always helped her sort through things.

*

The world had become a strange place for Charley Lumley. Every day it was getting harder to find unfiltered Camels, and he didn't even want to think about how much they cost. And why, he wondered, was everyone always on the phone these days? What could they possibly have to talk about that's so important—in their cars, on the course, sitting on the crapper; for the love of God, couldn't it wait? Wouldn't it be cheaper to use a pay phone? Lumley spat and turned his attention to Franzen setting up his video equipment as Gretchen Schumacher took practice swings. Lumley realized they were about the ages he and Cybil had been when they'd met; the difference, of course, was that Gretchen was just about the best female golfer he'd ever seen, and he'd seen some great ones. Lumley knew that the first time he saw her swing. She had a short backswing for a woman but the way she lagged the club was perfect. And her finish position was a work of art. Lumley saw each part of her swing vividly, as clearly as if they were chiseled in granite. Gretchen was a natural; not even Franzen could screw up that swing. Lumley fished another cigarette out of his pocket and lit it without taking his eyes off Gretchen.

"Absolutely gorgeous."

He meant her swing.

*

Sunlight was fading and there was a slight chill in the air as Ketterman walked to his car. He had planned to hit balls after work, but the episode with Stokes had thrown his whole day off schedule. He settled for a couple practice swings in the parking lot. He could see Gretchen finishing her practice session with Franzen, and Lumley's cart in its usual spot at the far end of the range. As soon as Franzen and Gretchen drove away, Karl saw Lumley get out of his cart, grab an iron, and drop two balls. Two waggles and the first ball flew on a high right-to-left arc at the hundred-and-fifty-yard marker; two waggles and the second was on a left-to-right flight at it. A perfect draw, a perfect cut, both within ten feet of the sign.

Watching Lumley so mesmerized Karl he was a little startled by the noiseless approach of Franzen's electric cart.

"Hi, Mr. Ketterman!"

Gretchen's greeting made Karl feel he was wearing a tweed jacket with elbow patches and smoking a Meerschaum pipe. He smiled feebly as they rolled by.

"Can I take you out for something to eat, Gretch?" Franzen's oily words assaulted Karl's ears; Fabio, his target in sight: he shoots; he scores! They were moving too quickly for Karl to hear her answer. He watched until they came to her car. She put her clubs in the trunk and got in, but what of it? She could be meeting him at the restaurant... or his place.

Karl's heart was heavy and his mind confused by lust, devotion, and the soft scent of her sweat he'd caught as she rode by. There was no denying it: Ketterman was in love.

*

Gabriel Dunn sensed it in the evening air. Even though it was May, there would be a frost in the morning. It would come right after daybreak and he would be waiting for it, ready to turn on the sprinklers and dissolve the hoary silver blanket off the greens. The fairways he would monitor. He knew Mo Mittenthal wouldn't allow anyone to tee off until he gave the word. Alone in the maintenance building, under incandescent light, Dunn prepared to protect his golf course.

It would be the last frost Dunn would have to contend with until the fall. The golf season would soon be fully underway, with warm nights following warm days and the course swarming with golfers of every skill level, some conscientious about replacing divots and fixing ball marks, most not. But nothing deterred the indefatigable Dunn from doing his utmost to keep growing things green and thriving. His dedication and consummate professionalism, as it did every year, would counter the onslaught of hackers and once-a-year scramble golfers and, as it was every year, would go unappreciated. Most who played the ZPGC simply assumed it would be in good shape, crediting nature and the climate more than the greenskeeper for the above-average condition of the greens, the uniformity of the rough, and the well-manicured tee boxes. Few knew that it was Dunn, regardless of budget shortages and chronic understaffing, toiling from sunrise to late in the day, who kept the ZPGC in the best shape of any muni in the state, even better than many private clubs with twice the crew and thrice the budget. It was Dunn's acumen, his uncanny ability with turf and plant alike, that made this old muni with its bumpy fairways and hard doglegs one of the best tests of golf in the area. The mysterious Dunn, vigilant and ever alert, knowing every inch of the ZPGC and caring for it like a doting parent, made sure of it. Dunn said little, but his work spoke volumes.

SUMMER

10

June is the month of sweet and alluring scents, wisteria and rose, lilac and lavender. Those smells, unfortunately, never penetrate the dismal air of the Zebulon Pike Golf Course, especially along the fetid edges of the Winnehala Wetlands where the only scents that perfume the air are insect repellent and sunscreen. In this breeding ground for mosquitoes, black flies, and gnats, the air hangs heavily and heats up quickly and the swirling clouds of insects that fill the shadows are sure signs the golf season is in full blossom. This is the time when the ZPGC bustles with activity. Franzen, a pied piper in tartan trousers and frosted locks, herds his golf camp kids from the clubhouse to the range every morning, company leagues tee off weekday afternoons at four p.m., and the women's league swarms across the fairways on Wednesday mornings. There is a rhythm to it all, a timeless regularity that pleases the eye and soothes the spirit; the inconsistencies, false starts, and disappointments of spring golf are past, the clubhouse hums with activity from dawn to sundown, and revenue trends upward.

This ebb and flow gave Karl Ketterman a feeling of finally belonging, as if he were really at the helm and guiding the various activities of each day. In truth, the sheer momentum of seventy-five seasons carried the ZPGC along, regardless of whether Karl reviewed receipts at the end of the day, Cybil prepared her signature egg salad every morning, or Lumley scrutinized the comings and goings on the range late into the evening or not. Like the herds on the Serengeti, foursomes would still roam across the ZPGC from sunrise to sunset, day after day, week after week.

*

Sundbaum stared; Rankel leered; Armstead tried to act disinterested; and Hood thought he felt a vague vernal stirring in his loins as Gretchen Schumacher came roaring down the fairway, her rambunctious breasts bouncing along with the beverage cart.

"Can I get you guys anything?" she said as she hit the brakes.

Armstead searched for a ribald rejoinder but could only come up with, "A hug would be nice."

Gretchen gave him the look a mother gives a child as a first warning. Armstead smiled weakly and turned to fiddle with his golf bag.

Into the lull charged Sundbaum. "So, I hear you and Franzen are an item, Gretchen. Is that true?"

Gretchen frowned. "We've had dinner a couple of times and he's a nice guy, but we're not an 'item,' whatever that is."

"Water," Hood croaked. Gretchen fished a bottle out of the ice and handed it to him. Rankel continued to leer. Gretchen took Hood's money and was off.

"Fabio Franzen, you lucky bastard," Hood said, taking a deep, satisfying swig.

*

The Halling brothers were looking for a game and that was not an easy task. They had a reputation, not for cheating or poor sportsmanship, but for annoying their opponents with their mindless chatter and, as they saw it, good-natured taunting. Whenever they walked into the clubhouse, a dozen sets of eyes lowered, suddenly finding a newspaper article or the grain in the tabletop riveting, because once the Hallings made visual contact they locked in like a heat-seeking missile. They swept the room with eager eyes. One man's met theirs. Tom Crupshaw smiled and waved them to his table.

The Halling brothers were more than brothers; they were twins. And not just twins, but fraternal twins, the sneaky kind of twins that look enough alike to be taken for siblings yet different enough to leave you wondering which was the elder, which the younger. Their mother, a woman who read the Bible daily, felt she'd overcome that ambiguity with the names she had chosen; after all, who doesn't know Jacob was the younger brother of Esau? Their father, a freethinker and fanatical baseball fan, wanted to call them Joseph and Dominic, in honor of the DiMaggio brothers; besides, he argued, they were names everyone could pronounce. Mrs. Halling nixed that idea. She had no problem with Joseph but Dominic sounded a little too Italian and definitely too Catholic for her tastes. One can only imagine her chagrin when Mr. Halling ran off with a laicized nun three years later leaving his parenting responsibilities to his hymn-singing wife and the soothing gray glow of their twenty-inch television set.

Ten is an impressionable age, a time when a new experience can shape a young mind for life. That experience came to the Halling brothers on April 10, 1960: left alone while their mother attended an afternoon Sunday service, the boys sat in front of their black-and-white Motorola, Esau spinning the dial between the three local channels. When he hit the CBS affiliate, Jacob shouted at him to stop. Something caught his eye; the image of a lean, tan man who reminded him a little of Roy Rogers. He was taking a violent slash at a small ball with an oddly shaped stick of some kind. Jacob was hypnotized and soon so was Esau. They spent the next hour, mouths agape, faces inches from the flicking screen, watching Arnold Palmer win the Masters. Jacob and Esau, like all boys of their generation, had many sports heroes, but after that Sunday, Palmer, Finsterwald, Hogan, and Player usurped the thrones of Mantle, Mays, Unitas, and Chamberlain. Mrs. Halling would live to rue attending that afternoon service.

The brothers grew up just a few blocks from the ZPGC, and on the first warm weekend that May they walked down the drive to the clubhouse for the first time. The following weekend they started caddying; this was before the dawn of the motorized cart, when golfers walked and even municipal golf courses had caddies. In July they had enough money to buy their first set of clubs—they shared a bag that first year—and started taking lessons with Lumley. They were good athletes and picked up the game quickly, yet they lacked something essential, something Lumley found himself incapable of instilling in either of them, a basic connection with the spirit of the game. They were brash and bullying, and Lumley could see they could barely repress the urge to shout, "hey, batter, batter...!" in other students' backswings. They were thoughtless, self-centered boys without being intentionally mean-spirited or cruel. These days such behavior is defined more clinically; back then it was called "being a dipshit."

The Halling brothers grew in skill and years, becoming above-average golfers with a keen sense of competition and an obsession with the game. Everything else in life receded in importance. Although bright and intelligent, Jacob and Esau slept-walked through school, preferring to play golf all summer and hit balls into an old mattress they leaned against their basement wall all winter. Nothing else seemed to matter to them. After they graduated from high school they spent the entire summer at the golf course. This was in the late 1960s. When they got their draft notices they took speed and drank black coffee for three days before their physicals. With their deferments secured, they decided they had to find a way to make a living. They fell in with an old-timer at the course who had a carpet-laying business and hired them as installers. When he retired, Jacob and Esau, or Jay and Es, as they preferred to be called—which some wags at the ZPGC said were short for "Jackass" and "Shithead"—took over and, to everyone's surprise, didn't run the business into the ground. From that day to the present, The Carpet Kings van could be found almost every day the snow was off the ground in the parking lot of the Zebulon Pike Golf Course.

*

Merril Stokes strolled leisurely up the path from the driving range to the clubhouse, staying well to the side so the golf carts that sped by didn't clip his pull cart. Merril had been doing penance ever since his unfortunate incident with Rambo

Burchell earlier in the year, going out of his way to be gracious and accommodating and doing everything in his power to reform his image at the ZPGC. He went as far as chatting up Cybil whenever he was in the clubhouse, not an easy thing to do. Merril, nonetheless, charged into it with verve, figuring if he could make a friend of one of the least friendly people at the course he might soon be welcomed again into the company of men. All his efforts got him was an awkward word or two from Cybil and an extra handful of fries in his cheeseburger basket.

In reality, no one had ostracized Stokes. His little blowup with Burchell was seen as just that, a minor incident. It drew attention to him for a day or two then quickly faded out of mind. After all, there was nothing that unusual about Officers Clack and Spurgeon showing up on the course; true, it didn't often result in someone being handcuffed, but it had happened before and it would again. These incidents were usually triggered by slow play: someone gets frustrated and hits into the group in front of them, shouting follows, maybe someone assumes a karate stance, then suggestions of what persons should do to themselves or insert up their rectum are hurled from a safe distance. But once the minions of the law come bouncing down the fairway, moods soften, the issue resolves itself, and play resumes; on a few very rare occasions the conflagration rekindles in the parking lot, fists fly, and there is an arrest for assault—but even those events fail to stay in people's minds for long. Still, Merril Stokes brooded.

"I've been looking for you, Stokes." It was that voice again. He had avoided being within its beckoning since that fateful afternoon on the ninth fairway, but now Crupshaw loomed before him like the Angel of the Lord standing between Adam and the gates of Eden. "The Halling brothers are looking for a game. I thought we might take them on."

Crupshaw's exposure to the Halling brothers was limited to the ZPGC. Merril Stokes had been dealing with them since kindergarten. They had been the nemeses of his youth, and to him the Halling brothers were a double dose of everything negative, unpleasant, and threatening. It was impossible for Merril to decide which of them he hated most, Esau, the blockheaded hulk who'd crushed his favorite cat's eye marble with an eight-ounce steely out of pure spite when he was in the third grade, or the slightly taller slack-jawed Jacob who'd stepped on the toes of his brand-new wingtips at an American Legion dance in junior high. Both incidents were long forgotten by the Halling brothers; they had terrorized so many kids in their youth it was all a blur to them. They vaguely remembered having gone to school with Stokes, but that was as far as it went. The humiliation and anger, however, still seethed in the heart of Merril Stokes as fresh and palpable as it had been fifty years earlier.

*

"I don't know if I'm up to this, Crupshaw."

"Relax, it's going to be fine. They're six handicaps, so am I. I told them they had to give you a stroke a hole or we don't play; they accepted. Low ball wins, no team total, so all you have to do is come through on a couple holes and their asses are ours. Easy," Crupshaw said with a wink.

"So what are we playing for?"

"A simple Nassau, five dollars for front, back, and total. The most you can lose is fifteen dollars. You can handle it."

Stokes could handle it. He had worked for an insurance company, had retired at fifty-five with a good pension and sound investments, and he'd always been a frugal soul, so he was more than comfortable financially. Losing fifteen dollars wasn't the issue, it was the competition that got to him, dealing with expectations, pulling off a shot under pressure; he was just no good at it. That, after all, was at the root of the whole Burchell Incident. Crupshaw was there, he had seen how Stokes had snapped, why was he putting him in the same spot again?

The Halling brothers were waiting on the first tee. Crupshaw and Stokes stood facing them. Crupshaw threw a tee in the air. It landed pointing at the Halling brothers. They would hit first. Es went first, Jay followed. Both drives were down the middle and long. Crupshaw's rolled five yards past theirs. Stokes addressed his ball.

"Geez, I hope he don't go nuts on us out there," Es stage whispered to Jay. Stokes hooked his drive into the trees on the left. The game was on.

*

The front side went much as Stokes had expected. He floundered and Crupshaw kept them in the game. The match was tied when they got to nine. Stokes, as usual, hit the shortest drive, then hit a 5-iron down the right side of the fairway, as far from the water as possible. It landed twelve yards short of the green. Both Es and Jay hit the green in two. Then something happened, one of those quirky things that occur during a round that falls under the rubric "rub of the green." Crupshaw's second shot, an easy 7-iron from a hundred-fifty-five yards came down just short of the green, landed directly on a sprinkler head and sailed high and left and into the water.

"That one's for you, McAdoo!" roared Es over Jay's horselaugh.

But Crupshaw's shot wasn't the only quirky thing that happened. Stokes chipped in for a net two to win the hole and the front. The Halling brothers watched in disbelief as Stokes picked his ball out of the cup.

"Looks like McAdoo's shoe just went up your ass, boys." Stokes heard the words but found it hard to comprehend that they'd actually come out of his mouth.

Neither Stokes' chip-in or his quip was enough to ruffle the Halling brothers. They played like men possessed on the back, but the strength of Crupshaw's game and the hubris of giving Stokes a shot a hole was too much for them. They lost front, back, and total and walked off the eighteenth green down fifteen dollars each. They shook hands and paid up while bemoaning the series of bad breaks that had led to their demise.

As Merril walked off the green Jay shouted out at him, "Next time, no eighteen shots for you!"

"Let's have a beer. I'm buying," Crupshaw said, waving his fifteen dollars in the air.

They sat in the clubhouse for quite awhile, savoring the win. Merril especially relished defeating his ancient antagonists. He sipped his beer and felt at peace with himself and the world. When he got up to get the second round from Cybil he gave her a wink. She was not amused.

Later, sitting at the dinner table with his wife, it struck Stokes why Crupshaw had been so insistent Merril play with him today. Crupshaw didn't need Merril's help to beat the Halling brothers; he could do that easily enough by himself. He just wanted Merril to have some fun on the golf course for a change. And Merril realized that Tom Crupshaw wasn't such a bad guy after all.

11

Morning wasn't Dan Casserly's favorite time of day, nor was wandering around a rundown muni his idea of time well spent, yet here he was again, canoeing across the Winnehala Wetlands at the crack of dawn to do just that. He did have to admit that coming at it from this direction gave him a fresh look at the property and a better sense of its potential.

As he neared the shoreline Casserly hopped out of the canoe and pulled it on shore. He stepped out of his waders and covered the canoe with a camouflage net. The sun was just brightening the horizon and dew glistened on the fairways; bird song filled the air. It was cool and damp and he was tired, but at this ungodly hour at least no one would know he was here. Casserly grabbed his backpack and headed out onto the course.

*

A man takes pride in a thing he creates from nothing, and Welmont Washington took great pride in Boutiqué Afriqué, the chain of four gender-neutral hair salons he had built up over the last twenty-five years to serve the city's African-American community. On this lovely spring morning he sat in his office above his flagship store on Chicago Avenue studying the hulking frame of Tyreal "Fort" Sumter sitting across from him.

"So you want me to put *my* money in *your* golf tournament, is that right, Mr. Sumter?"

"Yes, sir, I do."

"And why would I want to do that?"

Sumter spread his arms and looked about him. "To widen your exposure in the community, Mr. Washington; to support the aspirations of black athletes," he paused slightly before delivering his knockout punch, "and to break down the color barrier in golf."

Welmont, a twenty-year member of Lochenberry Country Club and current chairman of its tournament committee, had always found money the great barrier-breaker; still, he nodded as if he were struck by the freshness of that remark. Sumter felt he'd found an opening.

"Look, man, I'm trying to bring the Ebon Invitational back to life. My daddy started this tournament and there was a time when it was a big deal for black folk in this town. I want to make it a big deal again."

Welmont turned to the mirror behind his desk and gently touched the top of his perfectly coifed silver hair before picking up a pair of scissors and giving his moustache a quick clip. He spun back to face Sumter.

"It's ironic, isn't it, Sumter? Integration was going to make the world right for us, and what happened? Everything that was truly, uniquely ours went away and what are we left with? Eighty years ago there were tens of thousands of black businesses; we were kept separate but we supported our own. Now we go to Wal-Mart like everyone else."

Sumter wasn't sure he was following Washington but he played along. "Yes, sir, you're right about that. Man, it's a shame, isn't it?"

"Yet you seem to think a golf tournament that's exclusively for blacks is going to draw a big crowd; don't know if that makes a lot of sense to me, Sumter."

An entrepreneur sees opportunity and seizes it; Welmont Washington saw one in front of him, but subtlety was required before seizure. The moment Sumter had walked into his office, Welmont could tell he was incapable of organizing a two-car funeral, much less something as complex as a golf tournament. Welmont had those skills; what was more important, he had a business to promote, a business that required the continuing patronage of black customers. With the connections he'd made over the years he could turn the Ebon Invitational into one of the biggest sporting and social events of the year, a three-day extravaganza of golf, entertainment, and business opportunities. But it wouldn't be only for blacks. Quite the contrary; of course it would continue to feature the best black golfers he could attract to it, but he envisioned an Ebon Invitational that was both inclusive and exclusive, one that would eventually become the most prestigious tournament in the state. Of course, he would set up a scholarship fund for deserving black youth in the community. He might even name it after Sumter's daddy. Why not? He'd still be the guy the media would show handing the scholarship out. Welmont smiled at Sumter and let him prattle on some more.

*

Gretchen Schumacher loaded her beverage cart in the shade of the overhang behind the kitchen of the ZPGC. Her mind was occupied with other things as she buried the beers, sodas, and sports drinks deep into the ice. She was hearing too much about Franzen and herself and she did not like what was being said. He was a good-looking man but he just didn't appeal to her; and he came on to every woman he met so it was difficult to believe she could mean anything more to him than just another conquest—which is why she made sure she did nothing to encourage him. Still the rumors bothered her; she wanted to believe Franzen was helping her because he saw potential in her game, not in her panties.

She was wiping her forearm with a towel when Karl came around the side of the building. He stopped and watched her, his heart pounding against his sternum. She moved the towel along one firm, strong arm, then the other, her free hand extended, fingers spread out in a gesture that could command a legion of men to halt. Her arms dropped; she flicked her golden braid over her shoulder and put her foot on the cart's bumper to tie her shoe.

Whether it was a gasp or a whimper, Karl made some sort of sound that startled Gretchen. She straightened and turned. The sun was behind Karl so she had to shade her eyes with one hand to see who it was. She looked positively Wagnerian, Isolde searching the horizon for Tristan.

"Sorry, I think I swallowed a gnat," he said.

"Hey, Mr. Ketterman, what's up?"

Her smile put him at ease and he felt less like a leering pervert. "Call me Karl, Gretchen. 'Mr. Ketterman' makes me feel as old as Lumley."

She laughed. Karl had never heard laughter so melodious, so contagious, so unself-conscious. What was it about this girl that captivated him so? She wasn't the most beautiful woman he'd ever seen and certainly no Rhodes scholar. He was no naïf and could tell when a woman was trying to get his attention, and Gretchen had never consciously tried to do that. So what was the cause of his obsession with her? He'd been told his mother hadn't breastfed him, so was it Freudian? Pheromones? Maybe it was some kind of nutritional imbalance, not enough vitamin D, too much riboflavin? What the hell was the matter with him?

"Gretchen." He heard his voice go up an octave on the second syllable. He swallowed and started over. "Gretchen, I've heard a lot about your game and I was wondering if maybe we could play a round some time."

Gretchen positively beamed. What better way to help convince the world she wasn't Franzen's concubine than to be seen in the company of another man? "Sure. I'm playing early Saturday morning before my shift. How about then?"

"Perfect."

"I'll tell Franzen you're joining us. See you then!" Gretchen got in the cart and drove away from the clubhouse, leaving Ketterman swaying somewhere between despair and elation; he would be with Gretchen but he would have to put up with Franzen too. He adored her and abhorred him. If only he could get Franzen out of the way.

*

"Oh, wow! Thanks, Cybil!" Tommy Doherty smiled blissfully as she slid the egg salad sandwich he didn't remember ordering in front of him. His brother Clayton waved Cybil down to the end of the counter and settled Tommy's tab for May. Fifteen years Tommy's junior, Clayton played to a four handicap and was a perennial favorite to win the Keegan Cap, although it had been ten years since he last lifted it in victory. He'd be the first to admit that the distance the young guys could hit the ball was making it harder for guys his age to contend, so nowadays he concentrated his energies on being part of the tournament committee and keeping the great event alive.

"Is the manager around today, Cybil?" She laid his change on the counter and hooked a thumb in the direction of Ketterman's office. Clayton found Karl standing at the window.

"How's everything look?"

Karl, surprised at first by Clayton's voice, smiled and waved him in. Seems like a nice kid, Clayton mused, a little odd but that should help him fit in around this place.

"I'm Clayton Doherty," he said as he took Karl's hand, "I'm on the Keegan Cap tournament committee this year and on its behalf I want to personally invite you to play in it." The Keegan Cap was an open event that anyone with a current USGA handicap could sign up for, but Clayton's invitation was more than just a courtesy. Every manager of the ZPGC, even the ill-fated McAdoo, had played in the Keegan and he didn't want to see a break in the tradition.

"Thank you. I'd be honored to play in it," Karl said.

Doherty felt he'd accomplished something important. He valued tradition very highly. That and family pride had brought him to golf. He was just five when Tommy was felled at the Keegan Cap, and Clayton had known him only as the gentle-hearted, befuddled soul who came out of the coma with two passions in life: University of Alabama sports and the Keegan Cap. The first was inexplicable. Tommy had never been to Alabama, never known anyone who went there, and had never shown the slightest interest in the school before his accident. Still, the first words out of his mouth when he walked in a room were, "Roll Tide." His second fixation was understandable. His last fully cognitive moments took place during the Keegan Cap. His brother Clayton, a man of fierce loyalties, had learned to play golf and competed in the event every year, not out of passion for the game, but to give his big brother something to look forward to, something to focus his addled wits upon. No one but Clayton knew that, although his devotion to his brother was evident to all.

"Then I'll put your name on the sign-up sheet. The manager has always gone out in the first group; that's been the tradition. It doesn't matter whether you're a good player or not; we just want you to be part of Keegan Cap and have a good time. You good with that?"

"That works for me."

Good. We'll see you then." And, after a quick handshake, Clayton Doherty was out the door.

*

What Karl had been watching out the window when Clayton came into his office was the rear wheel of Fort Sumter's golf cart. It had just come to a stop near the clubhouse and Karl was fascinated with how far the distance between the wheel well and the tire increased when Tyreal got out to walk the fifty feet from the clubhouse to the first tee; it was his way of getting loose before a round. As soon as he got out, Scrumpy Scroggins pulled ahead, teed up a ball, and got back in the cart. This little ritual was to save Tyreal the physical contortions required of him to bend over and peg up a ball; it was a hybrid movement, part curtsy, part a lineman's three-point stance, and as uncomfortable to watch as it was for him to do. Tyreal didn't mind teeing his own ball on the course, but he preferred the "Scrumpy Option" on the first and tenth tees where prying eyes might witness his struggles to swoop to the ground and gain altitude again.

Tyreal waggled his driver and started his backswing, his belly orbiting around his axis like a small planet, then smashed into the ball, finishing with an abbreviated follow-through that pointed his driver down his target line. The first shot of the day had been fired by Fort Sumter; he lumbered back to the cart and jammed himself behind the wheel. Pleased with his drive, Tyreal watched Scrumpy's with unusual interest, even complimenting the shot, an occurrence so rare Scrumpy assumed it was meant to be sarcastic. The pat on his back when he got in the cart assured him otherwise.

"Scrumpy, my man, guess who I was talking with this morning?"

"I'm no mystic, Tyreal, so why don't you tell me?"

"Mr. Welmont Washington. That's right, the dude with the money, the brother with all the pull. Fool thinks he looks like Billy Dee Williams and acts like his first name was Denzel. But that's all right. I'm this close," he pinched two pudgy fingers together in front of Scrumpy's face, "to getting him to kick some serious cash into the Ebon. Yes, I am!"

As the cart went over the lip of the paved path and onto the fairway, the left rear tire rubbed against the wheel well, making a plaintive groaning sound.

"Can't they get some decent carts at this goddamned place?"

12

The valet caught the keys and smiled. He parked a lot of nice cars at Lochenberry Country Club, but Welmont Washington was one of the few members with a Bentley and he looked forward to the thrill of driving it, even if only for a hundred yards. Washington winked at the kid. "I better not hear squealing tires when I get inside."

Welmont strode through the clubhouse and into the men's locker room. There was no Midge in sight so he moved on to the grillroom. His man was seated at the bar surrounded by sycophants, guys who scraped and saved to make their monthly dues in the hope that someday they'd make a business connection that would make it all worthwhile. Such men gravitated to Midge; he was the man to know at Lochenberry, the guy who could make things happen, or get his father to make happen. There was no one in town more connected to professional athletes, politicians, and movers and shakers than Midge, and the Lochenberry Country Club was the centrifuge that flung his influence out to every point in the community.

"Excuse me, gentlemen, but I see Mr. Washington is here for our meeting. Maybe we can pick this up again this weekend. Carly, bring Mr. Washington whatever he wants and put it on my tab." Midge grabbed his Diet Coke and Welmont's elbow and guided him to a booth in a far corner of the grillroom. He leaned in and spoke softly, although there was no one else nearby to hear what he was said.

"Welmont, I'm working on an idea, a *big* idea, and I want you to be part of it."

"You're too good to me, Midge; what did I do to deserve it?"

Midge studied him for a moment; Asians, blacks, Latinos, mimes, Mormons, women: they were all inscrutable to Midge.

"All right, I *need* you to be part of this. It's going to be the biggest thing to hit this city in decades; it's something that people with money are going to want to be part of, and you're going to be in on the ground floor. That means you're going to make money on this deal, too."

"I'm all ears," Welmont said with a smile.

Midge leaned in and lowered his voice to a whisper. "I can't go into details right now, but let me leave you with this thought: imagine a brand-new, high-end, and totally first-class—let's just say at this point—destination that draws in the most affluent and influential people around here; and here's the kicker, it's inside the city limits not out in the lily-white suburbs."

Welmont nodded sagely; he lived in the same suburb as Midge. "I don't know if this is the best time to be building a new home, Midge."

It was Midge's turn to smile. "Don't jump to conclusions, just focus on the general idea. In a week or so I'll lay it all out for you and it's going to blow you away, believe me." He raised his glass and waited. Reluctantly, Welmont clinked Midge's glass.

*

Welmont had come to the Lochenberry to tell Midge about his plan for taking over the Ebon Invitational and get his family to contribute to the scholarship fund. Realizing it's never a good strategy to try to trump someone else's big news, he decided to keep his under his hat for the moment. He told Midge he looked forward to hearing more about his mystery project. Midge put a finger to the side of his nose and winked, then rejoined the group at the bar. After finishing his Arnold Palmer, Welmont walked outside and had the bag boy bring up his clubs. He went out to the range and hit a small bucket. There was no one on the range but older members—not the type he wanted to play a round with—so he waved the bag boy over and went back into the clubhouse. As he waited for the valet to bring up his Bentley, Welmont saw Midge driving away in his convertible. There were two others in it with him. He recognized one of them, Frank Chartreuse; the other guy he didn't know. Chartreuse had built Welmont's home, so Midge's big idea must be to get him to build a new place in the city. He chuckled to himself as he handed the valet a crisp five-dollar bill and got behind the wheel.

*

He repeated it three times to himself, just to be sure: *Ralph like safe, Ralph like safe, Ralph like safe.* "Ralph"—when he heard himself say it a burden was lifted from his heart—"glad to see you again. Are you playing or is this official business?"

Milbank placed a flaccid hand in Karl's. Karl tried to gently squeeze some life into it, to no avail. When he released it, it fell to Milbank's side like a flounder on the seabed.

"I'd categorize it as more of a casual visit than official business," Milbank said. "I make an effort to get out of the office every so often and visit a variety of Parks facilities." He walked out onto the verandah overlooking the first tee. Ketterman followed at a respectful distance.

"Not very busy today, I see."

"Thursday mornings tend to be a little slow."

Milbank nodded knowingly and scanned the grounds again. Pointing at two groundskeepers working next to the first tee, he said, "What are those fellows doing, Karl?"

"Just sprucing up the grave."

Milbank gave Karl a sharp look. He had no idea Ambrose Keegan was buried at the ZPGC and assumed the kid was becoming a little cynical about the ZPGC's future. That attitude certainly played into Milbank's hands but, nonetheless, he needed to keep Ketterman in his place.

Karl missed the look but caught the tone of Milbank's next remark. "The flowers are lovely, but they may not be the wisest use of the limited funds you have to run the golf course; some might even see it as frivolous."

"I couldn't agree more, but as you are aware, Ralph, that's a groundskeeper's decision and an expense that comes out of his budget." Karl knew his parry hit home. He studied the clouds and enjoyed the moment.

Milbank reddened. He had made a slip and the kid had caught him. He prided himself on knowing the little things, never missing a detail. He felt as if the fly on the suit of his authority were down. It was time to get to the point.

"Do you know how many acres the Zebulon Pike covers, Karl?" He didn't wait for a response. He had to reestablish his place in the Parks Commission pecking order. "I'd guess that this golf course takes up about a hundred-twenty acres; I'm just talking about the course now, not the clubhouse and everything else on the property. How many golfers do you have out there at your busiest time, let's say a Sunday morning?"

"I suppose somewhere between seventy and eighty," What, Karl wondered, was Milbank's point?

"For argument's sake, let's say eighty; that's about one-and-a-half persons per acre, correct?"

Without checking the math, Karl agreed. Milbank gestured to a bench. They sat down and he turned toward Karl. "The Parks Commission has many constituencies, Karl, and few friends. Everything we do is scrutinized and criticized by a dozen different special interest groups: the black, Latino, GLBT, Muslim, and atheist communities; Democrats and Republicans; dog owners, cyclists, softball leagues, soccer clubs; lefties who want more land under public control and capitalists who want less. I'm the guy in the middle, Karl; I'm the guy who has to deal with them all. And what do I hear from one of those groups just about every single day? 'You've got a park'—because that's what this really is, Karl, a park—'you've got a park that's being used by one-and-a-half persons an acre to play an elitist Anglo-Saxon game; is that justifiable, is that proper stewardship of a public space? Is that fair? Should that much city property be set aside for the exclusive use of so few who represent such a small part of this community?'" He paused, waiting for Karl to respond. Never too fast on his feet, Karl had to let it soak in before he ventured a comeback.

"I'm not sure I know what you're getting at."

Milbank gave him a paternal smile. "I'm not getting at anything, Karl, I'm just unburdening myself a little and letting you in on what a Parks Commissioner deals with: people coming at me with crazy ideas to turn all of this into a softball complex, bicycle and walking trails, a gigantic dog run, wildlife sanctuary, and heaven knows what else. Golf doesn't have a lot of fans, Karl, not in a city with all the issues this one is dealing with." He stopped and studied Karl.

"I guess I wish I had known all this before I took the job."

Milbank slapped him on the knee and stood up. "Karl, I'm sorry. I didn't mean to distress you. I guess I'm just having a tough day, forget what I said. You're doing a good job here; don't worry about things you can't control. Keep up the good work." He left Karl sitting on the bench, looking at nothing in particular, shoulders slumped, mouth slightly ajar. *"Moron meditating his fate"* was the caption Milbank put on the scene. Mission accomplished. Milbank wondered if Ketterman would start sending out resumes this week or wait until next.

*

Charley Lumley guided his cart into unfamiliar territory, taking the path that ran from the west side of the range and skirted the boundary of the property. He crossed the driveway and followed the dirt path all the way to the maintenance building. He hadn't been there for years, more years than he could reckon right now. Dunn was working on a mower when he pulled up. Charley hit the brakes and the tires skidded in the gravel. The unflustered Dunn gave him a leisurely glance and turned his attention back to the mower. He had a vague notion of who Lumley was: the guy who hung around the driving range all day. That was typical; that two people could work at the ZPGC season after season and seldom cross paths. The organizational structure was so convoluted that there was little communication and less cooperation between employees: Mo Mittenthal, Rambo Burchell, Karl Ketterman, Cybil Stumpher, Gabriel Dunn, and Charley Lumley had never been in the same place at the same time, never encouraged to work together toward a mutual goal, never even been introduced to one another. At some point, they found themselves sharing the same space and gradually, begrudgingly, acknowledged one another. This, then, was a seminal moment, although neither Lumley nor Dunn saw it as such.

Lumley dismounted and fished for a smoke. The snap of his Zippo lighter made Dunn look up again. He set down the wrench and toweled off his hands.

"What can I do for you?"

Lumley exhaled, wreathing his head in a cloud of smoke, and barked out a short, phlegmy cough.

"You the greenskeeper?" Lumley asked.

Dunn followed suit. "You the rangekeeper?"

Charley had never heard his job referred to as that; he liked it and acknowledged it with a nod and a wink. Dunn gave his head a slight tilt and waited for Lumley to move the conversation forward.

"The guy, the one wandering around the course early in the morning: you heard about him?" Dunn nodded, so Charley continued. "I think I know what he's up to."

"Step into my office." Dunn walked into the maintenance building. Charley took a final drag of his cigarette, flicked it, and walked into the darkness.

*

Twilight was falling as Midge finished out the ninth hole. This was his favorite time of day, when he could get out by himself and play a leisurely round with hardly another soul on the course. As he placed the flag back in the cup, he took a moment to study the white clapboard splendor of the Lochenberry Country Club. illuminated by the lowering sun.

"God, what a pile of shit," he muttered.

Robert Midge had a very low opinion of the Lochenberry, the club his grandfather helped found, the club where both he and his father had been introduced to the game, the place where many of their business and political machinations were hatched. Even though it was the third-oldest golf club west of Chicago and the site of some great moments in the game's history, Robert Midge loathed the place. He hated the creaky hardwood floors, the beamed ceilings, the cherry paneling, the mahogany bar, the twin stairways just inside the front doors that led up to the creepy old ballroom with the red-velvet-curtained stage, the library filled with leather-bound books that hadn't been cracked in his lifetime, the huge oriental carpets, the oil paintings of Great Britain's most famous links courses, the black-and-white autographed photos of Bobby Jones, Walter Hagen, Tommy Armour, Jimmy Demaret, Cary Middlecoff, Byron Nelson, Lloyd Mangrum, Ben Hogan, and a dozen other golfers no one under seventy recognized that lined the hallway leading to the men's locker room. He hated the flowerbeds in front and the wide verandah that ran the full length of the back; he hated the gravel driveway and the commemorative plaques in the entryway. He hated the trophy case in the grillroom with its tarnished, dust-coated cups. He hated the small lockers and the white-tiled showers. He hated everything about the Lochenberry. Where others saw tradition, heritage, and history, Midge saw only tired, stagnant remnants of things best forgotten. Lochenberry was not Robert Midge's idea of a country club. To him a country club should be overstated, ostentatious, and reek of over-sized excess; it should have vast, marble-floored rooms, glittering chandeliers dangling from high ceilings, thousands upon thousands of opulent and unnecessary square feet, bright, dazzling spaces that echo laughter and tinkling glasses, massive flat-screen televisions and digital connectivity everywhere, a gleaming, seductive pleasure dome of luxury and bullying wealth; that was Robert Midge's idea of a country club, not the quiet, dignified, properly proportioned building in front of him.

As Midge drove his cart toward the clubhouse he could see the setting sun through the corner windows. He imagined it as a ball of fire inside the building about to engulf the whole thing in flames; the thought pleased him.

13

The pencil made a neat check mark on the left side of the column. Mo Mittenthal admired it for a moment before picking up the microphone and pressing the key. "The 7:12 group is now on the tee, 7:12; 7:24 is on deck and 7:36 is in the hole." He put the microphone down and leaned out of the starter's shack, a clapboard structure slightly larger than a phone booth standing just across the cart path from the first tee. The 7:12 group's carts were pulling up to the tee box. Mo, always on the job by five a.m. sharp on summer mornings to make sure no deadbeats snuck out early, was now in desperate need of another cup of coffee. Double-checking the tee sheet to make sure all was in order, he stepped out of the shack and dashed to the clubhouse for a refill.

Cybil was serving up breakfast plates and waved him off when he raised his cup at her; that caused him to worry. A fussy man who took a simple job too seriously, Mo was anxious to get back to his shack. Gretchen came in and, seeing Mo pacing, walked behind the counter, grabbed a pot from the coffeemaker and filled his cup.

"What you doing here this early, Gretchen; playing?" He said, blowing across the top of his cup.

"Yep. Seven-thirty-six with Franzen and," Gretchen paused so briefly Mo almost didn't catch it, "…Karl."

Mo arched his brows and went back to his shack. Saturday mornings in June were a busy time at ZPGC and he had to keep things moving along. Besides, he enjoyed kibitzing with the customers and answering the usual questions about course conditions, the weather forecast, and how the greens were running. Mo answered them all with a self-confidence and authority that assured his interlocutors they were getting the true scoop. But Mo was really making it up as he went along, for he had never played the ZPGC or any other golf course; in fact, he had never even picked up a golf club. Some things he had learned by observation. He could tell a good golf swing from a bad one and whether the bad ones would send the ball left or right. He knew a group of once-a-year-players at a glance and how to politely instruct them before they teed off on the need to stay up with the group in front of them. He knew that once a group was inside the hundred-fifty-yard marker it was usually safe for the next one to tee off. He knew what time to expect the first group out to come up the hill from the ninth green on their way to the tenth tee. And he knew the moment he set eyes on Fabio Franzen that he was a horse's ass.

*

"Shorten your backswing a little."

The cart came up so slowly Karl didn't hear it. He turned to find Lumley, cigarette in the corner of his mouth, both hands on the steering wheel, looking at him through a whirling veil of smoke. Which, he wondered, carved more of those wrinkles in Lumley's face, cigarette smoke or sunlight? He pulled a range ball away from the basket and hit another shot, this one with a shorter backswing.

"When you take the club away, push your hands a little farther from your body." That bit of wisdom was followed by a chest-rumbling cough.

Karl hit another. His trajectory was lower and the ball had more zip on it.

"Thanks, Charley."

Lumley touched two fingers to the front of his straw fedora. "You playing this morning?"

"Yeah, with Franzen and Gretchen Schumacher."

"You want to beat him?"

Lumley's deadpan delivery made it difficult to tell at first if he was posing a question or making an accusation. Karl decided to be evasive. "It's just a friendly game, Charley."

"There hasn't been a friendly game since Cain asked Abel to play tag," snarled Lumley. He turned the wheel of his cart sharply and hit the accelerator, coming so close to Karl he clipped the basket of balls. He hit the brakes when he was alongside Karl and pointed the two fingers pinching his cigarette at Karl's face. "I've seen his game. He's good; he'll probably outplay you from tee to green but that's okay. The key is to make him putt everything out. That's his Achilles' heel. No gimmes and you got a chance."

Lumley locked eyes with Karl and he felt some weird transference of confidence. Mittenthal's call for the 7:36 group brought an end to the standoff. "Hop in. I'll give you a lift." Karl grabbed his bag and plopped down next to Lumley.

*

Karl hopped off Lumley's cart and joined Franzen and Gretchen on the tee box. He was pleased to see they were walking too. Karl hated carts. He'd grown up using them and it wasn't until college that he realized how they destroyed your concentration.

"Karl, glad to see you could join us."

Karl picked up the slight sarcasm in Franzen's voice. Fabio was making languid practice swings with his driver. Gretchen, sunglasses set on top of her head, had hooked an iron behind her back with her elbows and was slowly rotating her upper body. This posture forced her shoulders back and pushed her breasts forward; they strained against her shirt. What amazed Karl more than the magnificence of her body was her nonchalance in putting on this show; she was completely oblivious to the effect her warm-up was having on every man near the tee box.

"What do you play to, Karl?" Franzen said in an offhanded way as if he were only mildly curious.

"I haven't played much lately. I was a four in college."

Franzen's head bobbed subtly. "You played collegiate golf?"

"Division II."

"Well, what do you say to a little game?"

"I'm in," said Gretchen before Fabio's words had barely passed his lips. Karl dittoed her remark.

"All right. Let's say a buck a point, one for hitting the fairway, one for green in regulation, one for low score on the hole, and one for closest to the hole on par threes." Franzen looked at his playing companions for their agreement. Gretchen came back first. "Let's say a buck for sandies and chip-ins." Karl and Franzen agreed, then Gretchen and Franzen looked at Karl for his input. He hesitated a moment. "How about five bucks for fewest putts. Of course, that means no gimmes; everything to the bottom of the cup." Gretchen was for it. Franzen gave Karl a narrow look and nodded. "Ladies first."

Karl knew Gretchen was a good player, but she surprised him when she teed up at the back tee; that meant playing the course at a little over sixty-six hundred yards. That's a paltry distance on a modern course but a big challenge for even the best women golfers, especially at the ZPGC. Karl wondered if she might have taken on too much until she hit her drive. He tried to watch her ball but couldn't take his eyes off her. Her finish position was perfect. He didn't realize she'd out-driven him by ten yards until they were out on the fairway. Franzen was a good fifteen yards past her. And so the contest began.

By the third hole Karl could see Lumley was right about Fabio. He hit the first two greens in regulation but didn't come close on two reasonable chances at birdie. His putting stroke was a disaster. On long putts he took it back too far and decelerated into the ball; on short putts he made a short, abrupt stroke that had a faint odor of fear about it. Karl was off to a slow start but he knew things were going to change as the game went on. It was obvious Franzen's game depended on gimmes.

The sixth hole at the Zebulon Pike is a short five-hundred-ten-yard par five. The tee box is slightly elevated and the landing area generous but there are ponds on either side. "Pond" being a bit of a misnomer since they're really orphaned offspring of the Winnehala Wetlands; murky, reed-lined, fetid bogs from which no golf ball returns unless you go out in the winter when the vegetation is dormant and the foul-smelling ground frozen, a task only the oddest of the course's ball hawks undertook. It was not a difficult tee shot, especially for someone with Franzen's distance, and he easily drove his ball well past the trouble and straight down the fairway, as did Gretchen, but Karl, forgetting his tip from Lumley, got too long in his backswing and cut his drive near the hazard on the right. When he got to his ball he found it was playable, but just barely, lying inside the red stakes on soggy, uneven ground. The smart play was to hit a 9-iron and get the ball safely out and down the fairway, which he did.

Gretchen complimented Karl's shot as he walked up the fairway. He acknowledged it with a wave and stood still while she hit her second. He was impressed by her aggressiveness; no shot seemed to intimidate her. She either pulled it off or she didn't, either way she didn't linger over the results. She had about two-hundred-forty-five yards to the green and pulled her 3-wood without hesitation. She went through her pre-shoot routine, took a deep breath, set up to the ball, and hit it. Karl watched it start off down the right side of the fairway, then turn back to center, land, and roll within ten yards of the putting surface. She turned to Karl, hands raised in comic-serious celebration. Her exuberance was contagious and both Karl and Franzen gave out a whoop. Franzen followed with a 3-iron that carried to the back of the green. Karl hit a 6-iron for his third shot that came up just short.

The conversation between Karl and Franzen had been limited up to this point in the match: good shot, nice drive, the usual polite banter. Most of the time each did his best to monopolize Gretchen, a strategy she tactfully neutralized by a series of brilliant conversational maneuvers: When Karl asked if she'd seen a movie she responded by asking Fabio if he had; when Fabio was curious about what she would be doing next weekend, she was curious about Karl's plans, thus leaving each with the strong suspicion she was fending him off. Nonetheless, they pressed on.

Gretchen frowned down at her lie. Her ball had come to rest in a divot. Now she had to rethink her options. Seeing her dilemma, Franzen suggested she roll it out of the divot. "No one replaces divots on this goat ranch, Gretchen. This isn't a tournament, so kick it out of there if you want."

Gretchen transferred her frown to Franzen. "No gimmes on the green and no rolling the ball in the fairway, right Karl?" He, seeing an opportunity to put himself on the side of the angels and the USGA, concurred. Franzen smiled weakly and shrugged. Gretchen pulled her sand wedge and played the ball a little back in her stance. It came off the clubface low and ran twenty feet past the pin.

Ketterman's ball was just off the fringe. He walked up to the pin and looked at his line. He had about thirty feet to the cup; the decision was whether to putt or chip it. His putter had kept him in the game so far so he went with it. He made a couple practice strokes looking at the hole and asked Fabio to pull the pin. Stay down and accelerate, he said to himself as he took the putter back. It was a perfect stroke and the ball felt like a marshmallow coming off the putter face. His eyes stayed fixed on the spot where the ball had been, his ears straining. He wanted to look up, but he didn't. Not until he heard the ball rattling in the bottom of the cup.

"Great putt, Karl!" His head was barely up before Gretchen's arms were around his neck. She gave him a squeeze and his face nestled behind her ear, the soft scent of sweat and soap and the heavenly touch of soft blonde hairs on his cheek. She had leaned into him so there was no body contact below the shoulders, but Karl threw caution to the wind and brushed his lips against her neck as she broke away. She gave him a quick, curious look, as if she were trying to decipher what had just happened: was it a fumbling attempt at a kiss or unintentional? He avoided her eyes and walked away to retrieve his ball.

Franzen simmered at the back of the green. He gets on in two and nothing; Ichabod Crane rolls in a lucky birdie and she's all over him. Franzen was more annoyed than jealous. He had every intention of bedding Gretchen before the month was out even though she was far from his type. She was a goal, like breaking seventy. The hug she'd given Karl, however, he took as a slight to his prowess as a golfer and seducer. As far as he was concerned, there was no empirical basis for a woman preferring Ketterman to him, and anything to the contrary—even a gesture as meaningless as that hug—was an affront to his sensibilities. The only proper way to respond was to make this putt for eagle.

Observed objectively, putting should be the easiest thing in golf.

You don't have to get the ball in the air and you don't have to hit it very far. You simply have to roll it along the ground and at the cup. At the very least, it would seem to require very little skill to two-putt every green. But that analysis fails to factor in the power of our imagination, how quickly we can conjure up a variety of negative outcomes before we take any action, and the influence of adrenaline on our motor skills; how it can fire fast-twitch muscles that short-circuit large muscle motion. Then there is our capacity to remember, our uncanny ability to recall similar moments in the past and how they played out. All of those factors came into play as Franzen looked over his putt for eagle.

The sound was the first indication that it had gone wrong, a muted clank that told him the putter had made contact with the ball above its equator. The sound sickened him. He turned to follow the ball. It seemed to be on line and rolling down toward the cup. Franzen's knees buckled and his butt cheeks almost hit his heels. He watched the ball pick up speed as it went wide of the cup, coming to rest twelve feet below the hole. He looked for sympathy and got none. He was the pro and Karl and Gretchen wanted to beat him. Franzen marked his ball and waited for Gretchen. She made her putt, punching the air with her fist as she walked to the cup. Franzen seethed. He set his ball down and picked up his marker. He tried to control his breathing. He couldn't. His stroke was short and quick and he pushed the ball right, leaving it a foot above the hole.

Karl smirked a secret little smirk as he watched Franzen's facial muscles spasm. Then Franzen made his fatal mistake. He said, "Good?" and gave Karl a pleading look. Karl didn't know how to respond. He didn't have to.

"Everything to the bottom of the cup." Gretchen's voice was cold and critical; it was like a knee to Franzen's groin. He gave her a sheepish grin and tapped in but the damage had been done. He had begged for a gimme. The great sin had been committed and from that day forth a metaphorical archangel stood with a flaming sword of scorn between Franzen and Gretchen Schumacher.

That was the only three-putt Franzen had that day and he finished with a seventy-six, but Karl ran away with the putting contest with just twenty-two and was medalist with a seventy-five. Franzen was begrudgingly graceful in defeat. Gretchen shot seventy-eight and was the big winner, hitting the most fairways and greens and getting closest on all four par threes; with their points subtracted, she ended up taking five bucks from Karl and six from Franzen. She was magnanimous in victory and offered to buy drinks. Karl accepted but Franzen had a lesson waiting on the range and, still stinging from her reaction to his plea for a gimme, begged off.

Gretchen went for the drinks and Karl grabbed a table. He found one in the corner by the fireplace. This was the first time he would have Gretchen to himself and he wanted it to be as private as possible. She slalomed through the empty tables with the drinks held high.

"Couldn't find one farther away?" She said. He reddened. Was it that obvious? "You want to move?" She shook her head and sat down.

They sat and talked. She told him about herself and the more she spoke the more infatuated with her he became. He learned Gretchen was naturally optimistic; he liked that. Of course, she was younger and hadn't seen as much of life as he; she hadn't known the pain of losing fifteen hundred dollars in Las Vegas, the ignominy of failing to get in a fraternity at college, and now the unavoidably depressing thought that he'd taken the wrong job. But she made all of that go away, at least for a while. He felt comfortable with her, at ease. So much so he found the courage to ask her out. She accepted. They agreed on a time when he could pick her up. Gretchen looked at her watch. It was time for her to start her shift on the beverage cart. She touched Karl's hand as she got up and said she'd see him later. Then she was gone.

When Karl got up from the table he noticed Keegan's putter in its place of honor over the fireplace and it reminded him of Lumley's wise counsel. Before he left the course, he drove down to the range and handed the scorecard to Charley.

"No gimmes," he said, as he rode away.

14

Casserly was hunkered down in his hotel room toiling away on his computer when his mobile phone rang. He saw the call was from Midge and set it back down. He'd check his voicemail later. Right now he had to get his thoughts on the ZPGC down while they were fresh. He brought up the calendar and checked his schedule. He sighed. He had one more week before he would be out of this backwater town. He was an architect, not a spy. He didn't enjoy all this subterfuge. Canoeing across a swamp at dawn. Sneaking around a golf course. It was humiliating. If he'd known just how silly it would become he would have passed on the project. But there was no turning back now. Besides, the worst of it was over. One more visit to the course and he could finish his report and get home.

*

When Casserly beached his canoe that morning and crept out of the ooze like his primordial ancestors, he had stopped to listen for the sound of mowers or golfers; hearing neither he moved blithely about his business. But focusing on what he could hear left him blind to what he should have seen: Lumley's cart parked in the tree line not more than forty feet away. Lumley, a closet amateur ornithologist, often came out to this far point on the golf course just after dawn to commune with nature. Paying little attention to the hawk floating above the trees and the ducks drifting among the reeds with their young trailing behind them, Lumley studied the branches above for the rarer species that summered along the Winnehala Wetlands. Sometimes he might sight a fox, or ferret, or one of the muskrats or beavers that lived along the edges of the swamp, but Casserly was the first human he'd spotted out here at this hour. Charley had heard the story of the early morning intruder and had dismissed it. He had been coming out here for years and had never seen a soul. This was his spot, the quietest, most remote place on the golf course. That's what he loved about it. It was so peaceful, so removed from the world that it was hard to believe sometimes he was still in the city.

Lumley was between cigarettes as Casserly came out of the swamp, so there was neither the smell of smoke nor his raspy cough to signal his presence. Casserly walked off in the opposite direction, following the shoreline toward the tenth green. Lumley pondered what had just seen. Then carefully, gingerly, he stepped out of his cart and retraced Casserly's path. He didn't notice the camouflaged canoe until he bumped against it. He pulled the cover away and looked through the gear Casserly had left behind. He found a map of the golf course, but there was something different about it. He studied it for a moment before he put it back. He replaced the camouflage cover and went back to his cart. He lit a cigarette and sat thinking, moving his right hand to his mouth every so often to take a meditative drag; when he finished his smoke he flicked the butt into the swamp and waited, as still and silent as a gargoyle, for Casserly's return. He lowered himself in the cart when he saw him coming back. Lumley checked his watch. He'd been gone about a half hour. Charley watched enraptured as Casserly uncovered his canoe, slipped it into the water and disappeared into the bulrushes.

"Well, I'll be goddamned," he said softly.

*

Dunn sat impassively as Lumley told him all of this. They were alone in the maintenance building; only Lumley's low grumble disturbed the silence. When he finished his story he looked at Dunn, whose lean, angular face was passive and blank. He was wondering why Lumley had chosen to share this information with him, but he didn't want to give the satisfaction of showing curiosity. Lumley, no stranger to silence, waited him out.

"So, he canoes all the way across the Winnehala to get here." Dunn said. "What do you think he's up to?"

Lumley knew he had to tell Dunn about the map. It was the only way to get Dunn's help. Dunn studied the ground while Lumley told him about what he had found in the canoe. When he finished, Dunn didn't say a word.

"What's on that map, what that guy is up to, is the future of this golf course, Dunn, and I don't think that future has a place for either one of us."

They rose spontaneously and stood facing each other.

"Well, it seems there's only one thing to do." Lumley waited for Dunn to finish his point. "Before we go around telling everyone who works here the sky is falling, we've got to confront this fellow and get all the facts."

This made perfect sense to Charley. The only way to get to the bottom of this was to trap the varmint.

*

When Cybil Stumpher first saw Gretchen, she thought of herself at the same age and took an immediate liking to her; when Gretchen first saw Cybil, she thought she was scary and did her best to stay away from her. Time and proximity modified that opinion and Gretchen came to like Cybil, even to understand her a little. She didn't know about her star-crossed love affair with Lumley, but she instinctively knew there had been a great tragedy in Cybil's life, something that had stunted her emotionally and made her the taciturn, brooding, and blunt short-order cook she was today. They never had a talk, never shared their feelings, yet they grew close over the three years Gretchen worked at the ZPGC, first as a counter helper, then as cart girl. They were a study in contrasts, a rose blossoming against a ruin; but a ruin that nonetheless could protect the rose from bitter winds and scorching sun.

Seeing Gretchen and Karl sitting together near the fireplace earlier, happy in each other's company, Cybil felt a pang as memories of moments long ago came back to her. She and Lumley had once sat together like that, maybe at the very same table. She sighed and flipped a burger onto an awaiting bun. How different things might have been had she taken to that idiotic game like Gretchen did; if she could have struck that damned little ball straight maybe the years would not have been so lonely. The man at the counter waiting for his burger attributed the tear on Cybil's cheek to the slice of onion she was setting on his plate. She wiped her face with a coarse white towel and went through the kitchen and out back. Gretchen was just getting into the beverage cart for her first run around the course.

"Saw you and Ketterman gabbing away in the corner. You getting sweet on him?"

Gretchen scrunched up her nose. "I don't know. He's nice. Not a bad golfer, either."

"Be careful, girl. You don't want to end up like me, spending your whole life hanging around this place."

Cybil went back inside. Gretchen, puzzled by the emotion in Cybil's voice, stared at the greasy screen door long after it closed. What did she mean by that?

*

Leaning out from his perch, Mo Mittenthal waved Burchell over. "So, how's it going out there today?"

Burchell parked his cart in front of Mo and nodded. "Not bad. I had a slow group on seven, but I jacked them up." Burchell raised his tattooed forearm to check his watch. What the hell is a "Divel Dags," Mo wondered. He'd have to ask Burchell about that someday.

"You been down sixteen lately?"

Burchell shook his head.

Mo jerked a thumb in the direction of the clubhouse. "The group that just came off eighteen said a sprinkler head by the green is leaking. I haven't seen any of the grounds crew around lately; maybe you should swing by maintenance and let someone know about it."

Burchell saluted and rode away. Mittenthal went back to his crossword puzzle.

*

Lumley and Dunn were coming out of the maintenance building when Burchell pulled up. They turned jaundiced eyes on him; he responded in kind. The scene aroused his suspicion. How could it not? Here were two notorious recluses suddenly chumming around. Burchell smelt a rat; it was the lion lying down with the lamb, Rush Limbaugh lunching with Hillary Clinton: something was up. The click of Lumley's Zippo broke the silence.

"What brings you down here, Rambo?"

Burchell pulled down the brim of his bush hat. His first thought was to laugh and toss Lumley's question back at him. He chose to stick to the purpose of his visit and give himself some time to ferret out what these two zombies were up to.

"There's a broken sprinkler head by the sixteenth green. Mittenthal couldn't find any of your guys around the clubhouse, so he asked me to come down here." He ignored Lumley and focused on Dunn.

Dunn pulled the walkie-talkie from the holster on his hip. "Jorge, over."

Over the static and squelch, Dunn directed one of his crew to sixteen in a pastiche of Spanish and English.

"He'll take care of it," Dunn said and waited for Burchell to ride off. He didn't.

Intuition is an amazing thing. It strikes without warning and, at times, with a clarity that can take one's breath away. Burchell sat up straight in his cart. A smile crossed his face as he scrutinized Lumley and Dunn.

"You guys know something about the homeless guy, don't you? Don't bullshit me; I can see it in your eyes."

Lumley took a drag but stayed tight-lipped, exhaling out his nostrils. His strategy was to stand there, say nothing, and wait Burchell out, even if it took to sundown.

"And what if we do?"

Charley couldn't believe Dunn hadn't picked up on his lead. He took Dunn by the arm and walked away, giving Rambo a wave indicating they'd be with him momentarily.

"Why didn't you dummy up, like me?"

"It seemed pointless. He's got a pretty good idea of what we're up to; I don't think we can shake him now."

"Fine, but do *not* tell him anything more, especially about the map." Charley's throat was beginning to hurt from whispering so loudly.

Dunn looked down and nodded. They walked back to Burchell and told him how the man was getting on the course and where they planned to intercept him. Rambo's eyes brightened.

"I served in 'Nam. I know how to set up an ambush," Burchell said, setting his forearm on top of the wheel to put his tattoo on full display.

"We've got a plan, Rambo, and we're going to follow it," barked Lumley. "If you want to help, fine, but we're not putting on grease paint and camouflage and crawling around in the weeds. We're going to meet here in the morning, have a cup of coffee, go where I know he's going to be and ask him exactly what he's up to. It's as simple as that. No big deal. So just shut up about this. We don't need anyone else knowing about it."

They agreed on a meeting time and Burchell left.

"When he gets here, we'll be gone. We don't need that doofus underfoot."

Dunn shook his head. "Bad idea. If we cut him out he'll tell everyone what we're doing. The only way to keep him quiet is to keep him close."

Lumley shrugged and ground his cigarette under his foot.

*

They reconvened at the maintenance building just before sunrise. The morning was damp and cool. Burchell and Charley rode out to the peninsula in Charley's cart, Dunn in his John Deere Gator; they were in position to intercept the canoeist just as the sun came over the tops of the reeds. It was a perfect morning, cloudless, calm, and, aside from the cacophony of birdcalls, quiet. If they listened very carefully, they could make out the faint sound of traffic from the other side of the Winnehala Wetlands, but for the most part peace and serenity ruled.

It was not unusual for Dunn or Lumley to be on the course at this hour, but it was for Burchell. He had violated his routine to join them at this ungodly hour, and now he sensed the onset of a process that usually took place about this time in the comfort of his upstairs bathroom. It started as a vague inkling, quickly developed into a distinct sensation, then erupted into an irresistible urge. Nature, which usually whispered softly as he sat upon the commode, now shouted out a sharp and clear message that the moment was nigh; it sounded like a low note from a muted trumpet.

"Judas, Burchell," Charley whispered, giving him a withering look, "would you mind getting out of my cart before you do that?"

"Lumley. I got to go. I got to go *now!*"

Dunn shook his head in disgust. "Charley, let him take the cart back to the clubhouse." A second, more sustained bass note was sounded.

"I don't think I can hold it that long."

"Are you shitting me?"

"Goddamn it, Charley, I'm about to shit myself!" Burchell's face was flushed and sweaty. He crouched over as he got out of the cart and stumbled down into the brush. Charley, repulsed by Burchell's lack of self-control, kept his eyes on the swamp. He whispered to Rambo to move further away so he wouldn't tip off the canoeist. Dunn went near the brush, but not too close, to make sure Burchell was all right. What he could hear told him the problem was being resolved. Then Burchell whispered something Dunn couldn't quite make out.

"What?"

"Toilet paper!" Burchell said in a harsh whisper. "I need toilet paper. You got any in your vehicle?"

"Why the hell would I have toilet paper in my Gator?"

"Kleenex? Napkin? A towel?"

Dunn looked at the golf bag on Lumley's cart.

"I'm not giving him my towel."

"We can't leave him down there. That guy is going to be paddling up here any minute. Hey, how about a glove?"

Charley went to his bag. He took out a golf glove and held it out to Dunn with two fingers as if Burchell had already used it. Dunn tossed the glove over the brush and then, hearing a sound not too far away, froze. It was the thud of a paddle hitting the side of an aluminum canoe. He crept back to Lumley's side.

The canoe glided out of the reeds and ran aground in the shallow water about thirty yards south of them. Casserly stepped out and pulled the canoe ashore. He unloaded his gear, covered the canoe, and walked up to the golf course. He looked right and left. Dunn picked up a rock and threw it in the bushes to Casserly's left. Casserly turned, staring intently into the brush. He never heard Dunn come up behind him. There was a sudden, sharp pain at the back of his neck. He tried to turn around but his knees were buckling under him. He staggered forward, trying to regain his equilibrium. There was a shrill ringing in his ears. He started to put his hand on the back of his head where the pain seemed to be centered. Then the grass rushed up at him.

*

Lumley ran up to the canoeist as he hit the ground. His eyes darted between the sap in Dunn's hand and the prostrate figure as he struggled to get the words out of his mouth.

"Shit, you killed him!"

Dunn gave Lumley a look that told him he was next if he didn't shut up.

"Help me get him in the Gator."

Burchell came out of the brush buckling his belt as they were laying the body in the back of Dunn's vehicle. Burchell's eyes pleaded for an explanation.

"We'll talk back at the maintenance building. Get all his stuff out of the canoe," Dunn said placidly.

Dunn put a bag of grass seed under the canoeist's head and drove off, Charley and Burchell right behind him. Burchell had missed seeing Dunn knock the canoeist out but he was still in a mild state of shock. If this guy were dead he and Charley would be accessories. That meant arrest, trial, disgrace, and maybe years in prison. Hadn't he heard rumors about Dunn, that he had some sort of criminal past? Maybe this wasn't his first murder. Maybe when he and Charley got to the maintenance building they'd be next. He looked over at Lumley. His face was grim.

"What do you think, Charley?"

Charley hit the brakes and gave Rambo a steely stare. "I think you owe me a new goddamn glove," growled Charley.

He sped up to keep them within a few feet of Dunn's Gator. They could see the man's feet hanging over the top of the gate. Dunn took the long way back to the maintenance building, keeping off the fairways and out of sight of the clubhouse.

*

Contrary to popular belief, most first dates go swimmingly. Both parties are usually on their best behavior and anxious to make a good impression so there are few chances for things to go awry. Even if one of them is convinced at the outset that it's a one-time event, a first date can be a pleasant experience for both of them as long as the rules are observed. The first rule is to make sure the setting is appropriate. Secluded locations, personal residences, or anything suggesting an overnight stay are not good choices. The second rule is to keep the conversation general. Childhood trauma, previous relationships, phobias, physical scars, and medical histories should be avoided. The third rule: keep it simple. Dinner and a movie, or a movie and a drink are good options. Asking your date to attend a family event, pose for "artistic" photos, or play Twister are not. A successful first date is a lot like a business lunch, a chance to learn more about the other person in an inviting public place. And both should end much the same way, with a handshake and an agreement to possibly do this again.

Ketterman's evening with Gretchen Schumacher followed these general rules. As the evening processed, he learned her father was an insurance agent and a Shriner. She learned that he had two sisters and his mother was born in Canada. They learned they had things in common: neither could understand the infield fly rule; the appeal of NASCAR, the Kardashians, or *Dancing With the Stars*; or the fairness of 6-6b of the *Rules of Golf*.

Karl, already smitten with Gretchen, was smitten even more after an evening with her. It was the first time he'd seen her in a dress, a casual summer frock—sleeveless, scoop-necked, falling just above her knees—that he knew instinctively she had put no thought into selecting. It was just what she felt like wearing at the moment; it was feminine, casual, simple, and suited her perfectly. Her hair, always in a thick braid at the golf course, fell like a golden mantilla over her shoulders. He'd never seen such hair in all his life, thick, blonde, lustrous, simply brushed out and left to fall how it may. The only other changes in her appearance were a light application of pale red lipstick, a faint whiff of perfume, a silver bracelet on her left wrist, and thin-strapped sandals. He tried to imagine her in high heels without success; he wondered if she wore flats for fear that heels would make her taller than him; not that he would have cared. He was infatuated with every Teutonic inch of her and she already towered over him from the pedestal on which he had put her.

Karl couldn't help being mildly disappointed with her parents. While Karl could see Gretchen bore some resemblance to her mother, neither parent had her physical presence. They were friendly and engaging, but he had expected them to be more imposing, more like Odin and Freya. Her father was a tall, thin, rather timid-looking man; her mother wore an uncomfortable smile and said very little the whole evening. They didn't seem capable of producing something as magnificent as Gretchen.

They had dinner at a restaurant in the neighborhood, sitting outside under a vine-covered trellis. Gretchen ate daintily, pausing between each bite to look around and take it all in. He was happy his choice pleased her.

"You going to stay here, Karl?"

"At least through dinner."

She gave him a look. The question seemed odd to him; didn't she know he'd moved halfway across the country for this job?

"Yep. I like it here."

"You like the ZPGC? Really?"

"Well, for the time being, yeah. I've always wanted to work at a golf course. If the Lochenberry offers me a better deal, I suppose I'll take it."

She laughed at that; like everything else about her it was big and bright and attractive. There was a vase of flowers on the table. Gretchen gave Karl a conspiratorial look, took a cornflower from the arrangement and put it behind her ear. The cornflower accentuated the blueness of her eyes. He tried not to stare at her but it was hard not to after that. They ordered dessert and she ate it with the relish of a five-year-old. "What an amazing girl," Karl thought as he watched her tipping the dish to scoop the last remnant of melted ice cream from the bottom.

They had planned on going to a movie but there was a long line in front of the theater and Gretchen suggested an alternative.

"Let's go for a walk in The Willows."

Karl felt his heart rate jump. Was she luring him to a secluded place to seduce him? She took his hand, innocuously, like a mother takes a child's, as they walked to the car. She directed while he drove, taking him through a part of town he hadn't explored yet. He had no idea where they were going until they pulled up in front of the gates.

"This is a cemetery."

"Hey, you're quick."

Gretchen was out of the car as soon as it came to a stop. "C'mon, I'll show you around."

For the next hour they wandered among the mausoleums, tombstones, and obelisks, Gretchen pointing out the resting places of MacMullens, Pallisers, and Draydens, the pioneers, industrialists, and merchants who had built our fair city. Karl learned she'd spent hours here as a child, wandering around, lounging on the cool porticoes of grand granite tombs, dreaming of palaces and princes. Karl tried to look interested but couldn't overlook the fact that even though the summer sun still shimmered in the leaves and the shadows were still penetrable they were wandering aimlessly about a necropolis. The gravel path crunched beneath their feet and swallows swooped around them. Karl walked closer and their shoulders brushed. He stopped and took her hand. She turned and looked at him.

"Gretchen."

"Yes, Karl?"

He knew what he wanted to say, yet sensed this was neither the time nor place for saying it. She cocked her head ever so slightly, waiting for him to speak.

"What do you say we hit a few golf balls?"

A smile radiated her face. He wanted to kiss her more than ever but she was already in full stride down the path on her way to the car.

"Let's get going! I love hitting under the lights."

He kicked himself for being such a coward and hurried to catch up with her.

There were still cars in the lot when they arrived, and the lights were just coming on down at the driving range. Karl was relieved to see Franzen's car was gone. Cybil was just leaving as they got out of the car; she gave Gretchen a soft, melancholy look as she passed by. They sat on a bench near the putting green and watched a young father herding his two children as they whacked golf balls around with little plastic putters. A soft breeze moved the warm air around them. Karl watched as Gretchen combed her hair behind her ear with her fingers. He wanted desperately to whisper into that ear.

"Gretchen." When she looked at him he lost confidence in words.

"What?"

"I'd like to do this again." He felt sick. That was all he could muster?

"Maybe next time we should go to the movie first." She was smiling at him. He felt good.

Gretchen jumped to her feet. "Your clubs are in the car, right?"

He got them out of the trunk as she sat in the passenger seat pulling her hair back into a ponytail. They went down to the range and hit a small bucket. Her swing looked even better in a dress. After that he took her home. It was still early but she had to be up early for work.

On the drive to his apartment Karl reflected on his decision to take the job at the Zebulon Pike Golf Course. It had more issues than he'd bargained for; repairs were needed to the clubhouse, the entryway was uninviting, the staff was an odd lot, the divided management of the clubhouse, food and beverage services, and maintenance crew was a major stumbling block to change, and, most discouraging of all, it seemed as if the Parks Commission could care less if the course flourished or failed. Maybe he should have stayed in California. At least he had friends there.

As Karl was getting out of the car, something on the floor caught his eye. It was the cornflower from Gretchen's hair. He picked it up, put it to his nose, and closed his eyes. Maybe things weren't as bad as they seemed.

15

It was dark. His head throbbed and the air was stifling and smelt of burlap and rotting vegetation. He heard people moving about. A new smell invaded the darkness. Someone was smoking a cigarette.

"We have a few questions for you, Mr. Casserly."

"Yeah, start talking."

"Am I bleeding?" Casserly whined through the sack.

"Bloody thou art, bloody will be thy end;
Shame serves thy life and doth thy death attend."

It was the first voice again; there was a long pause.

"What the *hell* is that supposed to mean?" said the second voice.

The bag came off suddenly, the light stinging Casserly's eyes; he squinted and blinked, the abrupt change from pitch black to daylight making it hard to focus. He could see two older men—one with a cigarette in his mouth and a burlap bag in his hand—and a younger guy, quiet and ominous-looking, wearing a green jumpsuit that didn't fit him very well. Casserly took a deep, calming breath before he dared to speak.

"What happened? Where am I? Who are you?"

"How about you answer a question first? What are you doing on our golf course?" It was the other older guy. Casserly noted his bush hat and tattoo. They would be part of the police complaint he would file when he got away from these lunatics.

"Is it a crime to be on a golf course? Does that give you the right to kidnap me like this?" Casserly looked pleadingly at his captors. He was becoming more and more frightened. The more he studied his abductors, the greater the odds seemed that they were about to murder him. The smoker pulled up a chair and sat in front of Casserly.

"Skip the crap, Casserly. You didn't just wander onto the course, you paddled all the way across that goddamned swamp at the crack of dawn to get here; and it's not the first time you've done it. You've been spotted before. That's why we were waiting for you." Lumley paused to take a drag. "We've gone through your canoe so we know what you're up to, the only thing we want to know is who's behind this? Who hired you and why?"

Casserly looked at his potential murderers and pondered his options for a moment. "Cut me loose and we'll talk," he said, studying their faces, trying to detect a glimpse of compassion in any of them. The smoker turned to his companions and gave the creepy one in the jumpsuit a nod. When he walked behind the chair Casserly wasn't sure if he was going to cut his throat or free him until he felt the rope go slack across his chest. His first act as a free man was to rub the lump on the back of his head.

"Who do I thank for this?"

The lanky gargoyle produced a homemade sap from his back pocket. Casserly gave him the evil eye.

"A guy named Midge hired me. I'm working for him. There are two other guys who I think are in on the deal with him named Chartreuse and Mil...brook, Mil...." Casserly could see the name he was struggling for was getting their attention.

"Milbank? Was the guy's name Milbank?"

"That might have been it. I only saw him once."

"Was he balding, about fifty, smug; kind of a pretentious prick?" Dunn leaned in toward Casserly.

"Yeah, that sounds like him. Like I said, I only saw him once. Midge brought up his name a couple of times, said he works for the city, but I don't know anything more about him than that. Midge said he was important to getting the project done."

The smoker dropped his cigarette and ground it into the concrete. "Maybe you should start from the beginning."

*

A man in love is much like an ox in a slaughterhouse just as the poleax hits his forehead; for a split second he seems unfazed, then he's down. From that point things go from bad to worse. Thus, metaphorically, we find Karl Ketterman. It is the morning of Casserly's capture, the Monday after his date with Gretchen. He sits at his desk, sipping his morning coffee, the details of the course's weekend business spread before him; all seems normal on the surface but his mind can focus only on fleeting images of the golden Gretchen. Ketterman is no longer in sole possession of his faculties. Emotion has displaced reason, sentiment has co-opted commonsense, and passion has pushed clear thinking to the curb, yet even with his mind dimmed by the blunt force of love's poleax, Karl is vaguely aware of his predicament. He stands up and rubs his temples vigorously. He knew he needed to clear his head, to go outside and get some fresh air.

*

Karl didn't notice Clayton Doherty waving at him as he crossed the grillroom and barely felt his hand on his shoulder as he was walking out the door.

"Hey, Karl. You ready for next weekend?"

Karl turned to Doherty and smiled, envisioning a weekend alone with Gretchen somewhere far from the ZPGC.

"I can't wait."

"Great. I just posted the starting times on the bulletin board. You're off at 7:35." Doherty could see Karl wasn't following him. "The Keegan Cap, Karl; next Saturday. You committed to playing in it. Remember?"

Karl started like a sleepwalker. "Oh, sure, Clayton, sure. I guess I'm a little distracted. Of course I'll be there. Absolutely. You can count on me."

Doherty gave him a fraternal pat on the arm and left Karl to his morning airing. As Karl walked around the east side of the clubhouse he saw Lumley coming up the path from the maintenance area with a passenger in his cart. It was a rare thing to see Lumley this far away from the range. Karl didn't recognize

the man in the cart with Lumley. He clearly wasn't dressed for
golf, even by the casual-to-nonexistent standards of the ZPGC. He
wore a khaki shirt and quasi military-style pants with pockets
everywhere and muddied boots. He looked very displeased with
Lumley and rubbed the back of his head as if it were a magic
lantern. As they drove by Karl thought he heard Lumley say, "Don't
be such a pussy," to the man. He watched the cart as it went across
the parking lot then down the driveway to the street. "That's
strange," thought Karl, but he lost interest in Lumley and his
passenger as he came around the clubhouse and saw the spot where
he and Gretchen had parked Saturday evening; he sighed and
wandered down to the driving range. He stopped at the top of the
hill and looked down the tenth fairway. In the distance he could see
the Winnehala Wetlands stretching for hundreds of acres beyond
the course. The ZPGC never looked so placid and inviting. Then it
struck him: Lumley had driven up from the maintenance area. Why
would he be down there? Karl shrugged. Maybe Lumley and Dunn
were pals. He paused to take in the course again. Love made it all
so beautiful.

*

Lumley turned right at the entrance and drove his cart down the
sidewalk. He took another right at the corner and drove down the
north side of the golf course all the way to the eastern edge of the
Winnehala Wetlands. Casserly's car was alone in the parking lot.
   "What about the canoe? It's a rental."
   "Dunn's putting it in the maintenance building; it'll be fine."
   "You know, I have every right to press charges."
   Lumley rolled his eyes. "Yeah, you do that. But maybe you
should know we're not the only ones that have noticed you skulking
around here. Golfers have reported a suspicious character to the
manager; they were referring to *you*. It's not a park; it's a golf
course. You have to pay to be on it. Otherwise you're trespassing.
And we have the legal right to detain trespassers."
   "With a blackjack to the back of the head? That's bullshit and you
know it."

"So, call the cops. But you're still going to have to explain to them why you paddled all the way across a swamp at the crack of dawn to get on a municipal golf course open to everyone; I bet they're going to find that kind of fishy. They'll probably start asking you all sorts of questions. Before you know it, this whole project will be out in the open; it'll probably make the papers and the evening news. I don't think your employer Mr. Midge would like that."

Casserly stared at Lumley; Lumley stared back. Casserly blinked.

"I want that canoe and all my stuff in it back."

"Go home and get some rest. Come back this evening and we'll load it up for you. This time come in the front gate like everyone else."

Lumley couldn't see Casserly giving him the finger as he drove away; he just took it for granted.

*

Clayton Doherty was a man of unimpeachable integrity and had spent many hours setting up the foursomes for the Keegan. No one dared ask to be paired up with a friend or for an early tee time; those decisions were his and his alone and he guarded his prerogative as chairman of the tournament as an eagle does its young. Clayton also valued ritual and pageantry, and continuing the traditions of the Keegan Cap were a sacred duty to him. His father had played in the Cap, his brother had been disabled in it, and Clayton himself had won the Cap three times. The only person who had won it more was Crupshaw. But he took even greater pride in the fact that his grandfather had been in the foursome that fateful day when Ambrose Keegan's head had left his body and his soul this world. For all those reasons and more, Clayton was both judicious and scrupulous in setting up the field for the Keegan Cap.

The Keegan Cap had standards. It was not open to any and all; participants had to have a current USGA handicap of fourteen or less. In putting together the foursomes Clayton tried to mix up the players as much as possible. He assigned a number to each one then drew them to form the foursomes; the exception was the first group, which comprised Clayton, Crupshaw, Karl, and Billy Lupus.

Ketterman may not have noticed Clayton that Monday morning but everyone else in the clubhouse had; they knew this was the day he would post the foursomes and starting times for this year's Cap. A hush fell over the room as he walked in with his brother. "Roll Tide," chirped Dan as he strolled merrily to the counter. Sundbaum nudged Rankel, who cleared his throat to get Armstead and Hood's attention. All eight eyeballs followed Clayton to the bulletin board. Without fanfare, he posted the single sheet of paper and went to the counter to join his brother. Armstead, with an artificial air of nonchalance, rose and walked to the bulletin board, casting his eyes over the "for sale" and other random postings before fixing his gaze on the sheet. The less subtle Rankel, Sundbaum, and Hood were already crowding around it, their fingers sliding down the list to locate the player they had pegged to win this year.

"I like the Hallenbeck kid; hits it a mile, good short game."

"Nah. Jay Halling. He was close last year and, after Crupshaw, he's the best putter and the greens are in the best shape they've been in all year. He's the guy."

They were soon joined by others; some to find out when they played, most just curious to know what the field was like this year. There was someone perusing the list for the rest of the day. The Keegan Cap was fast approaching and the Zebulon Pike Golf Course was abuzz with expectation.

*

Cybil watched the hubbub around the bulletin board and gave it a dismissive snort; silly old men and misguided young ones wasting their lives fixating on an equally silly game. She scoured the grill with her wire brush, occasionally looking up to take in the world around her and seeing nothing good in it. She thought about an article she'd seen in the paper the other day about modern reproductive medicine and how it could someday make the male's role in perpetuating the species totally unnecessary; she looked out at the motley assortment of men lounging around the clubhouse and imagined the whole lot of them going the way of the dodo bird.

The thought warmed her heart almost as much as the sight of her now gleaming grill.

*

Gretchen stopped her beverage cart behind the tenth green and rested from her labors. There was a scramble tournament underway; that meant plenty of once-a-year golfers on the course and lots of beer sales. She'd replenished her supply three times and was almost empty again. She already had over seventy dollars in tips; it meant putting up with the usual come-on lines and "unintentional" touches, but nothing she couldn't handle. She'd been fending off wandering hands since she was thirteen.

Gretchen took the sunscreen out of the console and reapplied it to her forearms, neck, and face. The sun could find her even under the roof of the cart and she was a cautious girl. As she slathered more on her neck she mused about her future. This fall she'd be in college and playing NCAA golf; she felt suddenly melancholy at the thought of leaving the ZPGC. She'd practically grown up here. She had been Women's League champion for the last five years and represented the ZPGC in the state amateur since she was fifteen, and would do so again this year. It was perhaps a bit threadbare and overplayed, but she was proud to claim the Zebulon Pike as her home course. She'd played a lot of different golf courses but there was something special about this old track. Gretchen took a deep breath and sat up straight. There was no reason to be melancholy; wonderful things awaited her in the future, she knew it. She hit the accelerator and rumbled off toward the eleventh hole.

16

Welmont Washington walked briskly through the Boutiqué Afriqué acknowledging with a nod and a smile the men and women sitting in the chairs and taking the stairs up to the corporate offices on the second floor two at a time. He closed the door to his office and sat down at the computer. He had asked the woman who did his advertising to come up with a poster for the Ebon Invitational and she had phoned him on his way into the office to say she had one ready for him to review. He opened his email and studied the design for a minute. He liked it. He fished his phone out of his jacket pocket and dialed her number.

"Make the logo bigger."

He hung up and looked at the design again. Yes, he liked it. But he was even more pleased with the idea of sponsoring a golf tournament, especially one with so much potential. It had so many possible tie-ins—black history, black sports, and the local black community—and, of course, corporate partnerships. And now his company was going to be front and center on the whole deal. He was confident that under his leadership it wouldn't be long before the Ebon Invitational became a huge local, even regional, event with professional athletes, celebrities, and politicians begging to be part of the field. He imagined the best young golfers in the country playing it. And the impresario of all of that would be Welmont Washington. He couldn't help but smile. Of course, he would have to find a better venue, a course with more prestige, more impressive surroundings, better facilities, but this year and next he had to reconcile himself to the Zebulon Pike. The key was patience. Rome wasn't built in a day.

The only bug on the windshield marring the vista before Welmont was Tyreal Sumter; dealing with that fool was going to be a trial, but he'd handled guys like him before and he knew how to subtly—or not so subtly, if necessary—move them to the side. Welmont ran a finger along the bottom of his moustache and pondered at what point it would be best to squeeze that fat brother out of the picture; but first things first.

*

Welmont circled the lot twice before he found a place where he felt the Bentley would be safe. He hadn't been at the Zebulon Pike for years, maybe decades. He caddied here as a kid, but only for a couple of weeks. Then he moved on to the old White Elk Country Club where the wealthy, socially conscious membership always tipped a polite young Negro kid well. Now he played there every year in the member-guest tournament and always gave a big tip to the polite young white kid who carried his bag.

The smell of greasy food, sweat, and stale beer assaulted him as he entered the clubhouse. An angry-looking heavyset woman eyeballed him from behind the counter. Something about her seemed vaguely familiar. Had she been there when he was a kid? Two surly-looking men who looked like they could be brothers stood scowling at a piece of paper on the bulletin board. The rest of the occupants were equally odd and off-putting. The people, the shabby state of the once elegant room, somehow it all seemed a little sad to him. He walked quickly through the door to the screened-in verandah. There, ensconced in a chair created for a less substantial man, sat Tyreal with his faithful sidekick Scrumpy next to him. Tyreal's hand was immersed in a large basket of fries that he had liberally sprinkled with salt. He had eschewed the catsup; he was committed to losing weight before this year's Ebon.

"Mr. Washington! Well, well, well! It is good to see you. Join us won't you?"

Welmont gave the chair a close inspection before sitting; he didn't want to stain his linen trousers.

"Thank you, Tyreal. I thought I'd drop by and take a look at our venue. My, my, the old ZPGC isn't what she used to be, huh?"

"The clubhouse surely has seen better days, sir, there's no denying that. But the course is still a challenging track. These young kids may be able to hit it a mile, but the guy who set up this course must have seen them coming because not too many of them go low here. That's why the Ebon always attracts the best."

Welmont gave Tyreal a look that Tyreal deftly avoided by studying the fry he'd just pulled from the basket. Welmont turned his eyes toward the first tee in time to see a guy in cut-off jeans and a tank top take a wicked swing and completely miss the ball. This definitely was not the place for his Ebon Invitational; it was far too accessible to the unwashed masses for Welmont's tastes.

"I've been considering your proposal, Tyreal. Here's what I would like to do. I'll handle all publicity and promotions for this year's event, including registration and entry fees. All you have to do is manage everything here the day of the Ebon, meet and greet the players and act as master of ceremonies. I will also provide a one-thousand dollar scholarship for a deserving young black person under twenty, and I'll make sure there are lots of prizes donated from local businesses; no one who signs up for this tournament is going to walk away empty-handed, I guarantee you. I can also assure you at least one player from every major league team in town will play in this year's Ebon. And no later than thirty days after the event is over, you and I will sit down and review everything; at that time I'll decide whether or not to continue my sponsorship of the Ebon Invitational."

Scrumpy Scroggins clapped his hands and grinned broadly. Tyreal drove the toe of his shoe into the side of his foot. Scrumpy winced; he got the message and settled back in his chair. Tyreal did his best to keep his emotions in check. He wiped his fingertips daintily with a paper napkin, allowing himself time to think through his response. The Ebon was held on the second weekend in September and the clock was ticking. This was the chance to resurrect his father's event that Tyreal had been praying for; he knew he had to jump at this offer but he felt it was important to keep his cool.

"Well, Mr. Washington, that is indeed generous of you, however, as the son of the founder of the Ebon Invitational, I've always had input into every element…"

"That's my offer, Tyreal," Welmont said, standing up. "I've given it a great deal of thought and it's really nonnegotiable. If you choose not to take it, I understand. No offense taken. Business is business. But if we're going to breathe some life into this event, given the limitations of time," he extended his arms to take in his surroundings, "and the fact that the course itself doesn't have any drawing power, we've got to get moving. But I don't want to rush you. Think it over and let me know your decision by noon tomorrow."

Welmont extended his right hand. Tyreal struggled to his feet and grabbed it with both of his.

"No need to waste time thinking about it, Welmont. We've got a deal."

Welmont called his lawyer in the parking lot, telling him what he wanted in the agreement and to start drafting it immediately. The lawyer repeated the stipulations, caveats, and addenda Welmont wanted as he calculated the hours he could bill for his time on a legal pad. He told Welmont the contract would be ready within the week.

"Make sure it's airtight."

*

After icing his sore head for an hour, Casserly decided it was time to break the bad news to Midge.

"They hit you on the head and tied you up for walking on a public golf course?"

"They seemed to think it was within their rights."

"They're out of their minds; you going to sue them?"

"I haven't decided yet. But I thought I better let you know what happened first."

"So what's the problem?"

Casserly was a little baffled by Midge's response. He had kept everything about this project so close to the vest that Dan assumed he would be upset at the possibility of it all suddenly being out in the open. Midge clearly didn't understand the import of what he was telling him.

"Well, they didn't just get me, Mr. Midge, they got everything that was in the canoe, my maps, my notebook, the layout; everything about the project." The silence on the other end of the line told Casserly that Midge got it now: a couple of Parks Commission employees were about to blow two years of work to smithereens.

"Have they talked to anyone else about this?"

"I have no idea."

"Well, get an idea! You're the one that told them about this!"

"I'm not a covert operative or your employee, Mr. Midge," Casserly fired back. "And I'm pretty sure the contract the company has with you doesn't say anything about what I reveal under torture."

"All right, all right, take it easy. Don't get dramatic on me." Midge paused for a few moments. "Where's your stuff now?"

"They've got it in the maintenance building. I'm going back there this afternoon to get it."

"I'm going with you."

Midge said he would be by the hotel to pick him up around five. Casserly hung up and sprawled out face down on the bed, a wet washcloth on the back of his head. As bizarre as this project was, he never imagined it would lead to him getting hit with a blackjack. It would make an interesting story back at the office.

*

The map was unfurled on the desk in Dunn's office at the back of the maintenance building, one end held at bay with a chunk of concrete, the other with the head from an old 3-iron. Dunn, with Burchell and Charley on either side of him, stared down at it as his grimy finger slowly moved across the surface. It was late afternoon and no one was in the building but the three of them.

"I don't get it," Burchell muttered.

"What's not to get? This is exactly what Casserly said he was working on. It's obvious. And you can bet there are other big money guys and politicians behind this. Obviously, they want to keep this hush-hush until they have everything ready, every detail covered; looking at this I'd say they're just about there. The days of Zebulon Pike Golf Course are numbered, boys, and I'm going to be out of a job." Dunn lifted the chunk of concrete with a flourish and the map rolled up.

Lumley and Rambo looked at each other. They knew the closing of the course was an even worse fate for them. Dunn, odd as he was, was still a relatively young man who knew what he was doing on a golf course. He wouldn't have too much trouble finding a job as the greenskeeper at another course—but what about them? What could they look forward to when the ZPGC closed? Where would they spend their days? What would they do? Burchell could see long summer days spent with his wife, puttering around the house and yard. The thought made him shudder.

"We got to do something about this," Charley growled.

"Like what?"

"Talk to Ketterman. He'll want to fight for his job, won't he?"

"A guy who hasn't been on the job for a year is going to save the day? What can he do to stop Midge, a guy with lots of money and plenty of pull? Don't kid yourself, there's nothing Ketterman or anyone else can do." Lumley had no answer for Dunn.

There was nothing more to do than sit and wait for Casserly.

*

History had always fascinated Karl, so it was a pleasure for him to close his office door for an hour every afternoon and page through the material on his shelf, learning more about the Keegan Cap, the Ebon Invitational, the club championships, and the men who had preceded him. The dust and musty odor that permeated everything told him he was the first person in decades—maybe ever—to go through all this stuff. Some of his finds made it all worthwhile; like the photo album that documented the building of the course. He was surprised to see how little had changed. He'd been told that acres of wetlands had been filled in to create the course, but these photos showed most of the dirt brought in was used to build the tee boxes and greens. The fairways were mostly just cleared off with a slight contour or berm added here and there. Karl took a photo of the first fairway out of the album and went outside. Standing at the same vantage point behind the first tee box as the photographer had in 1934, Karl saw virtually the same scene that had been captured decades earlier. The tree line on either side of the fairway had changed some—hardly surprising after so many years—but the hole was essentially the same. The album made clear that whoever had laid out the course had not altered the existing topography very much, letting the holes emerge from the landscape, allowing nature to reveal its own design. Maybe that's why the course was still so challenging after all this time.

As Karl contemplated these things walking back to the clubhouse, two men hurried across his path. He recognized one of them. It was the man he'd seen in Lumley's cart that morning. The other, much bigger man seemed familiar too, someone he'd seen on the course. They walked briskly past Karl and down the path to the maintenance building. Karl assumed they were sales reps and went back to his office. With the Keegan Cap fast approaching, he wanted to learn all he could about it.

*

"Who's there?" Dunn asked. With the bright daylight behind them, he couldn't make out the two figures standing just inside the door; he had assumed Casserly would be coming alone.

"It's me, Casserly. This is the man I work for. He wants to talk to you guys."

"Come on in, then, and let's talk," Dunn said.

It took a moment for Midge and Casserly's eyes to adjust to the dark interior of the maintenance building. Dunn stood by a lawn mower; Burchell and Charley were sitting on a bench, their backs against the wall, arms folded, frowning at the intruders. Dunn gestured Midge and Casserly into his office.

Dunn's office was a small plywood structure with a large window looking out onto the shop and a smaller one to the outside. All that was visible through the outside window were the leaves of the elm that had taken root next to the building. Dunn sat behind his desk and Midge took the one chair that faced it; Burchell and Lumley flanked the desk, Casserly stood like an aide-de-camp behind Midge.

"Well, fellas, I'm no lawyer, but I think you may be in a bit of trouble, abducting Mr. Casserly here and holding him prisoner..."

"Let's not pussyfoot around, shall we? We know what's going on here. How we found out isn't going to matter much to the media when they get wind of it; political intrigue, backroom deals with the city power brokers, a rich man grabbing up city property; they're going to eat it up. The three of us have absolutely *nothing* to lose. You, on the other hand, Mr...?

"Midge. Robert Midge."

"You, Mr. Midge, have a lot to lose." Dunn leaned back in his chair, Lumley and Burchell nodding solemnly.

Midge squirmed and the chair creaked. "Hey, I have nothing to hide. I am a developer looking into a *prospective* project—a prospective project—and there's nothing unusual about keeping such things on the down low."

Dunn, Lumley, and Burchell stared back at him. Midge decided it was time to get to the point.

"Okay, it's important to me and my partners that this deal be kept a secret for a while. There's nothing crooked going on here, it just takes a lot of time and effort to move these things forward and if word gets out too early then people get cold feet. We asked Mr. Casserly here to keep out of the public eye and not draw any attention to his work." He paused to glare at Casserly. "For obvious reasons. I mean, you guys are a perfect example of what I'm talking about; you get wind of what he's up to and you automatically assume it's all bad; your golf course is gone and you're out of a job; right away, it's a worst-case scenario." He paused to study his audience. He knew he'd found his theme. "No one wants to lose their job, I understand that. So here's the deal: I'm prepared to offer all three of you jobs at the Lochenberry Country Club, with a reasonable increase in what you're currently being paid here, of course. And I will put that in writing. All I ask in return is that you give Mr. Casserly's property back and don't say a word of this to anyone."

Midge sat back and waited for a response. He could see the wheels turning; he had the greenskeeper's attention for sure. The other two were a little harder to read. Regardless, Midge saw the best strategy was to wait them out. A fly trapped in the office buzzed furiously as it banged itself over and over against the window behind Dunn.

Midge swung his arms out wide. "Guys, this project is a good thing for everyone. I'm not putting up an apartment complex or a shopping mall. This is going to be a very good thing for the city, believe me."

Dunn unrolled the map and studied it closely. Midge knew he was the guy who was going to make the decision for all of them.

"And, it goes without saying, if you play ball, " Midge added, impatiently, "Mr. Casserly will forget about everything that took place earlier today."

Dunn locked eyes with Midge. This was the type of guy she had chosen over him, he thought, the kind with the breezy confidence and facile tongue that always comes out on top; a man who can insinuate himself comfortably into any situation; smug, arrogant, and at ease in the world, everything Dunn wasn't. He decided he didn't like Mr. Midge.

"We'll think about it," he said. Without looking at Dunn or each other, Lumley and Burchell nodded in agreement.

"Fair enough. But keep this in mind, guys. You know as well as I do that the days of this golf course are numbered. Let's say you blow the lid off this deal; all that will do is bring the viability of this place into the light of day. You're right, the media will eat it up, but are you really that confident they're going to see the situation your way? This project could bring a lot of money into the city, much more than this course ever could. Think about it. And let me know by Friday if we can do business or not." Midge rose and pulled out his wallet. He took out a business card and slid it across the desk to Dunn, then he and Casserly walked out of the office. Lumley and Burchell moved closer to Dunn, studying the card on the table.

"What a collection of boneheads," Midge whispered as they walked back into the sunlight. Casserly wasn't so sure.

17

Clayton Doherty stood in the center of the clubhouse, watching solemnly as the morning sunlight struck the bronze plaque, the unflinching stare of Zebulon Pike brightening under his feet. Not once, he had been told, in its long and storied history had the sun failed to illuminate the hero on the morning of the Keegan Cap. Clayton turned to the crowd of mostly older men who stood around him, men who reminded him of his father, and his throat tightened with emotion. He took a deep breath.

"The first group in this year's Keegan Cap will tee off in fifteen minutes."

The Keegan Cap was officially underway; the clubhouse hummed with energy. Cybil, who had come in an hour early to prepare for the breakfast rush, looked out the pass-through as she buttered toast in the kitchen, barking directions at the two kids working the counter. Her eyes followed Karl as he came in the back door and went into his office. She still felt a twinge of conscience for having talked about him behind his back to Milbank, reporting on him every other week, and her conscience was beginning to bother her. There was nothing damning in what she communicated to Milbank, just a litany of banal activities that reassured him the ZPGC was moving slowly, inexorably, steadily toward its demise.

*

Charley Lumley was ready for the Keegan Cap. This would be

his fortieth appearance, and although he knew he had no chance of winning, he looked forward to it as much as anyone. He had, in fact, never won it, holding the dubious distinction of finishing second eight times. He warmed up at the far end of the range with a small basket, pausing between shots to watch others on the range. He was familiar with all the good players in town and recognized most of those hitting balls; one in particular got his attention. Charley shaded his eyes with one hand and squinted. "I'll be damned if that's not Murlofsky," he mumbled.

Charley hit another ball and watched it fly. The wedge felt like an extension of his will. He was glad he'd regripped his clubs last night.

*

The field for the Keegan Cap was one of the best in years. Twelve foursomes were on the tee sheet, each with at least one player with a legitimate chance to win and, even though no one other than a member of the Zebulon Pike Men's Club had ever hoisted the trophy in victory, each of the city's three other municipal golf courses was represented by at least one player.

A few minutes after watching the sunlight strike Pike's brass visage, Clayton ducked his head into the doorway of Karl's office.

"It's time."

Karl put down his newspaper and followed Clayton outside. They turned right and walked to the flagpole on the south side of the clubhouse between the putting green and the tenth tee. The color guard from the local VFW was already in place, the sun glinting off their chrome helmet liners. Karl felt slightly embarrassed for the overweight, aging veterans in their tight-fitting uniforms. Clayton, familiar with the ritual, guided Karl into position next to the flagpole and nodded to the NCO in charge.

"Detail...ten-hut!"

The color guard did their best to assume the erect posture of their younger years. The NCO marched over to the flagpole, loosed the halyard, and began to slowly raise the flag held by two other veterans. In the distance, Karl could hear the first mournful notes of "Taps." He put his hand over his heart and watched as the flag reached the top. The veterans, eyes riveted on the flag, held their salute until the last doleful note faded away. The first volley took Karl completely by surprise. No one had told him about the twenty-one-gun salute. Like the trumpeter, they were somewhere nearby. Clayton waited until the other two volleys were fired.

"They're down by Keegan's grave," he whispered.

Karl nodded. As the last volley echoed away, the NCO loosed the halyard and lowered the flag to half-mast, then walked briskly back to the color guard. They did a crisp right face and marched off. The flag would remain at half-mast until the last group of the Keegan Cap came off eighteen.

"The gunfire was a little unexpected. I hope the neighbors don't think we're under siege."

Clayton laughed. "They're used to it. Besides, it's only once a year."

Alerted by the twenty-one-gun salute, carts started coming up from the range. Even those who had later tee times liked to see the first group go off; this year that was Clayton Doherty, Tom Crupshaw, Billy Lupus, and Karl Ketterman. Traditionally, the chairman played in the first group so he could be off the course early to supervise the posting of scores and deal with any disputes, rules questions, or unforeseen problems that might crop up. Crupshaw liked to play early, and although Doherty claimed no one was shown any favoritism in tee time assignments, he made sure Tom was always in one of the first two groups. No one had won the Cap more times than he, so who could argue if he got the first tee time? It was also tradition for the manager to go out in the first group; Billy Lupus was the only one there purely by the luck of the draw.

"The first group of the Keegan Cap is now on the tee."

Karl tapped in on the putting green, retrieved his ball, and walked to the first tee. Mo Mittenthal, microphone in hand, leaned out of the starter's shack and gave Karl a nod. "Mr. Karl Ketterman, the manager of the Zebulon Pike, as is the tradition at the Keegan Cap, will hit first. Mr. Ketterman, the tee box is yours."

Karl pulled his driver from the back of Clayton's cart and stepped onto the tee box. He shook hands with the rest of the group and teed up his ball. Some people, even good players, get nervous on the first tee, but not Karl, even with all the players and hangers-on gathered around the tee. He relished taking that first swing. His nerves never came into play until later in the round when the potential for a low score started to come into view; on the first tee his mind was free and his hands steady. He set his driver behind the ball, aligned his body, and hit a high draw down the center of the fairway. The Keegan Cap was underway.

*

Mo Mittenthal watched pensively as the last foursome of the Keegan Cap left the tee box. He checked his watch. It was almost ten thirty. There was a gap in the tee sheet to allow for slower play in the biggest event of the year; the next foursome wasn't due to tee off for fifteen minutes so Mo took a stroll down to Keegan's grave. The groundsgcrew had mown it and planted flowers around its edges as they did every year to prepare it for the Keegan Cap. Mo spotted a spent cartridge that the honor guard had overlooked lying among the flowers. He picked it up and pondered Keegan's grave. Mo couldn't understand the mad devotion people had to this game; and to be so obsessed with it that you would want to be buried where it was played struck him as very odd indeed. Was it, he wondered, really Keegan's wish to be here? Mo didn't know whether that was the case or not; he knew from the stories he'd heard about Ambrose Keegan that he had had no immediate family, but if he left a will, did it actually say he wanted to be buried at the Zebulon Pike or had others made that decision for him, post mortem? For whatever reason, here lay Ambrose Keegan, a man who left the land of the living to become a legend, an institution, an event. Mo bent over and brushed a leaf away from Keegan's marker. Suddenly, he remembered standing at his father's graveside reciting the mourner's Kaddish. He had died when Mo was a young man, not yet twenty-five. His father was a distant and difficult man and they had not been close. Had he ever gone back to clear away his father's marker? Maybe, Mo thought, it made sense to be buried in a place where people are, where they can't help but pass by and be aware that you were once one of them, living, complaining, sure of your importance and immortality. At least here Keegan had visitors, even if unintentional. And he did serve as a sort of memento mori, a reminder of the frail grip we have on life; at least to those who took the time to notice he was buried here.

The sound of a golf cart braking brought Mo back from his reverie. The next group was on the tee. He wished Keegan well and walked back to his shack.

*

Tyreal Sumter was two over par after five holes and he felt fine. Without Scrumpy in his group he had been put in the awkward position of teeing up his own ball on the first tee, but that onerous task hadn't affected his play so far; not even playing with the Halling brothers was bothering him. He was inured to their taunts and mindless chatter; besides, Tyreal had never known a black golfer who didn't like to talk trash, who wouldn't try to get under your skin during a round; as a matter of fact, he was one of the best at it and the Halling brothers knew it. They couldn't match him when it came to biting gibes but were confident they could outplay him any day of the week. They knew Tyreal was good, and far more athletic than his size would lead one to believe, yet they didn't hesitate to offer a wager on the first tee: the brothers versus Tyreal and the other member of the foursome for two bucks a hole, low score only.

Tyreal took them in for a moment. "Can we press?"

"Naturally, Tyreal, whenever and as often as you like."

The brothers and Tyreal looked at their fourth, John Murlofsky, a five handicap from Withering Heights Golf Course, the muni on the north side of town. He signaled with a subtle wink he was in. Sumter played Withering Heights and was familiar with Murlofsky's game; he was a money player. The Halling brothers knew he was a five handicap but that's all they knew about Murlofsky; with both their handicaps hovering around six and Tyreal closer to a ten, they figured it would be an even match. Besides, no one knew the subtleties of the ZPGC better than they did.

This was Murlofsky's first appearance at the Keegan Cap. Doherty lived not far from Withering Heights and played there often and, always keen on getting the best local players into the Keegan Cap, had been trying to get Murlofsky to play for a long time. He'd signed up this year hoping he'd be in Crupshaw's group. He and Tom had played in events around town for years. Unlike the Halling brothers, Crupshaw knew all about "Johnny the Mouse," as Murlofsky was known at Withering Heights. He'd earned that moniker for his uncanny ability to "steal the cheese," to come back strong on the closing holes, to hit the shot that had to be made, and to drop the putt that kicked the guts out of his opponent on eighteen. The Halling brothers didn't know about his nickname nor about the black leather sack with the drawstring top in Murlofsky's golf bag, the one that held a wad of bills he wouldn't count up until the end of the season, and the small spiral notebook in which he neatly entered what he won and lost. The "won" column far outpaced the "lost" column; it had for the last seventeen years.

Tyreal struggled to an upright position and stood behind the ball for a moment. He knew Johnny the Mouse was one over par. The Halling brothers were both even par. Tyreal could see it was time to make a move.

"Unless you got a problem with it, partner, I think it's time to press. What you got to say to that?"

"Press early and often, I always say." The Mouse said in a voice barely above a whisper.

"Press accepted; hit away, fat man," Jay barked.

Recounting the round later that afternoon to Scrumpy in the clubhouse, Tyreal described his drive on six as the beginning of the end, the pivotal moment that sealed the doom of the Halling brothers. He spent so much time regaling Scrumpy about the agony he and Murlofsky put the Hallings through he forgot to tell him he'd also won a thirty-dollar gift certificate in the tournament.

*

Shortly after the last group left the first tee a small crowd of course regulars began to gather on the slope behind the ninth green. Dan Doherty was the first on the scene, alerted by Cybil as he sat at the counter that his brother's group would soon be coming down nine. The four horsemen of the Apocalypse—Sundbaum, Rankel, Armstead, and Hood—followed him down; Merril Stokes and Scrumpy Scroggins sauntered onto the scene a few moments later.

"They're on the tee!" Dan said, peering down the fairway through his binoculars. Although the players were visible to the naked eye, he wanted to get a read on their faces. Dan's mind seemed clearer when he was on the course and attentive to the smallest nuances in a player's demeanor, especially during the Keegan Cap. "The kid's got honors." They all knew he was referring to Billy Lupus. "Everyone still looks loose."

The group of spectators came closer together and sat down on the still-damp grass. They shaded their eyes against the morning sun and watched all four drives hit on or near the fairway; all were respectable, leaving the player a decent shot into the green.

"Crupshaw's the oldest guy out there and his tee ball is still up with the rest of them," Rankel marveled.

Officers Clack and Spurgeon, assigned to the course the entire day of the Keegan Cap, looked down on the ninth green from the parking lot. Rambo Burchell raced down the left side of the fairway, bouncing up and down in his cart.

"Damn the hemorrhoids, full speed ahead," quipped Armstead.

The crowd around the green, anxious for news on what was happening on the course, gathered around as Rambo's cart pulled up behind the green. Merril asked the question on everyone's mind: "How are they doing?"

All eyes were on Rambo. He took a swig from his coffee cup and took a deep breath. "Lupus was one under after seven. Tom and Clayton are even par and Ketterman's three over."

Every head turned at the sound of a ball hitting the green. It was Ketterman's. It took one hop and settled within ten feet of the cup.

"How about eight? What did they do on eight?" Hood barked at Rambo.

"No idea. I hung back on seven to watch the Halling brothers get their asses kicked."

The gallery wasn't listening. They were watching Billy Lupus go through his pre-shot routine.

"What's that? Gawd almighty! Remember Julius Borus? He'd just pull a club and hit a shot; none of that *crap*," Rankel said to no one in particular. "Nowadays everyone on the PGA Tour farts around before every shot; that's where these kids learn it. What's the point? Hit the ball!"

"Shut up. He knows what he's doing." Sundbaum believed in Billy. He'd bought him in the Calcutta, certain Billy was a future star at the ZPGC with a real chance to win the Keegan Cap this year.

Billy was just off the fairway but his ball was in a deep divot left by a hacker. He could either knock it down the fairway with a wedge or try to hit something low and hard to the green. He was playing well and that shot was not impossible. The group around the green had no way of knowing the tough spot Billy's ball was in. They could tell he was pondering the shot but assumed he was just trying to gauge how much spin the rough would take off the ball. Billy's swing threw a large clump of grass into the air. He had gone for it, but the ball came out low, hooking sharply.

"That one's for you, McAdoo," Rambo muttered as Billy's ball took one hop in the fairway before being swallowed up in the pond.

"Shit!" Sundbaum hissed through clenched teeth.

Billy, still shaken by the unfairness of his bad lie, took a drop on a line from where his ball had last crossed the margin of the hazard, put the ball on the green and two-putted for a double bogey. Ketterman got his birdie; Crupshaw and Doherty made par.

While they were putting out, Armstead wandered over to Doherty's cart to sneak a look at the card. He waited until they drove away before he reported to the gallery.

"After that double Billy is one over. The birdie gets Ketterman to two over. Doherty and Crupshaw are still even par."

Rambo drove off toward the back nine. Dan Doherty, Armstead, Rankel, Sundbaum, Hood, Stokes, and Scroggins turned their attention back to the ninth fairway. There was no one any of them were rooting for in the next two groups but they hung around to see how the Halling brothers were doing.

"Here they come," Dan whispered, binoculars pressed against his eyes.

Down the fairway they could see the Halling brothers, Murlofsky, and Fort Sumter about to hit their second shots.

Sumter and Johnny the Mouse had started to make their move on the sixth. Standing in the ninth fairway Tyreal was still two over but his partner, having birdied the sixth and eighth holes, was now one under. The Halling brothers were both two over, but with Tyreal and Murlofsky declaring a press on each of the last three holes, they were now down in the money game.

Scroggins pointed down the fairway. "See Tyreal hitching up his pants before he pulls a club? That means he's up," chuckled Scrumpy. "He's feeling *good*!"

Tyreal's second shot showed how good he was feeling, landing inside twenty feet. Jay and Es were right with him but Murlofsky flared his to the right side of the green, a good thirty feet from the pin. The faces of the Halling brothers showed that the game was indeed on. Tyreal was all smiles. Seeing he had an audience around the green, he needled the brothers as they lined up their putts.

"Now, partner, don't put any pressure on yourself. Just roll one close. I'll take care of the birdie on this hole. You're looking good; you could win the Cap, baby! Just get your two-putt and head to the back nine. Old Tyreal will take care of the Terrible Twins."

Johnny gave Tyreal a nod, marked his ball and walked to the hole, studying the contours of the green, trying to see the path the ball would take. It didn't take him long; ten seconds at the most and he was back to his mark. He replaced his ball, took one practice stroke looking at the cup, then set the putter behind the ball. His head didn't move until the ball was halfway to the cup.

"It's in," whispered Rankel when the ball was five feet away. Almost simultaneously Es spit out an F-bomb. A second later the ball made a throaty rattle at the bottom of the cup.

"Oh, Lord! Good God! Can the man putt, or can the man *putt*? Oh, I'm *so* sorry, fellas! I had no idea this guy was a *killer*!" People up at the clubhouse could hear Tyreal's booming voice. The scales lifted from the Halling brothers' eyes. They could see they were going down hard, that their fate was sealed. They'd been hustled. All they could hope to do now was to minimize the damage. Jay glared at Es when he missed his putt and cursed when his lipped out. They stood brooding shoulder to shoulder as Tyreal putted. It meant nothing so they felt no glee when he missed it badly to the right. They were walking away when they heard Murlofsky say, "We press the back."

Es wheeled around. "You can't press the back! You're up! You can't press when you're up!"

Jay grabbed his arm. He knew what was coming next.

"Didn't we ask if we could press whenever and as often as we like on the first tee? I believe we did." Tyreal said, his voice dripping with sarcasm. "And you fellas agreed, did you not? Now it seems my partner wants to press the back. And I'm with my partner all the way. That means, Hoss, the back is pressed." Fort Sumter put a massive hand on Es' shoulder. "I don't know why you're complaining; he's giving you boys a chance to get back in this game."

"We accept," Jay growled as he pushed his brother toward their cart.

Scrumpy Scroggins grinned and shook his head as the two carts drove off toward the tenth tee. The unwritten etiquette of the Keegan Cap was that no one was allowed to follow players on the course—unless there was a playoff—so while Stokes stayed to watch the next group coming down nine, the others made their way to the clubhouse where they would keep close track of the time so they could be behind the eighteenth in time for the final fireworks.

18

About the time the last group in the Keegan Cap was making the turn, Ralph Milbank sauntered down the corridors of the Lochenberry Country Club, his mood positively effervescent. Things were beginning to fall into place. He believed he had the rest of the Parks Commission poised to make a decision about the future of the Zebulon Pike in the fall. They knew nothing of the planned housing development, of course; Milbank wanted them to make their decision about whether the Zebulon Pike Golf Course stayed open or closed solely on its merits, and he was confident of the outcome. Did it really make sense to keep a money-losing municipal golf course going at a time when there were so many other needs the Parks Commission could be addressing? And if the ZPGC did close, wouldn't the city still have three courses in operation? Surely, that was more than enough. He didn't have to manipulate the facts; they were already in his favor.

Ralph Milbank stopped a moment to study one of the oil paintings on the wall, a large landscape of a links golf course somewhere in Scotland, at least that was his supposition; a bleak plain of heather and gorse with a glimpse of fairway or green here and there, stretching along a barren coastline. He didn't have his reading glasses on so he couldn't decipher the brass plate on the ornate gilded frame even when he squinted. Milbank liked the painting, not for its subject matter but because it exuded money and privilege and status, the things he valued most in life, the very cornerstones of Lochenberry Country Club. As a public official and political operative, he had acquired privilege and status; it was money he lacked. If he had that he could become a member here instead of just a visitor. He sighed and turned into the meeting room where Robert Midge and company awaited his presence.

"What's the news, Milbank?" Midge stood leaning over the conference table with Chartreuse at his shoulder.

"The news is the Parks Commission is in unanimous agreement with me; unofficially at this point, but definitely the majority is on my side of the issue. I've met with all of them individually, gone over the financials in detail, and they now can see the Zebulon Pike is a losing proposition for the city. I've helped them understand that even if we closed it down and did nothing with the land, the city would be better off. If a more lucrative use for it were presented to them at some point, I'm quite confident they would be receptive to such a proposal."

Midge's porcine lips split into a grin. He gestured to a chair and Milbank took a seat. "So," said Ralph, as he settled in, "how are the plans for the development going? I'd love to see them."

Chartreuse looked at Midge. Midge saw no reason to tell Milbank about Casserly's run-in at the golf course. He knew Milbank was a skittish character who might turn his back on this project the moment he felt any heat.

"They're going great," said Midge. "Casserly's done his preliminary study of the property and his firm is moving ahead with things. When do you think we should make our presentation?"

"In the fall; once the numbers for the summer are in I think the writing will be on the wall for the Zebulon Pike. Even though I have the majority of commissioners on board, there's still a process we have to go through, public hearings and all that. And you have to expect some pushback along the way; it's inevitable. Some people will want to preserve the course, others will want to turn it into a nature preserve or a gigantic doggie park, so there will be lots of hearings and the usual delays. There are procedures to be observed and..."

"We can handle all of that, Ralph. This isn't our first rodeo, is it, Frank?"

"No, no it is not," said Chartreuse, doing his best to look sage and wise.

Milbank had much more to say about the intricacies of the political process and didn't appreciate the way Midge cut him off. He was the one who came to Midge with the idea for finding a new use for the Zebulon Pike. Now he was beginning to feel Midge was trying to keep him on the periphery, but without Ralph Milbank pulling strings behind the scenes this project didn't have a snowball's chance in hell and it was about time Midge realized it.

"Robert," Milbank lowered the register of his voice, "the success of this project rests on politics, *city* politics, something I know a good deal about. It will not be a cakewalk; as I said, we will have obstacles in our way, difficulties to overcome, but if you let me take the lead on that and we trust each other and deal openly with one another, we will prevail. There mustn't be any secrets between us. Everything must be aboveboard," he made a circular gesture, "among us."

Midge gave Ralph a hurt look. "Why, of course, Ralph! There are no secrets here. Casserly's firm is on the job, Frank here is in charge of all construction matters, I'm lining up the financing, and you're handling the approval process. We're a team. We've all got the same goal in mind. And we're all going to benefit from it in the end. Everyone is going to come out a winner, Ralph. Especially you. When a political leader can make something like this happen in a city that, let's be honest, has seen better days, there's no telling where his career will take him."

Midge grinned. Milbank was mollified. With the business of the day concluded, Midge led his guest to the grillroom for a leisurely and convivial meal on him.

*

"Here she was wont to go, and here, and here,
Just where those daisies, pinks, and violets grow!
The world may find the spring by following her,
For other print her airy steps ne'er left.
Her treading would not bend a blade of grass,
Or shake the downy blow-ball from his stalk.
But like the soft west wind she shot along,

And where she went, the flowers took thickest root,
As she had sowed 'em with her odorous foot."

Gabriel Dunn closed the book and his eyes, Ben Jonson's words echoing back to him in the cavernous maintenance shed. He'd always liked to read poetry aloud, especially to her, although she had said he hadn't the voice for it. The memory made him smile. Maybe she was right. It seemed funny how what she had said, the things she had done so many years ago still held such power over him. He tossed the book on the workbench and surveyed his surroundings. Here he was, the boy genius of bygone days, reading poetry to lawnmowers and weed whackers—an uncritical audience, to be sure—in a dank shed, the air redolent with moldering grass and disappointment. Neither the irony nor the pathos of his surroundings was lost on Dunn. He went out into the sunlight. It was, he'd heard, nature's cure for festering wounds.

*

The playing of the Keegan Cap is secondary to the stories told afterward. Each year a moment of golfing glory would define the event as a whole, and that's how the regulars of the ZPGC would speak of past Keegan Caps: *The Year Crupshaw Won His Fifth*, *The Year of the Five-Man Playoff*, or *Dan Doherty's Braining*. This year's event—even though it had absolutely nothing to do with the outcome—would be known as *The Year the Hallings Took It in the Shorts*.

To describe a defeat as someone's Waterloo is a cliché. What the Hallings experienced was closer to the battle of Cannae where, using a brilliant tactical feint, Hannibal annihilated a Roman army. The analogy is apt: the Hallings, like the Romans, were overconfident and arrogant; Johnny the Mouse, like Hannibal, was canny and in control of events. Tyreal Sumter was like one of Hannibal's elephants, a lumbering mass in the midst of the mêlée, large, noisy, but in the end incidental to the outcome. That, however, didn't keep him from claiming credit for the win and never letting the Halling brothers forget it.

The victory, however, belonged entirely to John Murlofsky. It was his game that won the day. He wasn't as long as some off the tee, but seldom missed the fairway. He wasn't the best bunker player, but then he was rarely in one. And he didn't very often stick the ball close to the pin, which was the most frustrating thing about playing against him, because what made Johnny the Mouse so hard to beat was his putter. He wasn't just a good putter; he was an extraordinary one with an ability to make putts few players could match. Of course he gave the Halling brothers no indication of that on the first four holes, intentionally two-putting and letting them win, confident he could make up the deficit and, possibly, even win the Keegan Cap, by putting the hammer down later in the match. But it was the money game he focused on, for Murlofsky's avarice far outpaced his thirst for golfing glory; besides, winning the Keegan Cap gained him no prestige at Withering Heights. Money, on the other hand, was respected everywhere.

By the twelfth hole the Hallings were done. It was clear to them a repress on their part would be futile. If Murlofsky got on the green he was going to make the putt. Their confidence was shot. Minimizing their losses was their sole concern from that point on. Johnny had nine putts on the back with a chip-in for birdie on fourteen. He went about his business, soberly and silently as a mute in a funeral procession, once or twice giving Tyreal a wink as he plucked his ball out of the cup. Tyreal was giddy. Not only was he playing well, he was winning money, too. That did not sate his appetite to rub it in and he continued to hound the crestfallen twins until Johnny the Mouse's final putt on the eighteenth green.

"Hey, Es! What you think of my boy here? He sure can putt, can't he? Man, that cup must look like a manhole to him. I don't believe he had more than one two-putt on the back. Is that right, Johnny?"

Johnny gave Tyreal a little nod as he put his ball marker, glove, and divot tool back in his bag. He'd finished with a seventy-six, Tyreal an eighty. Neither Halling broke eighty. The Hallings trudged solemnly up to the clubhouse, calculating what they had lost: they had won four of the first five holes—one was a push. At two bucks a hole, that put them up eight dollars, but Tyreal and Murlofsky won that last three with a press that made them worth four dollars each, putting them four dollars ahead on the front. The real damage came on the back. Murlofsky's press made each hole worth eight dollars. The Hallings had only managed to tie two holes, losing fifty-six dollars on the back for a total loss of sixty dollars each. Jay suffered the added indignity of having to go to the ATM in front of a full clubhouse to get the cash to pay up. At that point their personal defeat became a public humiliation. Tyreal offered to buy them each a beer, but the dejected Hallings preferred to make a quick exit.

Johnny the Mouse took Tyreal up on his offer. He added his winnings to the roll in his black leather sack and entered the amount and the date in his notebook, then turned his attention to the board near the fireplace where Clayton Doherty was posting their scores. Scrumpy joined Tyreal and Johnny; they drank beer and watched the board until the last scores were posted. It looked like there was going to be a playoff.

*

Clayton and two other members of the committee double-checked the scorecards and the board one more time before listing all the players in order of their finish on a whiteboard by the front door. Murlofsky had finished fourth. Clayton would do no better than seventh, a little disappointing yet respectable for the chairman of the event. Ketterman's score was the biggest surprise of the event. Now that the last group was in, it was clear that he and Billy Lupus were tied for low score. Karl had blistered the back, making birdie on ten and eleven, then par the rest of the way in. Billy, on the other hand, hadn't finished well. Standing on the seventeenth tee, he'd been two strokes up but bogeyed the last two holes, missing a four-foot putt on eighteen for a seventy-two and tying Ketterman. Finishing one under on a par seventy-three as tricky as the Zebulon Pike was no mean feat. The indefatigable Tom Crupshaw, counterpunching youth and distance with course knowledge and accuracy, finished with a seventy-four.

"Nice finish, kid," Crupshaw said, patting Karl on the back. "For a guy who hasn't played here often you seemed to have figured the course out pretty fast."

146

Karl beamed. He might not know all the holes by heart like the rest of them, but this day he'd proven himself to be a ZPGC golfer.

*

Sundbaum groaned and turned away. It was clear even from his vantage point far behind the eighteenth green that Billy was going to miss the putt the moment it came off the clubface. He could tell by Billy's body language as he walked off that the back nine hadn't gone well.

Burchell, who'd taken Crupshaw in the Calcutta, came over to comfort him. "You might still be in it, Sunny. He's still going to put up a low number."

Sundbaum, always the pessimist, curled his lips and walked away.

Rankel wandered over to the cart Clayton and Tom shared to sneak a peek at the scorecard. Shaking his head in disbelief, he rejoined Hood and Armstead and waved over the pouting Sundbaum.

"Ketterman and Billy are tied! They're both one under. All you got to worry about, Sunny, is someone in the later groups shooting lower than that, and that ain't likely."

Sundbaum, buoyed by that news, waved over Burchell. He knew Rambo couldn't fight the urge to tell the others still on the course that two in the first group had shot one under. An unfamiliar surge of optimism washed over Sundbaum as he watched Burchell's cart bounce down the fairway, knowing the message he bore would add a little more pressure to every shot on the back nine and get him a little closer to winning the Calcutta.

*

Billy and Karl's tie held up. Forty minutes after the last score was posted, the playoff began. The rules were simple. The first player to win a hole would win the tournament. This was the fifteenth playoff in the history of the Keegan Cap, the most famous, of course, was the five-man marathon of 1983. It had taken fifteen holes to reduce the field to two players. On the sixteenth, the late

Walter Thompskemper hit it stiff for what looked like a kick-in birdie; his putt lipped out. Tom Crupshaw had already made a longer putt for birdie and Thompskemper's miss sealed Crupshaw's victory. Those there that day remember Thompskemper looking down at the cup for what seemed like an eternity before he straightened up, shook Tom's hand, and walked in. He didn't play another round at the ZPGC for the rest of the season. That fall, Walter, a man who had never been an outdoorsman, drove up north. After having a hearty lunch at a local restaurant, he parked his car and walked off into the woods. At the inquest the hunter swore he thought Walter was a deer.

Clayton stood between Billy and Karl and tossed a tee in the air. It pointed to Karl. His drive, like the first of the day, sailed off into the air and bounded down the middle of the fairway. Billy followed suit, out-driving Karl by ten yards. The atmosphere was different this time down the first fairway. They had a crowd. At least fifty people, some competitors, others course regulars like Sundbaum, Rankel, Armstead, Hood, and Stokes, followed them down the fairway in carts and on foot, keeping a respectable distance and watching every practice swing, every gesture for signs that one of them would falter.

They tied the first hole and the second. On the third, Karl's tee shot landed twelve feet above the flag. Billy, his nerves getting the better of him, hit his shot fat. It fell short of the green on a slight upslope, a clump of grass keeping it from rolling further down. Karl marked his ball and stood to the side of the green, gathering his thoughts, assessing his putt. Billy walked up to the green to see how far he had to carry his chip. He walked back to his ball and made several practice swings. They were stiff and awkward. Sundbaum looked pale. Billy took a deep breath and took the club back slowly. He felt the clubface make contact high on the ball; it came up on the green low and fast, crashed into the flagstick hard and disappeared. Billy leapt into the air and let out a whoop, echoed by Sundbaum's. The crowd turned its focus on Karl. He waited for Billy to retrieve his ball from the cup then replaced his ball on the green and walked below the hole to get a read. He either made this putt or the tournament was over. It didn't take him long to make a decision. He made a practice stroke, stood over the ball, and hit it. It was clear to Karl while the ball was still several feet from the cup that he'd misread the putt. He took off his hat and walked over to Billy to shake his hand. Oddly, he found it hard not to feel happy for Billy, winning the biggest event at his home course at such a young age.

The crowd and Billy started back to the clubhouse where the Keegan Cap would be lifted from its place of honor behind the counter, carried solemnly down to Keegan's grave, and, with all due ceremony, handed over to Billy Lupus. Within the week, the little brass plate with Billy Lupus' name, score, and the year of his victory would be added to the venerable oak base over which Keegan's bronzed cap rested.

A few lingered a moment to congratulate Karl. Dan Doherty, Tom Crupshaw, Charley Lumley, and Merril Stokes all shook his hand. Karl was pleased. He'd played well, better than he normally did, and he'd had fun; and he'd won the admiration of the people who played his course. He wouldn't feel as much of an outsider anymore.

As he was chatting with Stokes, a hand touched his forearm. He turned, hoping to embrace Gretchen but found himself in the arms of Cybil Stumpher. He returned her hug, touched by the gesture and doing his best to ignore the greasy hair and the body odor the afternoon breeze couldn't negate. Cybil's eyes welled with tears as she held him at arm's length.

"You're the best manager Zebulon Pike's ever had. The *best*. I've been here a long time and I know. And I'm not going to let anyone take you away from us," she said, then lumbered away.

"Thanks, Cybil," Karl said, after a moment's hesitation. He hoped Gretchen would be as proud of him.

19

Mo Mittenthal sipped his coffee and watched Cybil. He had noticed something different about her of late and he was trying to put a finger on what it was and what had brought it about; she seemed quieter and calmer and there was an aura about her he'd never seen before; she seemed to have softened, to be less formidable. Cybil came by and refilled his cup; her cheeks flexed into what Mo could only guess was an attempt at a smile. He smiled back. He could see it made her uncomfortable so he turned his attention to his coffee.

Mo was right. Cybil was indeed undergoing a change of heart. Maybe it was the presence of Gretchen and the memories of youth she conjured up; maybe it was Ketterman's earnestness and enthusiasm for the Zebulon Pike. Whatever it was, something had begun to iron out Cybil's furrowed brow. The change didn't stop there. She'd had her hair styled and cut, and even though the look was a little out of date, it was clear she was trying to improve her personal appearance. It was obvious she was bathing more frequently, too. Mo noticed all these things; few others did at first, probably because over the years Cybil had become as much a fixture in the clubhouse as the fireplace, the brass escutcheon on the floor, or Keegan's cap on its perch; she was just part of the surroundings that the eye took in without the mind registering. That was due in good part, of course, to her spending most of the day in the far recesses of the kitchen. Other than when she put an order on the sill of the pass-through, Cybil was seldom seen. But when she began singing softly to herself in a haunting, off-tune soprano as she worked, everyone at the ZPGC became aware that something was definitely up with Cybil.

Karl noticed the change in Cybil, too, even though they rarely saw each other and the longest conversation they ever had was after the Keegan Cap. Her enigmatic statement about not allowing anyone to take him away from the ZPGC was puzzling at the time, but he hadn't thought about it much since. He took what she said for what it appeared to be, a sincere outburst of affection after seeing him lose the tournament, even though that loss hadn't bothered him in the least. He'd made a good showing and now felt he had the respect of both the staff and the customers of the course; that was enough for him. As a runner-up in the Keegan Cap, he was part of the ZPGC's history and tradition and, he felt, the rightful heir to Odegaard, Smythe, McAdoo, et al. The only thing missing was Gretchen. She was the only trophy he truly longed to hold.

In the meantime, he busied himself going through the dusty ledgers and albums that filled the bookshelf in his office. Karl was captivated by all the arcane details the course managers and club chairmen had recorded about the golf events at the ZPGC. Nothing was overlooked: every participant in every tournament had been logged in, along with his handicap and gross and net scores. The irony being that this care and diligence, all this determination to faithfully record the facts and pass them on to posterity, had gone unnoticed and undisturbed until Karl came along.

Karl saved going through the drawer under the bookcase for last, mainly because it had an old lock on it and he hadn't been able to find a key for it in his desk or anywhere else in the office. Finally, with nothing else left to page through and goaded by curiosity, Karl made his way down to the maintenance building to see if Dunn had a bolt cutter or a hacksaw. Dunn was outside hosing the undercarriage of a mower, chlorophyll-colored water splashing into the air, sparkling in the sunlight, and rattling off the metal housing.

"Ah, the wonderful smell of freshly mown grass," Karl said, hoping to start the conversation off.

"Cis-3-Hexenal; that's what you're smelling."

Someone had told Karl that Dunn liked to read poetry in his free time; it seemed a prosaic response for a lover of verse. He nodded sagely to give the impression he actually knew what Dunn was talking about. "I was wondering if you have a bolt cutter I could borrow?"

"I do, but I don't lend out tools. Show me what you need cut and I'll take care of it."

For a moment, Karl thought about instigating a turf battle. After all, he *was* the manager of the course and the lock was in his domain. Then he recalled the arcane and complicated organizational structure he worked within. Dunn didn't report to him and Karl was on his ground. Seeing there was no other way to deal with it, Karl told Dunn about the lock in his office without a key and asked him to come by with his bolt cutter when he had a moment. An almost imperceptible nod told him Dunn was willing to do that...when he had a moment.

"Why isn't anything easy around this place?" Ketterman muttered as he kicked a pinecone off the path. It seemed his curiosity would have to wait.

*

"Got a legal question for you."

Officer Spurgeon squinted up at Rambo from the passenger side of the golf cart. Officer Clack leaned over the steering wheel to get him in sight. Rambo had pulled up next to them as they finished giving a group of college-aged players a warning about urinating in public. It was a pro forma ritual; at least once a month a group of female golfers or a nearby resident walking the northern perimeter of the course reported seeing a male peeing in public. These calls were beginning to annoy Spurgeon. Chasing down and reprimanding old men with faulty prostates or young ones with beer-filled bladders was not why she had put on the shield.

"Pay the ticket."

"Nah, it's nothing like that," said Rambo, waving off her suggestion. "It's kinda theoretical, I guess you could say. Supposing you knew about something that was sort of wrong; you know, not a crime exactly, but not on the up-and-up either."

Officer Spurgeon peered over the top of her sunglasses trying to get a read on Rambo. Her year-and-a-half on the force had given her insight into the criminal mind and she could see guilt written all over Rambo's face.

"Get to the point, will you? We've got work to do." Clack backed her up by giving Rambo a cold stare.

"We got wind of something; me and Charley and Dunn."

"Dunn?" Clack hardened his squint. He didn't care much for Dunn; too secretive for his tastes.

"There's a guy, a rich guy, and he's got plans for the ZPGC. He's in tight with politicians but they want to keep this real hush-hush. He had a guy scoping out the place real early in the morning, but we," Rambo measured his words before he spoke, fearful of incriminating himself too much, "found out about him."

"So what the hell do you want from us?" Spurgeon snapped at him. She'd lost interest in Rambo's story, but Clack, as tired as Spurgeon of answering public urination calls, sensed something big, an opportunity to make a name for himself and maybe earn a transfer to the regular city police force. He got out of the cart and walked over to Rambo.

"Maybe you should start from the beginning and tell us the whole story."

*

No one at the ZPGC could recall this kind of interest in the Ebon Invitational. It had been decades since it had a field like this. The Ebon was still a month away, yet big names in the community—professional athletes, business leaders, politicians, and local media celebrities—were already signed up. Welmont Washington's promotional efforts were clearly paying off and Fort Sumter was elated. Finally, the event his father had founded was starting to get traction again and, at least the way he saw it, it was all happening under his direction. He fairly burst with excitement as he posted a preliminary list of participants on the ZPGC bulletin board. His list of luminaries lost some of its luster next to the handwritten "clubs for sale" notices, outdated tournament results, and the ubiquitous EEOC poster; nevertheless, the Ebon Invitational was definitely rising to a new level and, albeit grudgingly, Sumter had to give some credit to Washington. There was no question he was responsible for the names on this list, but Tyreal was determined to keep the Sumter name front and center. It was a matter of family honor.

While Welmont made some phone calls, a summer intern he hired and assigned to the Ebon Invitation did most of the work. She was an intense and well-organized marketing major who attacked the project with gusto, cold-calling prospective participants and putting together a media package that included the first thorough history of the event. She'd written it after one interview with Sumter and a week at the public library where she'd gone through microfiche of the local paper from years long gone by; it was both a compelling and informative read for both Welmont, who knew little about the Ebon Invitational, and Tyreal, whose knowledge was limited to his father's anecdotes. This history made them aware for the first time that for a span of a dozen years or so the Ebon Invitational was one of the premier events for black golfers in the entire country, no mean feat for someone of Obadiah Sumter's humble origins.

Washington had never had a summer intern before; in fact, had never even imagined the need for one until he found Bernadette Clayfield sitting outside his office one morning. He was never quite sure how she got there, other than boldly walking past everyone in the Boutiqué Afriqué and finding her way up to his private lair, which is exactly what she had done. As soon as Bernadette was face to face with Welmont she got right to the point. "You're a busy man, Mr. Washington, and I won't waste your time," she said, handing him a one-page brief of her assessment of Boutiqué Afriqué's business, a first draft of projects she would take on, and her salary expectations. He gave them a once-over as he made his way to his desk, pointing to the chair he wished her to take.

"I thought the whole point of an internship was to learn something, so why should I have to *pay* for your education?"

Bernadette smiled and pointed at the papers in Welmont's

hands. "Mr. Washington, I've put together a list of very specific things that I know will add value to your brand; they're not make-work assignments. To do them without compensation would, in effect, be saying that is what they're worth—nothing." Her eyes never left his.

This lady, Welmont thought to himself, is going to be handling the Ebon Invitational for me. She left his office ten minutes later with an internship, a salary half the amount she'd asked for, and one item on her agenda: making the Ebon Invitational the biggest golf event of the year.

Besides Tiger Woods, Bernadette knew nothing of golf. She couldn't think of a single person she actually knew who played it, but she had a vague image in her mind, an amalgam of movie scenes and characters in books—blustering Judge Smails in *Caddyshack*, Shooter McGavin in *Happy Gilmore*, the cynical, dishonest Jordan Baker in *The Great Gatsby*, and the upper-class asses in P.G. Wodehouse stories—a world of privileged, self-indulgent white people. That image didn't quite square with what she found at the Zebulon Pike Golf Course. It was midday on a Wednesday and the parking lot was almost empty. Bernadette parked near the clubhouse and took a moment to look around. There was a certain aging elegance to the place and nothing of the wealth, exclusivity, and class distinction she had expected. A raven perched high on the slate roof cawed as if it sensed an outsider, a non-golfer, an enemy, approaching. Bernadette went inside. A peculiar woman came out of the kitchen and stared at her from behind the counter; four old men at a table in the corner hunched over a scorecard paid her no attention; the man behind a display case filled with golf balls where, she assumed, you paid to play golf never looked up from his newspaper. Bernadette turned to the woman.

"Hello, I'm looking for Mr. Sumter. Do you know where I could find him?"

"He's somewhere on the course; probably won't be back here for a couple hours," Cybil replied. Bernadette looked at her watch. "I can't wait that long. Is there anyone else who's involved with the Ebon Invitational I could speak with?"

Cybil pointed to Karl's office. The door was open. Bernadette knocked on the frame and looked in. Karl was standing behind his desk poring through an old photo album.

"Excuse me, the lady at the counter said you might be able to help me. I'm Bernadette Clayfield and I'm in charge of marketing and promotions for the Ebon Invitational."

Karl waved her in.

"Then you'll find this interesting. This is from the 1955 Ebon Invitational. Look at that crowd. And check out this one of all the players. It was a huge event back then; players came from all over the country. And it was right here at the Zebulon Pike; amazing, huh?"

Looking down at the old black-and-white photo, Bernadette tried to match his enthusiasm. "Yeah, that's something. Say, do you know Mr. Sumter?"

"Fort? Sure." For the first time, Karl took a good look at Bernadette. College girl, he guessed, bright, driven, and, even though attractive, not the kind that gets by on her looks alone. He couldn't imagine the circumstances that would have brought her and Sumter together. "Are you working for him?"

"In a way. I work for Mr. Washington; Welmont Washington."

The name didn't ring a bell for Karl. "Great. Well, I told Fort I'm willing to do whatever I can to help the Ebon be a big success."

Bernadette, head down, tapped away at her laptop. "That's good to hear. Give me your email address and I'll copy you on all communications about the Ebon Invitational going forward. I'm also going to send you a list of action items I'd like you to tackle. It will have my mobile number on it so we can discuss it whenever you like."

"Glad to meet you, Bernadette," Karl said as she rose and moved to the door. She turned, gave him a business-like smile and was gone.

*

"I've got a pack of morons holding up my project and I need you to make them go away; whatever it takes. Bribe them, threaten them with legal action, but get them off my back, Sid." Midge paced the floor, the ice in his drink rattling. The only other person in the room, an elegantly dressed woman in a dark tailored suit, sat serenely in a Morris chair, her face as expressionless as a Kabuki mask. "It was your guy Casserly that screwed this up. He's the one that got caught skulking around the course at the crack of dawn by these misfits. I went to see them, but I didn't get anywhere and I can't be mixed up in this anymore; there's too much at stake here. I need you to be the middleman on this deal." He turned to see if Sid was paying any attention to him. She wasn't. Her eyes were scanning the room, studying the furnishings. She despised the Lochenberry Country Club as much as he did. Their eyes met as she took a silver case from her purse, removed a cigarette, and methodically tapped one end of it three times on the lid.

"There's no smoking in here. Only on the verandah."

The corners of her mouth flexed ever so slightly. The butane lighter hissed into flame. She lit her cigarette and inhaled deeply. It occurred to Midge that she must be the last woman in North America still smoking unfiltered cigarettes.

"I'll keep that in mind, Robert, if I'm ever on the verandah of this museum." She leaned back in her chair, silently snorting smoke from her nostrils. She rested her elbow on the arm of the chair, the hand with the cigarette poised as if holding an invisible platter. "So, explain to me again how this is *my* problem? You asked us to prepare a feasibility study and a design for the site. You set some rather bizarre parameters. Casserly followed them exactly; in fact, so precisely he ended up being bludgeoned by the locals, yet he still completed the task and I have delivered to you this morning," she said, pointing at the elegantly designed package on the large oak table in the center of the room, "a hard copy of those plans and all the supporting materials for what will surely be the most stunning redevelopment project in the history of this windswept, godforsaken, two-bit town. That seems to me to fulfill both the letter and the spirit of our agreement," she said, punctuating her statement by flicking ashes on the carpet.

Midge was over a barrel and he knew it. He couldn't meet with that gaggle of twits again. He needed an intermediary and Sid Deathridge fit the bill. She was smart, relentless, manipulative, and from out of town.

"You have an hourly rate. Double it and bill me for a twelve-hour day; expenses, too, of course. Just take care of this. It's a simple negotiation, something you could do standing on your head." He paused; she stared him down. "Look, you're a smart, resourceful woman, Sid. They're the Three Stooges. All I'm asking you to do is to get them to take the jobs I offered, or cash, and shut up. It'll take you five minutes." He gave her a pleading look.

The cigarette sizzled as it landed in her glass. Sid Deathridge rose from her chair, slender, dark, impeccably tailored, and still stunningly beautiful at forty. Two strides of her long legs brought her face to face with Midge. Cigarette breath had never seemed so intoxicating.

"What's the name of this goddamned muni?"

"The Zebulon Pike Golf Course. It's just off..."

"I'll find it, Robert. Everything is going to be just fine."

Her long, cool hand patted his cheek. She turned and glided out the door.

*

A finger jabbed into Karl's back as he unlocked his office door. He turned to find Cybil's eyes fixed intently on his.

"We have to talk."

"All right." It was the only thing he could think to say.

"I met him again last night. I feel so terrible."

"Cybil, your personal life is really none of my..."

"No! It's not like that! It's Mr. Milbank. It's what I've been doing for him."

Karl directed her to a chair and took his behind the desk. He felt he needed some kind of a barrier between them. He said nothing, waiting for her to say whatever she had to say. Cybil studied her reddened rough hands for a moment.

"It's my fault. I went to him because I didn't like you, not at first. But he encouraged me," she said, looking at Karl pleadingly.

"Encouraged you to do what?"

"To spy on you. To report to him about what you're doing and what's going on here."

Karl was baffled. "But why? All he has to do is ask me."

"He wants you to fail. He wants the ZPGC to fail. I'm not sure why, but I know it's true." Cybil's eyes brimmed with tears. "And I'm sorry, so sorry for helping him."

Karl went to Cybil and held her in his arms as she wept. He thought about Milbank's visit and how he said there were interest groups that would like to put the course to different use; could he really be working with them? Then why had Milbank hired him? Why all the mystery? It didn't make sense.

Karl arrived at the Zebulon Pike the next day to find Dunn
waiting outside his office. He'd just finished the daily ritual of
moving pin positions and mowing greens and his work boots were
wet with dew and covered in grass clippings. He stood looking
down at his feet, softly tapping the bolt cutter on his thigh.

"Morning, Gabe."

Dunn gave him a frown. "Gabriel or Dunn, either one."

"Got it. Well, I see you've come prepared, so let's unlock the
secrets of the past."

A snap of Dunn's cutter dispatched the old lock and Karl pulled
the drawer open. It took a little effort; who knows how long it
had been shut—forty, fifty, seventy years? The drawer was filled
to the brim, a jumble of ledgers, receipts, memos, and yellowed
letters on official city stationery. A quick perusal made clear it all
dealt with the development of the course, the meetings and the
correspondence between the various parties prior to and during
construction. At the bottom of the drawer he found a stack of
photos tied with twine, below that, covered by a brown paper flap,
a watercolor of the clubhouse, or at least how the architect had
originally envisioned it. His version had a wing on the north side
and an arched driveway with a dark green canopy covering the
walkway from the curb to the front door with white lettering along
its length—Zebulon Pike Golf Course. Rosebushes were in bloom
all around the building and behind the clubhouse the course went
from sharp detail to a wash of soft color on the horizon line. Clearly,

compromises were made between the time the painting was done and the actual construction of the clubhouse; still, it was a beautiful watercolor by a skilled artist. Karl went to the window to get a better look at it.

"This is beautiful! I'm going to get this framed and hang it in here; no, maybe it should be out in the main room, over the fireplace. What do you think?" He handed it to Dunn, who took it and stared at it for some time before speaking.

"No white nor red was ever seen
So am'rous as this lovely green."

"What's that from?"

"Marvell."

"You got that out of a comic book?"

At first Dunn thought Karl was making a joke. How could someone not at least recognize the name of one of the Metaphysical Poets?

"*Andrew* Marvell. The poet." Dunn could see he had to make his point about the painting a little clearer. "It's idyllic, a vision of an ideal world. Unfortunately, this architect was forced to compromise his vision, but he knew what he was doing; that wing makes all the difference; it really gives the building the proper symmetry. I always felt there was something awkward about this place, something missing; now I know why."

Karl felt somehow offended. "It's still a great clubhouse. You're not going to find too many municipal courses in the country with a building like this. This place was built during the Depression; it's amazing they were able to do what they did."

Dunn handed him back the painting with an acquiescent shrug and Karl propped it up on a shelf behind his desk. When he turned back, Clack and Spurgeon were in the room. It looked to Karl as if they were tiptoeing. Spurgeon closed the door and rested her right hand on the butt of her gun. Dunn, seeing Karl's attention was drawn to something behind him, turned around. Clack pointed to a chair.

"Take a seat, Dunn, this involves you."

Gabriel went to one of the chairs near the windows. He sat very erect with both hands resting on his knees, his eyes on the two cops.

"So the rumors are true," thought Karl, "Dunn really is a fugitive and justice is finally catching up with him. What is he guilty of? Embezzlement? Murder? Rape?" Karl leaned over his desk, anticipating the naming of the crime and wondering if Dunn would try to make a break for it.

Clack and Spurgeon grabbed two chairs and sat down facing Dunn.

"It seems your greenskeeper is a kidnapper, Mr. Ketterman." Clack said.

Karl hadn't thought of that one. He looked at Dunn. He looked guilty enough, but said nothing.

"No reason to stonewall us, Dunn. Conrad Burchell has already told us everything."

"He's an idiot," Dunn said.

"All criminals are; now why don't you tell us exactly why you beat and abducted Mr. Casserly." Spurgeon paused, then, to give the accusation a more legalistic tone, added, "…the alleged victim."

Karl was beginning to feel uncomfortable. He didn't want a scene in the clubhouse: a struggle, furniture overthrown, and, finally, Dunn, handcuffed and screaming, being dragged out the front door. "Hey, is this really the place for this? Couldn't you have waited until he was outside the clubhouse, or down at the maintenance building?"

Clack and Spurgeon had almost forgotten Karl was in the room.

"We thought you'd want to hear this," said Clack, sounding a little hurt.

"Dunn doesn't report to me; his operation is completely independent of mine and his criminal past is none of my business."

Spurgeon nudged Clack and gave him a look that said she'd take it from there.

"The incident Dunn was involved in happened recently, right here on the golf course you manage. And if he doesn't work for you, I'm pretty sure Burchell and Lumley do and they were right there when Dunn thumped Casserly and hauled him off to the maintenance building, which is also on your golf course, where they interrogated him, holding him against his will for several hours and forcing him to talk."

Dunn rolled his eyes.

Karl was trying his best to make sense of what Spurgeon was saying. "*Who* is Casserly? I don't know anyone around here named Casserly."

"He's the guy wandering around the golf course; the one the early birds reported seeing out on the back nine," Dunn answered. "The one skulking around at the crack of dawn. The one you thought might be a homeless guy. He wasn't… he isn't; we didn't *kill* him. I gave him a little tap on the head," Dunn said, throwing his hands up to express his good intentions. "He was creeping around out there, doing his best not to be seen. I had no idea what he was up to, he could have had a gun or a bowie knife, for all I knew." He paused for a moment, trying to gauge his audience. "Hey, he went through a lot of trouble to hide what he was up to, creeping out of the Winnehala Wetlands like some kind of a commando; he brought it on himself," Dunn said, nonchalantly folding his arms and staring down his accusers.

Clack saw the opportunity for a snappy rejoinder and took it. "He didn't bring torture and a beating on himself, Dunn, that was your doing."

Dunn jumped to his feet. Both officers put their hands on their pistols and he sat back down.

"He wasn't breaking any laws, Dunn," Spurgeon barked. "He was just doing his job, trying to find out if this golf course could be redeveloped."

It was clear to Dunn that Burchell had been doing a lot of talking. "So why did he have to sneak around to do that? This is a *public* golf course open to everyone. There was no need to canoe across the Winnehala and sneak around like a thief. I don't know how you two got involved in this but I know Casserly hasn't complained to the cops… I mean the *real* cops." He stared at Spurgeon; her grip tightened on the automatic. "Midge told us he wouldn't, so I don't know why you two are making an issue of it. Isn't it obvious? The people Casserly works for don't want anyone to know what they're up to. That's why they're offering to pay us off to stay quiet about this. And they won't be too happy when they find out two Parks Commission cops are nosing around in something that's none of their business." Dunn looked at Karl. "I was going to tell you all of this, Ketterman; I felt you deserved to know, in case you wanted to start sending out your resume."

Karl closed his eyes, trying to get a handle on what he was hearing. A man canoes across the Winnehala Wetlands in the early morning hours, day after day, so he can survey the golf course undetected at the behest of people who plan on converting it into something else. Okay, so far so good. Then that man is intercepted, assaulted, and detained by Parks Commission employees for several hours in the maintenance building until he reveals his purposes. For some reason, Burchell has told Clack and Spurgeon all about this and now they're investigating. Karl opened his eyes. None of this made a lick of sense to him.

"*What* exactly was this guy doing again?"

Dunn raised his right hand to Spurgeon and Clack before reaching into his shirt pocket and removing a mobile phone. He tapped on it several times and showed it to Karl. A bewildered, disheveled face looked back at him.

"This is Dan Casserly. He was doing a preliminary site survey. I took this photo in case he tried to say we seriously harmed him; there was just a little bump on the back of his head, no big deal."

Karl took the phone from Dunn and looked at the face more closely. He'd seen this man before, but where? Then it dawned on him; this was the guy he'd seen in Lumley's cart. He handed the phone back to Dunn and turned to the cops.

"So Burchell tells you he, Lumley, and Dunn kidnapped someone, so you come here to confront Dunn; am I right so far?"

Clack and Spurgeon nodded in unison, like a pair of bobble-head dolls.

"But the guy, this Casserly, hasn't reported a crime or made a complaint; he may not even be in town for all we know, so what exactly is the point of all this?"

Clack looked to Spurgeon.

"The man was assaulted! Burchell was feeling pretty guilty about the whole thing and had to get it off his chest," Spurgeon said, the anger rising in his voice. "Dunn beat up someone on your course; doesn't that concern you?"

"This sure as hell doesn't concern you and if you don't drop this right now Midge and Milbank will make you sorry you didn't," Dunn barked back at her. "You're both going to end up being crossing guards."

Karl's head was beginning to spin.

"Who is Midge, and what does Milbank have to do with this?"

"He's working with Midge to make this whole deal happen," Dunn said. "Midge is a big shot in this town. A developer. Old money. Lots of pull."

A picture was beginning to come into focus. Now Karl understood why Milbank was so concerned with the financial state of the course and why he asked Cybil to spy on him. It was all a setup, an elaborate game that would lead to shutting down the golf course. Milbank had probably been planning it for years; his final gambit was to hire a kid right out of school and put him in charge, someone without the experience or know-how to turn a floundering golf course around, someone long-time staff might resent, someone from out of town without any local connections, someone it would be easy to pull the rug out from under after a year or two; it was perfect in every detail, and guaranteed to create the situation Milbank needed to argue that the only sensible thing to do with the Zebulon Pike Golf Course was to shut it down and put the land to better use. Karl jumped to his feet, his face red and his voice shaky.

"Get out of here. You've wasted enough of my time with this crap. You're right, Dunn, this is nothing we can do anything about."

Karl followed Spurgeon, Clack, and Dunn to the door, slamming it shut behind them. The police officers got the message. The smart thing would be to just walk away and mind their own business; trying to figure out what was going on here was starting to look like career suicide. The greenskeeper and the police officers went their separate ways.

*

A driving range is a theater where the stories are told in gestures and looks. Occasionally, the silence is broken by a snarling curse or a hoarse mutter; generally, expressions of opprobrium are limited to clubs slamming against golf bags or aggrieved glances heavenward.

After his meeting with the cops and Dunn, Karl sought solace on the Zebulon Pike's range; he wandered behind a line of golfers unnoticed, trying to think through it all without being disturbed. He walked slowly, aimlessly, his eyes to the ground, fixated by the myriad broken tees, like shattered corpses littering a battlefield.

"You look a little lost, Karl."

It was Gretchen. He hadn't seen her; it was the first time even a peripheral glimpse of her hadn't caught his attention. He feigned a smile. She turned the 5-iron in her hand around and poked him in the chest with the grip. "What's up with you?"

Where to begin? This was clearly not the time or place. "Right now, I'm trying to sort it out for myself. We'll talk later, okay?"

She walked closer, took his chin in her hand, and looked into his eyes. She could see something was troubling him deeply. Her hand moved to his cheek. Karl felt himself blushing. She nodded and went back to hitting balls. Karl watched her for a moment, held, as always, by the way her body moved, fascinated with the sheer power of her being, yet somehow today it was not enough to elevate his soul. He walked on.

The hitting stations were arranged in a gradual arc and as Karl reached its apex he could see Charley Lumley on his golf cart at the far end, chatting with Franzen and Rankel. Karl knew a conversation with Charley wouldn't last long; he slowed his pace, waiting for Rankel and Franzen's departure. By the time he got near they were driving off; they waved greetings to Karl as they sped past him. Lumley removed the cigarette from his lips and nodded to Karl.

"I just heard about your little adventure; you know, when you and Burchell and Dunn kidnapped the guy named Casserly."

Charley narrowed his glance and said nothing.

"Burchell got scared. Thought he was going to get in trouble, I guess, so he told Spurgeon and Clack all about it. They came to me."

"Has Casserly gone to the cops?"

"If he had, you'd know it by now. No, I don't think it's going any farther than this." Karl stopped to take in the range and take a look back at the clubhouse. It looked quite lovely this time of year.

He would miss this place. "So I guess this could be the ZPGC's last year; or next to the last, at best."

A low, rumbling cough rattled up from Lumley's chest. He spit and took a long drag of his cigarette. "Don't give up before the fight starts, kid."

It may have been an involuntary twitch or Charley may have just smiled at him; Karl wasn't quite sure which.

"Grab a club. Hit a few balls. You'll feel better."

Karl hit. Lumley watched. He was right. Karl slowly began to feel the world righting itself on its axis again.

*

"Something is going on here," Sundbaum said, setting the three coffee cups on the table. Hood and Armstead took a cup and waited for him to expand on his statement. "Dunn is waiting outside Ketterman's office first thing this morning. They go inside. Then Clack and Spurgeon go in and close the door. They're in there about a half hour, arguing about something. Dunn and the cops come out and Ketterman slams the door behind them. About fifteen minutes later Ketterman, looking like his dog just died, goes for a stroll." He paused for reactions. None were offered. He shook his head disapprovingly. "When is the last time you saw Dunn in the clubhouse, much less *waiting* for the manager; that ain't normal, and don't try telling me it is."

"Ask Clack. He's a chatty bastard. He'll tell you what happened." Armstead blew over the top of his coffee and took a sip.

"As a matter of fact, I did just that. I caught up to them before they got in their car. They both acted like they had no idea what I was talking about." Sundbaum waited. Hood and Armstead said nothing.

They were watching Cybil leave the protection of her counter and go to Ketterman's door and knock. She had a sandwich and a glass of milk on a plate. When he didn't answer, she went in and put it on his desk. They could see Cybil was crying as she went back to the kitchen.

"You're right," Hood whispered, "Something is definitely going on here."

*

Bad news, like a communicable disease, travels quickly. People begin to sense its malignant presence long before it manifests itself. Merril Stokes felt something was wrong immediately; a palpably dark mood seemed to have descended over the ZPGC. As he turned into the drive, Clack and Spurgeon, leaving in the opposite lane and looking right at him, didn't acknowledge his wave. When he went into the clubhouse, Sundbaum, Armstead, and Hood never looked up at him. Cybil was a gargoyle behind the counter. A strange, toxic atmosphere drove Merril out the back way as fast as his legs would carry him. Seeing Mittenthal serenely taking in the view from the starter's shack brought back a sense of normalcy. Crupshaw came up from the ninth green just as Merril got to the shack. Maybe, Stokes thought, they knew what was going on. They didn't. Tom invited him to play the back nine with him and he went to the car to get his clubs. The air on the back nine couldn't be as oppressive as it was in the clubhouse. Later, when they got back to the clubhouse, they heard all about what had happened from Hood.

*

Tiny sharp explosions, crisp pops repeated again and again, resonated throughout the clubhouse. Cybil's head shot through the pass-through. Mo, at the counter for a refill, turned around. Fort Sumter and Scrumpy standing at the bulletin board, usually boisterous and loud, were speechless.

Sid Deathridge's high heels cracked to a halt on the terrazzo floor. She pivoted toward Cybil. "Where would I find whomever is in charge?"

Cybil pointed to Karl's door.

"You are indicating that door over there, are you?"

Cybil nodded. Sid responded with a smile. Smiles usually are reassuring and make a person feel safe and unthreatened. Sid's had the opposite effect. Cybil's head, like a tortoise's, slowly withdrew into the kitchen.

Several more strides of her long legs brought Sid to Karl's door.

She knocked once and opened it. Karl, just finishing the sandwich Cybil had left for him, looked up from the plate.

"My name is Sid Deathridge." She strode to his desk with her right hand extended. The sunlight caught the brilliant red polish on her nails. It made her fingers look like bloody talons. Her handshake was firm.

"I'm Karl Ketterman. I'm the manager of the Zebulon Pike. How can I help you?"

Sid stood smiling benignly at Karl until he got the drift and came around the desk and brought a chair up for her. Waiting for men to open a door or bring a chair were among the tactics she employed to keep them off balance, her punch-counterpunch of ruthlessness and ladylike reserve.

"Ketterman," she said distractedly as she checked her mobile device. "Not one of the fellows I'm after, but I'm sure you can point me in the right direction." Karl had the same reaction as Cybil to Sid's smile, only he had no place to retreat to. "I'm looking for a Mr. Birch, a Mr. Lampy, and a third gentleman named," she paused to check her list. "Oh, dear, Robert! What handwriting. It looks like Don; is that right? I need to talk with them as soon as possible, so could you tell me where I can find them?"

First Clack and Spurgeon, now this sophisticated, attractive, disconcerting woman wanted to talk to Dunn, Lumley, and Burchell. He envied them. He sat taking her in for a moment. Sid Deathridge's impeccably tailored suit, understated yet undeniably expensive jewelry, her poise and elegance—coupled with her way of entering a room—overwhelmed him. It dawned on Karl that she might have something to do with Milbank's machinations. This could be his chance to get the whole story. He knew Lumley was on the range and Burchell was only a walkie-talkie call away.

"If you'll excuse me for a moment, I'll get them up here," Karl came around his desk. Her green eyes followed him. "Can I get you anything, a beverage or something?" He couldn't believe how stupid that must sound; he was like a kid at his first dance. She communicated her complete contentment by languidly closing and opening her eyes. Karl excused himself several more times before he got out the door.

"Cybil," he shouted as he went out on the verandah, "I need you to jump in a cart and go tell Lumley he's got to come to my office right away." He was at starter's shack seconds later. "Mo, radio Burchell, have him find Dunn, pronto, and get them to my office immediately; *immediately*, you got that?" He could hear the walkie-talkie crackling as he ran back to his office.

*

On its surface it was a simple request: tell Lumley to go to Ketterman's office. To Cybil it was a painful journey into the past. She hadn't been to the range in decades, since the summer when love filled her heart and she Lumley's arms, but she would do it for Karl because his days at the ZPGC seemed to be as ill-fated as hers.

Gretchen was arriving for her shift just as Cybil came out the kitchen door. Gretchen had never seen her moving so fast.

"What's up, Cybil?"

"I've got to get Charley. I've got to go get him right away."

Gretchen could hear the anxiety in Cybil's voice as she rushed by. It didn't take much effort to catch up with her. Cybil was already in a golf cart but so flustered she couldn't turn the ignition key. Gretchen pointed to the passenger side and got behind the wheel. "I'll drive, Cybil."

Lumley was giving a lesson, watching the divot after each swing, saying nothing, just kicking another ball from the spilled basket up to the student, a chatty, gangly twelve-year-old girl.

"My mom told me more people die from cigarettes than anything else, Mr. Lumley."

"My mom told me Dewey beat Truman," growled Charley.

The girl tilted her head like a bird and gave Charley a quizzical look. She had no idea what he meant but she liked him because he treated kids just like he treated everyone else. He didn't say much, but she could tell he always meant what he said. Except for the smoking she thought he was kind of cute.

Charley flicked his cigarette away and waited for her approbation. She gave him a big smile. He could go an hour without a smoke for that.

"Charley."

The voice was unchanged. It still had the vestiges of youth and beauty and sensuality in it. It still brought something to life inside him. Even when he turned to look at her, he wasn't disappointed. The years, the pounds, they didn't quite seem to matter that much to him. If only she could have taken the game seriously.

"Cybil? What are you doing here?" It was a question Charley was almost afraid to ask. Gretchen could feel Cybil trembling and knew she wasn't capable of saying more than his name right now.

"Karl wants you to come to his office. And," Gretchen said with a nod toward Cybil, "it must be pretty important."

"Her lesson's just started," Charley said.

"Destiny knows me; I bet she'll let me take over for a little while. You take Cybil back with you."

Charley, a man wedded to antiquated social norms, rose and lifted his hat as Cybil got in his cart, his white hair brilliant in the sunlight. Cybil smiled. He did his best to return it. Charley told Destiny to tell her parents he'd give her another lesson free, and drove off. It was an odd sensation, having a woman beside him.

*

Burchell was already in the office when Charley came in. Burchell had had the same reaction to Sid as Karl; so did Charley. She was standing now, next to Karl's desk, ramrod straight, her right hand on her hip. Karl was at the desk, his hands folded, looking at Sid, waiting impatiently to find out what she was up to.

"Good afternoon, gentlemen. I'm going to hold off until your coworker gets here. At that time, Mr. Ketterman, since our business doesn't involve you, would you be so kind as to leave us for a few moments?"

"He knows most of it," Charley growled as he took a chair by Burchell, "he knows we brained Casserly and he knows they're going to shut this place down."

Sid pursed her lips. "Anyone else I should know about?"

"Two Parks Commission cops," Karl volunteered, "but I don't think they're going to be any problem." Burchell lowered his head.

"They're not on my list; I will let Mr. Midge and his friends in city government deal with them." Sid wasn't about to try to bribe two cops. "All right, I don't want to go too far until everyone I need to speak with is here, so I'll just say this: I'm here on behalf of Mr. Robert Midge, the gentleman who came to see you with Mr. Casserly after you… interrupted his work. Mr. Casserly is an employee of my company and, I can assure you, he is not going to press any charges, so you can relax about that. That's the good news, now the *very* good news. I'm here to reach a concordance, a rapprochement, with you gentlemen." She paused and looked at Karl. "And I suppose, since I have carte blanche in this matter, this could include you, too, Mr. Ketterman. It certainly would make things simpler."

Karl gave Sid a perfunctory smile. There was a sharp knock on the door.

"Come in," said Karl. Sid, wanting to create a little mystery and make a more dramatic impression on the late arrival, turned her back to the door and took a book off Karl's desk.

Dunn came in and said nothing. Sid waited a beat after hearing the door close and then turned slowly around, pretending to be deeply engrossed in the book.

The sound of Dunn's body hitting the floor and the three others rushing to his aid brought her head up. She moved briskly over to the crouching figures and took command.

"Is he an epileptic? Give him some air! Move away!"

Karl, Charley, and Rambo moved away from the prostrate Dunn. He laid very still, his face ashen. His eyes fluttered and opened. Her gasp turned their attention to Sid, then back to Dunn. His eyes widened; he looked transfigured, like a mystic having a vision. Dunn's voice was barely above a whisper.

"Cressida!"

Karl, Charley, and Rambo looked at each other, then at Dunn, and then at the woman.

Her practiced façade fell as Sid looked down at the man she had been in love with when she was young and uncalculating and, for a while, unafraid of love. Stretched out at her feet was the brilliant scholar she had once planned to change the world with, the dreamer, the romantic she had cast aside when she realized money had no allure for him, the man she had spurned because his love could not match her ambition. For a fleeting moment, she was that girl again, vulnerable, gentle, and warm. But that moment passed.

"My God! Gabriel! A greenskeeper? This is how you've ended up? A goddamned *greenskeeper*?"

He stared up at her. All the years he'd thought about Cressida Deathridge, all the times he wondered what he would say if they ever met again, how he imagined she would look, and when it actually happens the first thing she does is start an argument. Just like old times.

"Cressida!" Dunn whispered her name as if it were a prayer.

FALL

21

"After he said her name there wasn't another peep out of him. He just got up and walked out. Pale as a corpse. She tried to talk to him, but he kept going, like he was in a trance. It was the goddamnest thing I ever saw." The smoke was drifting toward Cybil so Lumley moved the cigarette to his other hand. They found themselves in each other's company often now, tectonic plates inexorably moving toward each other. They were sitting on a bench by the putting green, Lumley's mind wrestling simultaneously with the bizarre reunion of Dunn and Cressida Deathridge and the incompetence of the man putting in front of them. He made a wristy, neurotic movement and it took all Charley's fortitude not to leap up, wrest the putter from the man's hands, and show the nincompoop the right way to roll the ball to the hole.

"I knew something bad was going to happen the moment I laid eyes on her," Cybil said. "But I didn't see Dunn leave the office; her, either. Who was she, anyway?"

After the meeting, Karl had asked Charley and Burchell to tell no one about what happened in his office that afternoon. His real concern was Burchell; he'd already blabbed to Clack and Spurgeon about the Casserly incident. Karl knew Lumley was much less likely to say anything. But now that it had been several weeks since the incident, Charley saw no harm in telling Cybil. Labor Day weekend was approaching and the little dramas of the year—Stokes' assault on Burchell, the strange figure wandering the back nine, the thumping the Halling brothers had received in the Keegan Cap—

had faded away. Dunn was no more or less an enigma than he had always been. Besides, Lumley was enjoying these chats with Cybil and knew she could keep a secret. He didn't go into the reason why Sid Deathridge was there and Cybil showed no curiosity about it. She knew there were dark forces working against the ZPGC; she didn't feel the need to know the details.

The change of seasons can have an effect on a person; even someone as taciturn and unreflective as Lumley could find himself suddenly ruminating on his life and times. Such was the mood that settled upon Lumley as he shared that bench with Cybil. He paused to take a drag before he answered her question, prefacing his remarks with an admonition for Cybil to "keep it under her hat."

Cybil was not a romantic. She was a practical woman who viewed the human condition in a very uncomplicated way—man wants to mount woman; woman wants to domesticate man. That was about it, as far as she was concerned. She'd seen movies, even read a book or two, all about love and passion, but she'd always taken it as just that: fiction, made-up stories, fairy tales. She had never, ever heard of anything in real life like the story of Gabriel and Cressida, even the abbreviated version Lumley shared with her.

"They went to college together. He was crazy about her. She broke it off. He snapped. Quit school. Disappeared. She tried to find him but he didn't want to be found. Then some twenty years later he walks in a room and she's standing there. Down he goes. When he comes to, they don't say much. They just look at each other, like they both can't believe what they're seeing. Finally, he gets up and walks out. After he's gone she tells us what I just told you. She's a tough cookie, but you could tell she was pretty shook up too. Then she left."

The similarities to his relationship with Cybil suddenly struck Charley. Feeling himself blush, he turned away, flicking his cigarette off into the long grass. Cybil said nothing. Charley was watching the man on the putting green again, flicking his wrists and missing every putt. He felt Cybil lean her shoulder against his. He didn't mind.

*

Kismet best describes how the brilliant young scholar and the campus beauty came to be a couple, a chance encounter in Copley Square outside Trinity Church. She was arguing with a boy who'd asked her out on a date and had assumed she would benefit from his insights into the state of the world. Her withering critique brought the date to an abrupt end and sent the young philosopher slithering away. She was known as Cress then, a young woman of singular ideas, a strange mix of the conservative and radical; an anomaly. She had a reputation as a disputatious and intense personality, certainly not most men's idea of a dream date, but Dunn, sitting on a nearby bench, watching her verbally eviscerate her companion, found Cress rather fascinating. She was obviously smart, and not just the kind of smart that regurgitates what she heard in the classroom. Hers was an informed intellect, the product of independent reading and a skeptical attitude toward received wisdom. Everything and everyone interested her—as long as they were as focused on achieving success as she. What Cressida Deathridge couldn't tolerate was inactivity, prevarication, and indecision. The Will to Power was her gospel.

Gabriel, usually not one to approach a woman he didn't know, found himself countering Cress' argument, defending the field her date had abandoned. She turned her imperious green eyes on him. He didn't flinch; she asked if he wanted to see a movie. Only, he said, if she picked it. She laughed and he rose up and went to her; at that moment he knew he would love her forever.

Love soon blossomed. Dunn, who had never had a girlfriend before, doted on Cressida and she, in her peculiar way, on him. Her dark beauty had always attracted men, but she'd never met anyone like Gabriel before, someone who could parry wits with her, withstand her constant barrage of ideas and opinions, and, on a rare occasion, actually cause her to rethink her position. Hers was a cold, hard mind; falling in love disconcerted Cress, it made her uncomfortable. She didn't know what to make of it. For Gabriel it was a much simpler thing. He had found his soul mate. She cringed at the term, but he couldn't find a better way to describe how he felt about her. Cress was beautiful, brilliant, and never boring. True, at times her intensity could become tiresome, but like Shakespeare's Dark Lady, she ruled his heart.

Their backgrounds were as different as their personalities. Gabriel was the only child of schoolteachers, reserved, kindly people who lived quietly and doted on their son. Cressida Deathridge came from a more affluent and troubled family. Her father, the only child of Armenian immigrants, picked a new surname from the Boston phone book when he left home at eighteen. He rose quickly in the construction business and married the shy, introverted daughter of an old New England family. Mr. Deathridge, an avid golfer as well as a rapacious businessman, was either at the office, on a business trip, or at the golf course throughout most of Cressida's childhood. Her mother was lovely, frail, and aloof, and a serious alcoholic by the time Cressida was a teenager. Her two brothers, Damon and Marcus, despised each other almost as much as they did their younger sister, pausing their internecine battles only long enough to mercilessly tease the gawky, introverted Cressida. She emerged from that crucible of cruelty and neglect with a rapier wit, analytical mind, and will to dominate. Raised wealthy and given everything in life except affection and understanding, Cressida Deathridge was unprepared for Gabriel Dunn. He had none of the vices she despised in men—jealousy, the need to control, self-pity, anger—yet, paradoxically, the more she grew to love him, the more the power of that emotion frightened her.

Perhaps she felt she and Gabriel were too different to survive the vicissitudes of life together; perhaps she valued money too much; whatever the cause, however she justified it to herself, Cressida made up her mind to leave Gabriel. Usually not one to shy away from confrontation, she did at that moment. Without saying a word to him, she went off to Florida with her family, leaving behind a note telling him she would not be back. She didn't go into her reasons. She knew the note was an act of cowardice and refused to compound it with lies; she had too much respect for him to make up a story about another man. She simply wished him well with his dissertation and much success in the future, and said goodbye.

When Gabriel found the note he thought it was a joke, then he looked around the room and saw she'd taken all her things and the scales fell from his eyes. The next morning he went to his dissertation defense, delivered the cryptic quote from Marlowe's *Doctor Faustus*, and walked away from Harvard and out of Cressida's life.

It only took two days in Florida with her family for Cressida to regret what she had done. She called their apartment, but Gabriel didn't answer. When she got back to Boston, she searched for him in vain. His academic advisor told her about his bizarre departure but had no idea where he went. She called his parents. They hadn't heard from him in weeks and were stunned to learn he had thrown his academic career away. Cressida panicked, fearing Gabriel might have harmed himself. She coerced her father into hiring a detective who, after a three-month investigation, reported that he'd traced Gabriel to a ship and that it appeared he had jumped overboard sometime after it passed through the Panama Canal. Cressida refused to believe it. She checked in with his parents monthly for more than a year until they, anxious and frightened for the son they never heard from, lashed out at her as the cause of their misery. As time passed, the insanity of breaking up with Gabriel and the cruel way she'd gone about it came into bold relief; pride, however, trumped humility. Cressida turned inward, became even more distant and terse with people, and concentrated all her energy on finishing her education. The year she graduated, her father divorced her mother and moved to Florida where he began developing over-fifty-five golf course communities. Cressida went to work for him, loathing him, loathing golf, and loathing herself. And so the years passed.

After Gabriel walked out of the oral exam for his dissertation, he took every cent he had out of the bank and booked passage on a freighter to the Far East. He slipped away from the ship as it passed through the Panama Canal. When the detective traced him to the ship, one crew member swore he'd seen Gabriel on board several days after they'd passed through the canal. He told the detective Gabriel had seemed depressed and had most likely waited for a moonless night and thrown himself overboard. That was the usual way it was done. And that was the story the detective reported back to Mr. Deathridge.

Cressida's intuition was right. Gabriel was damaged, depressed, and heartsick, but not suicidal. He simply disappeared into the Third World, putting his skills to work on plantations and farms throughout Central and South America; he walked on a golf course for the first time in Argentina. He liked being a part of the grounds crew and he liked the quiet and solitude of the course in the early morning hours. But while he sought anonymity, it was difficult for a tall Anglo in such a lowly occupation to go unnoticed for long; people eventually asked questions, so he kept moving. While working at a private course outside Buenos Aires, Gabriel met and became friends with Roberto De Vicenzo, the great Argentine golfer. Gabriel, of course, had no idea who he was, other than an affable older man everyone seemed to know and respect very much. One day, De Vicenzo approached Gabriel as he was cutting new cups on the putting green and struck up a conversation. Soon casual exchanges became long talks and those long talks became a regular occurrence. De Vicenzo became a sort of father confessor to Dunn. Gabriel told Roberto about Cressida, the letter that greeted him on that fateful day, and his escape into obscurity. It didn't come out all at once. Gabriel doled out his tale like a miser in stingy installments over the course of many weeks. It didn't matter; De Vicenzo was a patient listener.

"You know, Gabriel, we all have our disappointments in life," De Vicenzo said, when Gabriel had finally finished telling his tale, "I myself had a great victory slip through my fingers because I failed to pay attention to a simple detail. I think maybe you failed to pay attention too; you missed something you should have seen in this woman, something that would have told you this great misfortune was coming your way. It doesn't matter now, that's all in the past. You should forget about her, my friend. Don't let her make you an exile all your life."

De Vicenzo's words struck a chord in Gabriel. He thought about them for a long time. Then one day, he woke up and decided it was time to go back to America, to forget about the beautiful, intoxicating Cressida Deathridge and begin life anew. Roberto De Vicenzo was kind enough to lend him money for the flight home.

Gabriel came back to America but still kept moving, traveling around the country, trying to get up the enthusiasm to return to his academic pursuits, but it was no use; the interest just wasn't there anymore. He continued to wander from state to state, working in nurseries, greenhouses, and organic farms for a while, then moving on again. He visited his parents—he never mentioned Cressida and they were still so angry with her they never told him how hard she had tried to find him—and made an attempt at settling down, but the small town he had grown up in couldn't keep him. After six months he wandered off again, coming, for no real reason, to this Midwestern city and eventually gravitating toward the only place where he truly felt comfortable, a golf course. The moment he arrived at the ZPGC, everything about this quirky, tired, old municipal golf course appealed to him: its isolated location, the way the fairways meandered through the trees, the uniqueness of each hole, and how little he would have to deal with people here. Gabriel dedicated himself to breathing new life into the course. The memory of Cressida Deathridge lingered, less raw but still vivid, and still the happiest of his life. Gabriel Dunn settled in, believing he had found his home and never for a moment thinking she would ever show up at the Zebulon Pike.

*

The office was deathly silent after Gabriel walked out. Sid Deathridge watched him, a look of childlike disappointment seeping through the hard veneer she presented to the world. The men around her didn't know how to react to what had happened; they were more stunned than she and no one said a word for several agonizing moments.

"You all right?" Karl asked.

The less sensitive Lumley chimed in before she had time to respond. "What the hell was that all about?"

She told them the story of Cressida and Gabriel in a quiet, almost clinical voice. While there was sadness in her eyes, she sat tall and motionless in the chair Karl brought up for her. No one said a thing when she finished. They were all thinking the same thing: what did this woman ever see in Dunn? Everyone was feeling awkward, wondering what to do next. Go after Dunn? Cressida looked around. Shocked to find herself surrounded by faces filled with pity and concern, she stood up and straightened her suit.

"All right, back to the matter at hand! We still need to come to some sort of an agreement. I'm not sure how we'll handle..." she paused for a second, "Gabriel. I suppose..."

"You don't have to worry about us. We don't want anything. Tell Midge he doesn't have to do anything for us. We won't say nothing to nobody." Rambo felt he was speaking for everyone and he was right. They just wanted her to go away and then to forget about this whole mess.

Sid looked at them for a moment. "A charming gesture. I will, however, need to get it in writing. You understand, I'm sure. I'll have Mr. Midge put together a standard nondisclosure agreement and mail it to you. Just print your names on a piece of paper for me so I have them all correct this time. You feel confident you speak for Gabriel, too?"

Lumley nodded and Karl handed her a sheet of paper with their names printed neatly on it.

Cressida threw her head back and smiled. "Well, this certainly has been an extraordinary day. Goodbye."

And with that she was gone.

*

Dunn spent that night in the maintenance building, shame and melancholy keeping him company, the murky interior dulling the pain of the reopened wound. Even after darkness had fallen he felt exposed, observed. They'd all seen him collapse like a rag doll at the mere sight of her, but how could they understand what that experience was like for him? How else could he react to seeing her so suddenly and without warning after all these years? Dunn brooded until daylight began seeping under the doorway. He mounted his mower and rode away into the mist.

22

Sid Deathridge left out the part about Gabriel Dunn when she reported back to Midge. She preferred to leave him with the impression she'd negotiated a complete surrender based solely on her keen negotiating skills. She even provided Midge with a draft of the letter for him to have them sign. It was, in the main, a standard nondisclosure agreement specifying they would leave themselves open to legal action if they spoke to anyone about Dan Casserly's work, Mr. Midge and his plans, or Mr. Milbank and his involvement in those plans, or if they made any mention to anyone at any time about any possible alternative uses of the Zebulon Pike Golf Course in the future. Midge had been impressed with Sid's business acumen before; she now achieved Olympian stature in his mind.

But Cressida Deathridge, regardless of her manicured, tailored, and coiffed exterior, had been shaken to the core at seeing Gabriel Dunn again, far more severely than she realized at first. That realization shocked her, for if Gabriel had never tried to forget her, Cressida had done her very best to get over him. Within two years of their breakup, she married for the first time. It lasted three years. Five years later, she tried it again. That marriage was over in two years. Both husbands were handsome, charming, successful, and shallow as a sidewalk puddle. She had subconsciously chosen men who were what she had wanted Gabriel to be and found them wanting, yet she lacked the introspection to see it. Her forays into marriage left Cressida confused and angry; she could never comprehend what had gone wrong or why both husbands had become so disenchanted with her and left her so quickly. Sid was not a woman who accepted failure graciously, and after two failed marriages in ten years she became a sort of secular nun. A nun, who, on occasion, threw aside her vow of chastity for an evening or two, then resumed it without regret. She became reconciled to the fact that she could sleep with a man and not love him without grasping the source of her detachment; that is, until Gabriel Dunn walked into Ketterman's office and she beheld the gaunt, taciturn dreamer of her youth with the absurdly passionate devotion to growing things in front of her again, and knew in her heart of hearts she'd never stopped loving him. A greenskeeper and a golf course developer: it was laughable. Somehow, they'd both found themselves attached to a game neither had ever played, nor wanted to; and somehow it had brought them together again in a city neither of them was from nor had ever wanted to visit.

Cressida pondered these things as she flew back to Florida, and with every mile the memory of Gabriel Dunn began to weigh more heavily on her.

*

There was a sense of anticipation in the air as the Ebon Invitational drew closer. This year's event was going to be different. For the first time in more years than any ZPGC regular could remember, the Ebon was going to be a big deal again; as far as local awareness, it had never been bigger. And the quality of competitors was the highest in decades.

The preparations for the Ebon Invitational culminated in the "great cleanup," the grand housecleaning Karl had envisioned when he took the job as manager. Bernadette Clayfield instigated it, bursting into Karl's office one morning with the idea of organizing volunteers to spruce up every square inch of the clubhouse, both inside and out. Karl liked the idea. Even if the future of the ZPGC was limited, there was no reason it shouldn't go down looking its best, and it had clearly not been at its best in years. And so it came about: Karl checked the calendar and found the perfect day for it. He posted notices that the clubhouse would be closed on that date and sent out word volunteers were needed. To accommodate players on that day, greens fees would be collected at the starter's shack and Cybil would serve food from a tent near the putting green. The kitchen, of course, would not be part of the cleanup; Cybil kept it so spotless the health inspector held it up as a model of hygienic standards. But the rest of the clubhouse had to be emptied, thoroughly scrubbed, and aired out. Over fifty people responded to Karl's call for volunteers; even Art Castle, Karl's predecessor, came back to help. Merril Stokes, still fixated on restoring his tarnished image, took on the job of marshalling the volunteers into groups and assigning them areas of responsibility. Not even Karl's office was exempt and Hood, a retired painter, took on the task, with Rankel's assistance, of giving it a fresh coat of paint.

There was, of course, nothing in Karl's budget for any of this. Bernadette finagled three hundred dollars out of hers, the rest was provided by the volunteers. Hood passed the hat among his cronies for the paint for Karl's office and to touch up the exterior trim. Karl was heartened by the enthusiasm of the volunteers, even though he knew all their efforts could do nothing to save the ZPGC from its fate.

*

While Cybil had foresworn allegiance to Milbank, he was not so easily shaken off and when he called and asked her to his office again, her courage waned. Cybil was not a brave person but she was determined to say nothing that would hurt Karl's career. Milbank was his usual polite self, greeting Cybil at his office door and setting a chair for her in front of his desk.

"Well, it's certainly been a long time, Cybil. I was beginning to think you didn't like our little meetings." He grinned and paused.

"No, it's nothing like that. It's just that we've been busy, especially with the Ebon Invitational coming up."

"I'm afraid I don't know what that is; some sort of a golf event?"

Cybil was nonplussed. How could he not know about the Ebon Invitational? Wasn't he a Parks Commissioner? Cybil realized he knew very little and cared even less about the things she held dearest. The Zebulon Pike was her world. To her it was a magical place where time coagulated, where change came at a glacial pace, and that was just the way she liked it. The ZPGC was where things from out of the past, like the Keegan Cap and Ebon Invitational, lived on, no matter how things were going beyond its borders. The Zebulon Pike was the most important in Cybil's life but to this man, it was all too clear to her now, it was nothing at all.

"It's a tournament for black golfers," she said in a low voice, her eyes riveted on her shoes, "that's been around since the 1930s, I guess. Fort Sumter has run it since his dad died, but now Mr. Washington is trying to make it something special again, like it was when Obadiah was alive."

"Mr. Washington? Do you mean *Welmont* Washington?"

"Yep, that's him, Welmont Washington. I guess he's gotten all sorts of important people signed up. It's going to be bigger and better than it has been in a long, long time. Obadiah would be really proud."

Milbank had no idea who Obadiah was or what Fort Sumter had to do with anything; but the name Welmont Washington got his attention. He needed to know more and he'd need a better source than Cybil.

"Mr. Ketterman, I assume, is also involved in all this. "

"He's helping, but it's really run by Sumter and Washington and this girl Bernadette. Karl's helping with the renovation, though."

"What *renovation?*" Milbank's voice was almost a shriek. Cybil could see she'd struck a nerve.

"It's not really a renovation, just a lot of people coming together to scrub and clean the whole clubhouse, inside and out."

Milbank felt things slipping out of his control and he didn't like it. What on earth was Welmont Washington, a prominent citizen and successful businessman, doing getting involved in an event at the Zebulon Pike? He would have to look into this personally.

"When is this housecleaning taking place?"

"Tomorrow." Cybil felt a surge of remorse in revealing even such a trivial fact. Milbank brought his palms down on the desk and pushed himself up.

"Well, I certainly wouldn't want to miss that. Thank you, Cybil; it was so good to see you again."

Before Cybil knew what was happening, Milbank had her outside his office.

*

It was the perfect ear and the only way he could possibly respond to its perfection was to nibble it. Karl felt her body move closer, her cheek gliding over his lips until hers were on them. He sat up and looked at her, marveling at the stark contrast between the whiteness of her body and the deep brown of her legs and arms. He couldn't quite believe she was really here with him. He leaned down and breathed in the aroma of her glorious hair, unleashed and cascading over the pillow, shimmering in the shaft of moonlight. Karl Ketterman had never been so happy in his whole life.

"I love you, Gretchen."

She smiled without opening her eyes and put a finger on his lips. It was a simple gesture that left him feeling he'd somehow spoiled the moment. He couldn't help it; he did love her, yet she seemed to not want to hear it. He'd always thought girls liked being told they were loved; Gretchen seemed uncomfortable with it. He would be more careful after this. He didn't want to be the possessive, clinging, demanding boyfriend. Karl fell back on the pillow. Gretchen moved closer and squeezed his hand ever so gently and then the night enveloped them.

*

Milbank was on the phone to Robert Midge the next morning. Midge hadn't heard Welmont Washington was involved in the Ebon Invitational either, yet he didn't sound concerned.

"So Welmont wants to help run a golf tournament at the ZPGC; big deal. The Ebon has been around forever yet somehow you and ninety-nine percent of the people in this town have never heard of it. You think he's going to change that? If he thinks it has a pulse after this year, I guarantee he'll move it to a better course, probably the Lochenberry, where he's a member. Relax, Milbank. Just focus on your part of the bargain. Keep those commissioners in our corner and ready to re-evaluate the viability of the Zebulon Pike."

The conversation with Midge quieted Milbank's concerns until Roger Bakken and Xavier Lopes, the Parks Commissioners most interested in finding other uses for the city's golf courses, came into his office.

"Hey, Ralph, you heard what's going on at the Zebulon Pike today?" Bakken was waving one of the notices Karl had run off. He'd mispronounced Milbank's first name again; Ralph was starting to believe Bakken did it on purpose. Bakken—who lived close to the ZPGC and cut across it on his morning walk to the chagrin of Burchell and the other rangers—had snatched it off a windshield in the parking lot. "Lopes and I are driving over to take a look; want to join us?"

Milbank read the flyer with a touch of trepidation; he knew Lopes and Bakken were suckers for any kind of grassroots community activity like this. He would have to go along to monitor the situation and them.

*

"That's where we are, as of yesterday afternoon. I'm heading over to the course now." Bernadette tapped her papers into alignment and put them back in the folder. Welmont gave the top of his hair a final pat in the mirror and turned his chair around.

"Great, but the action is going to be on the course, not the clubhouse. How is the course looking?"

"The greenskeeper is a strange bird, kind of a recluse. I've had a hard time running him down. Ketterman assures me there's nothing to worry about; he says the guy will have the course looking great. We're having a cleanup because I want the clubhouse looking its absolute best. The condition it's in now reflects poorly on the tournament—and the sponsor. I can't let that happen."

Welmont shrugged. Fine. Clean the place up. That won't stop me from moving the Ebon to the Lochenberry, he thought to himself.

A half-hour later Bernadette was standing in Karl's office. She'd changed into jeans and a t-shirt; it was clear she meant to do more than just watch. Gretchen was already taking down photos, wrapping them in newspaper, and putting them in boxes. She was almost done; only a few portraits of past managers were left to be put away. Gretchen stopped to give Bernadette a hug. She had met her before and liked her very much, even though she didn't seem very interested in golf.

"I've just finished my meeting with Mr. Washington. The field is set. The local TV stations have all gotten back to me; I know two of them will be here for sure; their sports guys are playing in the Ebon. Now all we have to do is get things spiffed up around here."

"I need you people to clear out now." Hood stood in the doorway, Rankel behind him. Karl and the two women left the office. The last of the furniture was just going out the clubhouse door, leaving the dirt and grime that had accumulated over the decades painfully obvious: windows yellowed with tobacco smoke and grease; walls stained with god-knows-what; and the terrazzo floor a patchwork of sticky, unidentifiable spills and blotches. They went out the back way onto the verandah where Fabio Franzen hovered. He too had met Bernadette and had been trying ever since to make inroads with her. He smiled. She smiled back. He felt emboldened to speak.

"How's it going, Bernadette?"

Having seen the cleared-out clubhouse, Bernadette realized they had a daunting task ahead of them. "Ask me in a couple hours."

"I'm here to help," he said.

Bernadette looked intently at him for a moment. "Then, let's get to work."

Franzen stayed by her side all day, but the best his charm offensive got from her was a promise that she would try to free herself from her duties at the Ebon long enough to watch him tee off. Nonetheless, Fabio felt he was getting somewhere.

*

"Roll Tide!" Dan Doherty said, grinning broadly and leaning on his rake.

Milbank looked at Lopes and Bakken. They seemed as baffled as he. What in God's name did "Roll Tide" mean?

"C'mon, Dan," Clayton said," "let's get back to work."

The three Parks Commissioners continued around the building, watching the bustling mass of men, women, and kids swarm over the building like ants on a picnic table. Suddenly, an enormous black man carrying a push broom lumbered toward them.

"'Scuse me, gentlemen. Coming through!"

Bakken pushed his sunglasses up on his forehead and admired the army of volunteers attacking their tasks, caulking windows, pulling the seedlings out of the rain gutters, and sweeping the pavement. What he saw pleased him. This was community action at its best, the people coming together, answering the clarion call to service and pitching in to improve a public facility. He nudged Lopes. Milbank found it disturbing, almost perverse. He led Bakken and Lopes to the far side of the practice green.

"This is good to see, as I'm sure you both agree. We should not, however, lose sight of the big picture. As inspiring as this is, it's an anomaly; not something that happens with any regularity, for certain. You can tell that from the general state of the place."

Lopes wasn't listening. He was watching a group of women planting flowers around the perimeter of the parking lot with members of the grounds crew. He breathed in the democratic atmosphere. This was the progressive, egalitarian world he dreamed of making a reality someday as he evolved from Parks commissioner to councilman, to mayor. "Boy," he said, "this is *really* something."

Milbank felt nauseous.

*

Midge sidled up to Washington at the main bar of the Lochenberry Country Club. Welmont was just finishing a chat with two black members who were recounting their childhood experiences at the Ebon. They'd caddied in it and had fond memories of old Obadiah Sumter. One of them had carried Charlie Sifford's bag one year. Welmont was fascinated with their stories. He had never gone near the Ebon Invitational as a kid. He knew about it, but his father was a baseball guy who thought golf was a sissy white man's game and, while he didn't mind his son caddying at a country club, he wasn't going to let him hang around a municipal golf course wasting his time watching golfers of any color.

"I hear you're a philanthropist, Welmont. Putting your money behind a golf tournament at the Zebulon Pike; aren't we good enough for you?"

Welmont looked closely at Midge's fat face and conceded to himself that it would be just as ugly if it were black.

"It's not *my* money, Robert, the company is sponsoring it. My customers are black. The Ebon Invitational is one of the oldest black golf tournaments in the country. My interest in it is simple: to promote my business; explain to me how sponsoring a member-guest here is going to help me do that?"

Midge frowned as if hurt by Welmont's response, then his mood brightened. "Say, remember when I told you I've got something going that I want to get you in on? Oddly enough, your Ebon Invitational kind of falls in line with that. Let's go someplace a bit more private."

They reconvened in the very room where Midge had conferred with Sid Deathridge. Midge waited until Washington was comfortably situated. Welmont felt a sales pitch coming. "If you and Chartreuse think I'm interested in building a new home, forget about it. Bernice and I are happy where we're at."

Midge waved him off. "Hear me out before you blow me off. Chartreuse and I are working on something really big and you could be a part of it. And, believe it or not, what we're working on involves the Zebulon Pike."

Welmont hadn't become wealthy by telegraphing his punches. He waited patiently for Midge to continue.

"You've been hanging around that place. You've got eyes. What do you see?" Midge hadn't meant it as a rhetorical question but Welmont remained stone-faced. "Okay, I'll tell you: a runned down, tired dump. But," Midge paused for a second, "the Zebulon Pike happens to be a very desirable location. Freeway access to downtown and the suburbs is only a half-mile away, yet it's surrounded by the Winnehala Wetlands and city parks on two sides and set off from the street, so it's very secluded for being right in town."

Welmont couldn't restrain himself. "Midge, about half the golf course is built on a bog. You couldn't build houses on that land without bringing in tons of earth, which I doubt the DNR would let you do because, as I'm sure you know, the Winnehala Wetlands is a nature preserve. Besides, who's going to put up a million-dollar home in a neighborhood of eighteen-hundred square-foot houses built eighty years ago?"

Midge reached over and slapped Welmont's knee. "No one! Have I said anything about building houses? I've got a bigger idea than that. The Zebulon Pike is the municipal golf course that doesn't turn a profit. Not a dime; hasn't for years. It's an albatross that some in the city would love to get rid of." Midge tilted his head and winked at Welmont. "Okay, now what if a nonprofit organization offered the city, let's say, eight-and-a-half million dollars for that land? Suddenly the city gets rid of that albatross and makes a lot of money in the process. And," Midge lowered his voice and stabbed his pudgy right index finger down on the palm of his left hand, "what if that nonprofit could show that it would also help revitalize the surrounding neighborhood? Now the city not only gets rid of a broken-down old golf course but it sees property tax revenue around it rise. What politician isn't going to be all over that?" Midge grinned and fell back in his chair.

"What nonprofit? And what are they going to do with the land if they're not building homes?" Welmont said.

Midge spread his arms out and looked about the room. "The nonprofit is us, the Lochenberry Country Club! And we're going to move out of this mausoleum and relocate on the Zebulon Pike. I've already got plans for the clubhouse and the course." Midge pulled his Morris chair closer to Washington's. "Imagine that old pile of rocks torn down and replaced with a state-of-the-art building with all the amenities: beautiful marble floors and huge windows, bright, inviting rooms, world-class dining, flat-screen TVs everywhere, and a bar as big as the ballroom in this dump. In a nutshell, a place you'll be proud to bring your friends and business associates to. My God, Welmont, this is a priceless opportunity. And you can be right smack-dab in the middle of it."

Welmont Washington was a cool customer, but Midge's

revelation caught him completely off guard. The audacity of it was stunning. And he knew immediately why Midge was courting him. He would need a black face in the mix and he was the perfect candidate, a member of Lochenberry, an entrepreneur, and someone who owned a business in the city.

"Okay, I'll admit it; it's an interesting idea. But tell me, how are the politicians going to sell the idea of shutting down a public course and turning it into a private country club?"

Midge waved a finger at Welmont. "I told you. It doesn't make any *money*. I've seen the financials. It barely breaks even. And for years all sorts of wing nuts have bombarded the Parks Commission with ideas for the land—soccer or softball fields, mountain bike trails, whatever. The problem is, the state DNR not only limits the changes you can make, it's grandfathered the land's use. That means the city now has two choices: it's either a golf course that doesn't make money or it's a wilderness. Wouldn't you want to be the far-sighted politician who comes forward with a third option that puts the city up eight-and-a-half million dollars; an idea with the potential to revitalize the whole area?"

"I don't get it. If the land is grandfathered in as a golf course, why are people still trying to get the Parks Commission to convert it to other uses?"

Midge chortled into his glass. "Because they don't *know* the DNR grandfathered the land yet. It's buried in a piece of legislation dealing with conservation of state land my old man got through the legislature last week. It says no land abutting any wetland *anywhere* in this state can be repurposed. Period. That kind of puts the city in a bind, don't you think? Golf course, wilderness, either way, the city loses money. Then old Robert Midge and Welmont Washington and their merry band come to the rescue. No one on the Parks Commission or the City Council is going to stand up and say, 'Who cares if it's a money loser? Let's save the Zebulon Pike;' they'd have to be nuts."

"How about the members here?"

Midge waved him off. "The old man is handling that. But let me ask you something, Welmont. You ever play the Zebulon Pike?"

Welmont shook his head. "I have. It's rundown, overplayed, and it's still *ten times* the course this is; it won't take much money to turn it into a really great track. And we'll have plenty to work with; do you have any idea what the land we're sitting on right now is worth? Do you have a clue how much working capital we'll have to put into the Zebulon Pike, even after we give the city that eight-and-a-half million dollars? A very tidy sum, I can assure you." Midge folded his hands on his ample belly and studied Welmont.

Welmont had always considered Robert Midge a blowhard, a spoiled little rich boy who never did a thing on his own. He saw him in a different light now. This was a formidable Midge, a man to be reckoned with; and his plan for the Zebulon Pike Golf Course seemed watertight.

"My, my, my, Midge. You are a devious little rascal, aren't you?"

23

Not since the day it opened had the Zebulon Pike shone so brightly. Never in its history had it undergone such a thorough cleaning, both inside and out, and those involved in it took pride in the fruits of their labor. They breathed in the scent of Pine Sol and polish, fresh paint and lemon oil, and felt good. The half-inch of dust was off Keegan's putter and its ancient hickory shaft refreshed with linseed oil. Even the stone fireplace had been washed, revealing the natural deep gray hue of the rock. Every sill, every pillar and beam, and every inch of woodwork was freed from layers of grime and grease and restored to its former glory. The sunlight reflecting off the newly polished terrazzo floor illuminated the room and the hearts of all who stood marveling at its long-hidden character. The regulars were amazed by the transformation, even the oldest ones who'd haunted the clubhouse season after season for decades had never seen the charm hidden under all that dirt. They pointed at little architectural details they'd never noticed before. They stared at the patterns of colored light on the floor and walls the prisms in the beveled windows created. They paid homage to Keegan's Cap, newly polished and resting on its perch behind the counter, finally in surroundings befitting its dignity.

There was still work to be done. The tables were out in the parking lot and Hood and Rankel continued painting Karl's office; the ceiling and walls had had to be washed and patched before they could start. But much had been achieved.

Karl stood next to Bernadette as she reviewed her checklist. A massive object landed on his right shoulder. Out of the corner of his eye he saw it was Tyreal's hand.

"Tell you what, Hoss, you did a hell of job here. This is... something! This is what it must have looked like when my Daddy first came here. Congratulations, man."

"It wasn't me, Fort. Bernadette is the one that made this happen. I certainly thought about doing a cleanup but if it weren't for her, we never would have gotten around to it. You ought to be proud to have her working with you on the Ebon Invitational."

Fort grunted and walked away.

"I don't think Mr. Sumter and Mr. Washington are on the same page yet," Bernadette said. "I believe he feels a little threatened, especially since I don't clear everything with him first, but I work for Mr. Washington, not him. Whether Mr. Sumter wishes to acknowledge it or not, Mr. Washington is the one who's gotten all the celebrities and the athletes signed up. I'm doing the legwork on the details but without his involvement the Ebon would be the same event it's been for decades. Deep down, Mr. Sumter knows that's true and I think it bothers him a bit."

It did more than bother Tyreal a bit; it galled him. Ever since he left the Army he had tried to resurrect the Ebon and had failed miserably. He knew why. He was nobody in this town. He didn't know the important people, the big shots. He couldn't call on business leaders and expect them to do something for him because he had nothing to offer in return. And he knew Welmont Washington was going to pull it off because he was everything Fort wasn't: handsome, polished, confident, and well liked. Aside from Scrumpy, no one much liked Fort Sumter. Be that as it may, he wasn't about to let anyone wrestle control of the Ebon Invitational from him, not yet.

*

Welmont parked behind his flagship Boutiqué Afriqué and sat mulling over everything he'd just heard from Midge. He had to admire the sheer boldness of the plan and how Midge had thought through every detail. It was brilliant. The eight-and-a-half million dollars the board of the Lochenberry would toss at the city—a board Midge and his father had packed with their cronies—was chicken feed when you considered the potential value of the prime suburban lots the old Lochenberry could be turned into. Welmont knew Midge was right about the courses, too. Anyone who played them both knew the ZPGC's layout was superior, and it didn't take much imagination to see how a little landscaping and a modern clubhouse could completely change the character of the place. Transforming the ZPGC into the new Lochenberry would, as Midge said, also ignite a surge of redevelopment in the surrounding area, gentrify the neighborhood, and increase property values. And with his inside information on the deal, Washington would have ample opportunity to buy up property before anyone knew what was coming and make a lot of money in the process. Welmont had underestimated Midge. Ironically, his plan even dovetailed with Welmont's goal of moving the Ebon Invitational to the Lochenberry; everything about Midge's big idea was designed to win him over.

But Welmont still had a few nagging reservations. For one, he liked the old Lochenberry. He found the creaky floors and dark paneling that revolted Midge charming. Welmont took some comfort in knowing the old country club was safe a while; all of this was years away yet. The political wheels, even though they had been well greased, would undoubtedly grind slower than Midge anticipated. There would be setbacks—there always are—so there was no reason to invest much thought in his grand plan just yet. Right now Welmont had other things to deal with.

*

Dunn rumbled up to the seventeenth green on his mower as Merril was setting the flag back in the cup. Merril thought Dunn looked more melancholy than usual, his thin body almost undetectable in his oversized green coveralls. He had last seen Dunn at the cleanup helping with the landscaping around the clubhouse. He had a real talent for growing things, for arranging plants so each one complemented the beauty of the surrounding ones. It was odd Dunn wasn't in charge of the outside of the clubhouse. But who could understand the vagaries of civil service rules? Merril envied Dunn's green thumb; the only thing he could grow was hair in his ears.

Dunn too was thinking about the cleanup as he mowed the rough around the green. He had enjoyed supervising the work around the clubhouse, in part because there was so much going on no one seemed to notice him. He hadn't had to do much. He gave one of the women a list of plants to buy, then he laid out where they would go and made sure the volunteers planted them at the proper depth. He knew he wouldn't run across Charley and he kept an eye out for Karl and Rambo; the humiliation of what had happened when he saw Cressida still gnawed at him. He wasn't so much ashamed of having fainted as embarrassed they had witnessed it. He might have been able to say something to her if they'd been alone, but seeing them he just had to get away as fast as he could.

He wouldn't have helped at the cleanup if that girl hadn't come by and asked him. She'd just walked into his office, brisk and confident, while he sat at his desk contemplating the cosmic joke of he and Cressida crossing paths at this unlikeliest of places. He could see many of the traits he had found so charming in Cressida in the girl. She was pretty and bright and carried herself with the same self-confidence; he hoped, behind her efficient and terse demeanor, she had a kinder heart than Cressida's.

*

"My name is *Phil!*"

Rambo gave Mo an "I'm shocked!" look. Franzen, walking with the lovely business-like girl in charge of this year's Ebon Invitational, had suddenly taken umbrage at being called Fabio. Mo returned Rambo's wide-eyed stare, then leaned out of the shack to reassure himself that it was really Franzen who had just passed by.

"What's up with him?" Rambo asked.

Mo shrugged. "I guess he doesn't want the girl to know about his reputation. Funny. He used to take pride in it."

"Maybe she's different."

Mo leaned out again, taking a closer look at the girl. "She's too smart for him, I'll tell you that much."

*

"Phil, you seem like a nice guy, but I've got a lot going on right now. I appreciate your offer to teach me to play golf. I just don't have time for it."

Franzen felt himself redden. He'd never had this kind of trouble with a woman before. It was embarrassing. Could she be immune to the Franzen charm?

"I didn't mean right now, I was thinking after the Ebon is over when you don't have so much on your plate. You know, a lot of women, especially in business, are taking up the game."

She stopped and took him in. He certainly was full of himself; handsome, surely, but what sort of future is there in teaching golf? A man would have to have a little more ambition and higher goals than that to interest her.

"I'll think about it."

Fabio felt a thrill.

*

Ralph Milbank tapped the pencil on his desk and knit his brow. He did not like the way Lopes and Bakken had gushed over the cleanup at the ZPGC. He had spent months planting the seeds of discontent, nurturing the notion that the Zebulon Pike was a money pit, a black hole that was sucking in funds that could be better spent on other things. True, they hadn't left as proponents for keeping the ZPGC going, but Lopes and Bakken had given him the impression they might not be reliable allies, which meant more work for Ralph, more machinations to undercut the future of the ZPGC. And what about Midge? Milbank was beginning to feel he wasn't being completely forthright. There was a time when he had checked in almost daily, yet Milbank hadn't heard from him in weeks. Naturally distrustful, Ralph Milbank felt he would have to keep a much closer eye on things. The finish line was in sight; he wasn't about to lose the race now.

*

Midge was holding court in the grillroom when the barman came over to say he had a guest at the reception desk, a Mr. Milbank. Midge parted company with his cronies and lumbered out to the foyer, greeting Milbank like a long-lost friend.

"Ralph! So good to see you!" He told the girl at the counter to have the barman come into the library for their drink order and guided Ralph to the least-used room in the club. Midge, ensconced in a tufted wingback chair, a fresh drink in hand, gave Milbank his undivided attention.

"Sorry to barge in on you like this, Robert, but I felt we needed to talk. Washington is going a little overboard with his tournament; he's funded a cleanup of the clubhouse and his assistant corralled a brigade of volunteers for it. While in itself that may be harmless, I'm concerned he may be raising hopes, maybe giving people the impression that the Parks Commission is going to start putting money into the place."

Midge stirred his drink meditatively. "It's funny, a guy works himself up from nothing, gets into the most exclusive club in the city, and suddenly he's got an urge to pump life into an event that's already brain dead." He took a long drink. "I don't get it."

Milbank closed his eyes for a moment to gather his thoughts. "His motivations don't interest me. What I care about is that two Parks Commissioners, Lopes and Bakken, dragged me over there to see what looks like a hundred volunteers, hard at work cleaning up the clubhouse and planting flowers, all under the guidance of Washington's Girl Friday. I realize Washington wants the place to look good for his event, but it would be helpful to know it's a one-time-only thing so I could get Bakken and Lopes back in line."

The ice in Midge's drink tinkled as he set it down. He pressed his hands together in a prayerful gesture. "It's funny you bring this up because I was talking to Welmont about this just the other day. The fact is, Ralph, he is deeply committed to the Ebon

Invitational and plans on being involved with it for a long, long time, I wouldn't be surprised at all if, in a year or two, it becomes the Boutiqué Afriqué Invitational. Have you seen the people he's got playing in it this year? Everybody who's anybody, some of the biggest names in town, professional athletes, TV personalities, you name it. He's doing an incredible job, incredible." Midge picked up his glass and drank deeply.

"Don't you see the problem here, Robert? Our goal is to *shut down* the Zebulon Pike, to redevelop it, to turn it into a high-end community that generates property taxes, right? What Washington is doing is completely counterproductive. It could be used to strengthen the argument to keep the ZPGC open."

Midge rose and went to the window. He felt he needed to put a little space between him and Milbank before he broke the news to him. "Ralph, it's sort of ironic, you coming here today. I just got some news that may mean a change of plans. It seems larger forces have been at work behind our backs."

"What do you mean, 'our plans may have to change'?" Ralph stood up abruptly. "There aren't going to be any changes! I need that goddamned dump plowed under and those houses built. That has been the plan from day one; *that* is what we're going to do," he said in a calm but forceful voice.

"Ralph, larger forces are at..."

"What the *fuck* are you talking about?" Milbank shouted.

Midge resumed his seat. "Calm down, Ralph. There is no point in making a scene. The DNR boned us. Somehow they slipped through an item in a piece of legislation that grandfathers the use of any land bordering a protected area. Do you understand what that means? We can't put up houses on the ZPGC. The law says if there's a golf course there now, that's all that's ever going to be there. Yeah, you could shut down the course and let the land go wild, but who benefits from that?" He paused to let the news sink in. "Look, I'm as upset as you are, Ralph. But I haven't been sitting on my hands. I've been thinking about a way that could turn this around for us. I don't have all the details worked out just yet, but trust me on this."

Ralph Milbank had been a politician his whole adult life and the last person he would trust was someone who asked him to trust him. Milbank was no fool: there are no surprises. Midge must have known all about the legislation before it left committee; he probably masterminded it. Why else would he be so sanguine over the demise of a project they'd worked on for so long? Milbank saw clearly now. Midge had torpedoed the project, now Ralph had to play along and find out why.

"I apologize for that outburst, Robert; I've spent a lot of time and effort on this project, so I hope you understand my frustration. You're right; there is no way to circumvent the Department of Natural Resources. Who could have seen that coming, huh?" He studied Midge's face; it was a conniving rodent's. Now he was sure this little piece of legislative legerdemain was part of Midge's strategy from day one.

"You mentioned an alternate plan."

Midge's face brightened. "It came to me right after I heard the news. At first I was as pissed as you are, believe me, but then I thought, why not beat them at their own game?"

Ralph cocked his head in anticipation of Midge's big idea, then nodded approvingly as he laid it all out: the cash to the city, the jobs created building the new clubhouse, the improvements to the property, the contagious development of the surrounding neighborhood. As Midge blathered on Milbank realized what a first-class, backstabbing scoundrel he was dealing with; yet being an old hand at double-dealing himself, it was difficult not to admire what Midge had wrought.

"And this all came to you in a flash?" Milbank smiled: he knew Midge had no ear for sarcasm.

"I won't lie to you, I've wanted to get the club out of this haunted house for awhile. Okay, why not take advantage of the opportunity? It's not how we drew this up, sure, but you'll still get the development and the growth in property taxes you were after; it will just take a few more years to work it all out; meanwhile, you take credit for bringing eight-and-a-half million dollars into the city's coffers. At the end of the day this is still going to be a win-win for everyone."

Milbank knew any redevelopment in the neighborhood around

the ZPGC would be at least a decade off, and how was he going to take credit for the philanthropy of the Lochenberry's membership? There could be a few political points to be gained in it, but not nearly enough to feed his ambitions. Now, however, was not the time to bring that up. Ralph Milbank would be patient. The day would come when he would show Robert Midge he was not a man to be trifled with.

*

Karl didn't see as much of Gretchen after she went back to college. The university was only one hundred miles away but most weekends she had a golf tournament. When she did come home for the weekend, he was lucky if they spent a day together. Of course, Karl still treasured any time with her. The lovemaking was a big part of that, he couldn't deny it, but it wasn't just that. Gretchen was mature for her years, wise even, and Karl found it easy to confide in her. He valued her ideas and enjoyed sitting around his apartment talking with her about life, golf, and what was going on at the ZPGC. He was pleased when she skipped classes for a day to come back for the big cleanup without him even asking her. That had been a good day, especially when she'd nudged him, pointed out the window at Franzen trotting after Bernadette, and laughed. It was a small thing, yet somehow it made him feel that all his rivals for her affection were vanquished. Their relationship, even though they did their best to hide it at the golf course, was no secret to anyone anymore.

Cybil practically beamed when she set the sandwiches down on the counter in front of them. There was even something in the inflection of Tommy Doherty's "Roll Tide" that suggested he knew they were lovers. Gretchen didn't seem to notice and Karl didn't mind. After all, he was in love with her.

"This guy Welmont is really whipping the Ebon into shape, isn't he? And Bernadette is *totally* amazing," Gretchen said, taking a bite of her tuna fish on rye. "They're even talking about it at school."

Karl smiled. He hadn't told her about the dismal future in store for the ZPGC. He saw no purpose in upsetting her with the news; she had enough to contend with at school. She was no scholar and

Karl was helping her get through her English requirement. They had decided to take a study break and have lunch at the golf course, which was soon extended to a session on the range. No one was there besides a middle-aged couple and Lumley, as usual, at the far end of the range. He was smoking and talking to himself as they walked up.

"Lloyd Mangrum could have sat out the war teaching golf to generals at an Army base. But he didn't. He landed in France on D-Day, fought in the Battle of the Bulge, earned two Purple Hearts. Comes home and wins the 1946 U.S. Open. He was one tough son-of-a-bitch, not one of these country club wimps." He sensed there was someone within hearing distance and turned toward them. "Ever heard of Lloyd Mangrum, girlie?"

Gretchen shook her head.

"How about you?"

"Can't say that I have," said Karl.

Charley let out two lungs-full of smoke in one exasperated sigh.

"Nobody has. Sad." He got out of his cart and came closer. "How you doing at school?"

"Some of the classes are pretty tough…"

Charley cut her off. "I mean golf, kid. How's your game?"

Gretchen brightened. "I've won every match this fall and the team is second in the conference; coach thinks we have a good chance to make the NCAA tournament."

Charley nodded. "Good," he said, then, pointing at Karl, he added, "just remember, golf's not everything."

She blushed but said nothing; neither did Karl.

"Ebon's coming up, and it's going to be a great event again," Charley growled.

With that he walked back to his cart and drove away.

*

The Halling brothers and Tom Crupshaw put some sheets of paper in front of Fort Sumter. He was sitting on the verandah of the Zebulon Pike with Scrumpy, still quietly fuming over his loss of control of the Ebon Invitational.

"What's this?"

The three pulled up chairs. Crupshaw spread the sheets out in front of Fort.

"Pin positions, three days' worth. You got to get this to Dunn before the Ebon starts," Jay said.

"Nobody knows this course better than us," Es said. "This isn't a bombers' course, you know that. Too many tight doglegs, too much risk, but to really test these guys the pins have to be in the right places."

"Tyreal, you've got some real sticks showing up this year. You've got to make sure they have to work for a good score," Tom added. "You put the pins in these spots and it's going to take a real player to win this thing."

Tyreal pulled the pages closer. On each were drawings of six of the ZPGC's greens, three sheets for each day of the event. The pin placement for each day was indicated by a black dot, along with its distance from the nearest edge of the green. Tyreal could see they'd put a lot of work into this.

"I've been running the Ebon for years now. You never did a damn thing for me before. Why, all the sudden, are you guys so anxious to help?"

Before Tom could come up a tactful answer, Jay was talking.

"Because you never had anyone worth shit playing in it before," he said, rattling off the names of four players from local sports teams, men known to be serious golfers, who were in this year's Ebon. "Those are country club guys, scratch golfers who play big-money games. They're going to draw a crowd like you've never seen before and we want a tough setup for them."

Tyreal could feel his blood pressure rising. Scrumpy put a hand on his arm. He pulled it away, grabbed the papers and stormed off the verandah, bumping into tables and cursing under his breath as he went. It was time he had a talk with Mr. Washington.

*

The climb up the stairs left Tyreal breathless and forced a slight delay in his dramatic entrance. The girl at the counter had called

Welmont's office to see if he was available but Tyreal hadn't waited. He took several deep breaths and opened the door. Welmont was seated behind his desk, Bernadette across from him. They were both leaning in on a spreadsheet. Welmont arched an eyebrow.

"Tyreal. What brings you here?"

Tyreal let fly with a torrent of grievances. Bernadette was shocked, even a little fearful. She wondered if she should leave. Welmont took it all stoically. When Tyreal paused to catch his breath, he seized the opening.

"Sit down. Take a minute to calm yourself down and we'll discuss this."

Bernadette started to get up.

"Stay where you are. You're part of this, too."

Tyreal panted, his mouth wide, nostrils flaring. He found a chair and sat down. For what seemed an eternity, the only sound in the room was Tyreal's labored breathing. When he seemed to be under control, Welmont spoke.

"You and I have an agreement, Tyreal; in *writing*. It is a binding legal agreement. I was very clear from the start how I was going to run this tournament. I've done nothing underhanded. I told you I would handle everything leading up to the event and you would be our," he hesitated, searching a moment for the right word, "our host. Now, out of the blue, you come at me like I was doing you dirt; disrespecting you."

Tyreal was humbled. He knew he had no ground for complaint. He tried to explain himself but he wasn't a slick talker like Washington. His voice trailed off. He bowed his head, wishing he could disappear.

Welmont, angry at first, softened as he watched Tyreal slowly shaking his head back and forth. Sumter was a blowhard and a loudmouth and, yes, a bit of a tedious boor, but he wasn't a bad or mean-spirited man. And Tyreal's rant about his father, the tournament, and the ZPGC brought Midge's plan to mind. If Sumter was upset with what Welmont was doing with his father's tournament, wait until he found out what that rich, conniving, son-of-a-bitch had in mind for his golf course.

24

In the second week in September fall began to creep stealthily across the Zebulon Pike. Already a faint flash of crimson could be seen hidden among the maple leaves. The old-timers gathered on the verandah and reminisced about days long ago and, with summer fading away all around them, pondered the possibility of this being their last season.

On this weekday the putting green was empty and a street crew languidly filled potholes in the parking lot. A Parks Commission arborist wandered over the course inventorying the trees, marking some for trimming, others for removal. A ranger zigzagged the fairways in his cart to shoo away the Canada geese. They rose, wings flapping noisily, honking a curse at him as they followed their leader out into the Winnehala Wetlands. These were the familiar signs that the golf season was nearing its end.

But before it did there was one last grand affair ahead, the Ebon Invitational. Reinvigorated and better organized than it had been since Obadiah Sumter stood at its helm, the Ebon was poised to do what it hadn't in decades—assume the mantle of the big event at the Zebulon Pike. The clubhouse, glistening and refreshed and looking like a grand old dame dressed for the ball, stood ready to greet the contestants.

In recent years, with only three or four foursomes in the field, the Ebon had been reduced to a one-day event. This year the traditional three-day format would be resurrected; the size of the turnout demanded it. Seventy-two players would tee off for the

Friday practice round and on Saturday, the first day of actual competition. That number would be cut to the thirty-six players with the lowest gross score after Saturday's round. On Sunday, the player with the lowest two-day gross score would be declared the winner of the Ebon Invitational; there would also be a low net score winner and prizes for closest to the pin on par threes, long drives, long putts and other accomplishments during Sunday's round. A special oversized scorecard with space for all this data was printed for the final round and a volunteer scorer accompanied each foursome to record it all. After the scores were recorded, everyone who hadn't won something on the course would be entered in a drawing for prizes. At the end of the day, everyone who played Sunday was assured of taking home some swag; Welmont and Bernadette made sure of it.

Tournament logistics required a shotgun start on Friday and Saturday: eighteen foursomes, each starting on a different hole. This would ensure that everyone would finish the round in less than four-and-a-half hours; at least, that was the plan.

Most of the players were new to the event, personally invited by Welmont Washington and each paying a one-hundred-and-fifty-dollar entry fee. They were the cream of society; more importantly, there wasn't a hack among them. Every major sports team was represented, along with some of the top amateurs and club professionals in the area. The field was talented and well balanced; three-quarters of the participants were nonwhite and only a handful—mainly local politicians—with a handicap of fifteen or higher. Welmont, while pleased with the caliber of the players, was confident he could be even more discriminating next year.

Not one of Fort Sumter's cronies who had played in previous years was in the field. Nor was Fort.

*

Bernadette scheduled a final meeting on the Wednesday before the Ebon. Welmont, feeling generous and buoyed by the response he'd gotten to the Ebon, made it a dinner meeting at the Lochenberry Country Club. He reserved a large corner table where they would have room to eat and shuffle papers about. Bernadette felt they needed to review the foursomes, the logistics for signing in players and getting them out to their starting hole, and the process for collecting and tabulating scorecards—especially on Sunday—one more time. Welmont and Tyreal had learned it was best to defer to her on all organizational matters, so they deferred to her on the agenda for this meeting.

Tyreal had never been inside the Lochenberry before. He had applied to be a caddy there when he was fourteen but he was so physically imposing even then the caddy master tactfully suggested he pursue other avenues of employment. As he pulled up to the valet, Tyreal regretted he hadn't taken his Cadillac through the car wash. The receptionist directed him to the bar where Welmont stood in the center of a small crowd of admirers. Welmont waved him over and introduced him. Tyreal's bright yellow Hawaiian shirt festooned with contorted green parrots stood out among the more conservative casual apparel of the Lochenberry crowd. Tyreal, still humbled after his outburst in Welmont's office, was less than his usual boisterous self; he was a little intimidated by the surroundings. He felt like an enlisted man in an Officers' Club. Welmont took Tyreal by the elbow and deftly guided his gigantic protégé through the cocktail hour crowd into the quiet of the dining room.

"Good evening, Roger, this is my friend and the chairman emeritus of the Ebon Invitational, Mr. Tyreal Sumter," Welmont announced to the headwaiter and the room at large. "I am expecting another guest any moment, Bernadette Clayfield." Roger showed them to their table and assured Welmont he would keep an eye out for Ms. Clayfield. Tyreal was flattered Welmont had called him a friend and relieved they were at a table. Tyreal could manage to tee up his own golf ball in a pinch, but there was no way he could get into a booth. They ordered drinks and waited for Bernadette. There was an awkward silence Welmont broke by reminding Tyreal it was Bernadette's show from this point on. Tyreal would handle everything on the course, however Bernadette was in charge of the overall event. Any glitches, any issues, were to be handled by her. Welmont knew she had the smarts and the political sense to deal with any problems or get him and Tyreal involved, if necessary, and he wanted to clear that up before she arrived.

Bernadette arrived precisely on time. She wore a pencil skirt and white blouse accented with an oversized silver necklace and open-toed red heels. She strode to the table shoulder to shoulder with Roger, confident and alert, as always.

"Sorry to cut it so close," she said kissing both of them on the cheek before she took the chair Roger held for her. "The pro at the ZPGC has been pestering me about taking a lesson so I finally gave in. It ran a little longer than I thought. That little white ball is harder to hit than I thought, Tyreal!"

She waved off the offer of a drink and, after a few more minutes of idle chitchat, she reached into her bag and pulled out a stack of paperwork and got down to business. That's our Bernadette, Welmont mused, as he raised a silent toast to Tyreal.

*

Gabriel listened to the wind rustling through the trees. He was standing in the doorway of the maintenance building, having just gone over the day's assignments with his crew and sending them on their way. The leaves were starting to have a brittle sound, their motion stiffer, as if their hold on the branches was getting more tenuous every day. In another week or two, they would start to fall in intermittent, swirling showers of yellows and browns and reds. Winter was not far off. He had much to do to prepare for it. As he thought about these things he heard a new sound, the agonized groan of straining springs and tires rubbing against wheel wells.

"Hey, Hoss! I got to talk to you a minute."

Tyreal's cart came to an abrupt stop, kicking up a low cloud of dust. He held out a sheaf of papers.

"My tournament is this weekend," he said. Dunn nodded. "What you think of these pin positions?"

Dunn looked at the first sheet and then at Tyreal; then he began to study each placement closely. A faint smile played across his thin lips as he leafed back and forth through the stack. He knew the topography of every green and could visualize how inviting, how deceptive, how diabolic each placement would be, especially those for Sunday's round.

"These are good; really good. You do this?"

Tyreal beamed. "Me? Naw! But you think they're good, huh? I wasn't so sure. Crupshaw and the Halling brothers gave them to me. I whooped the Hallings' asses in the Keegan, so I thought those two might be up to something; you know, trying to sabotage things and bringing Crupshaw in on it so I'd fall for it."

"Why would they want to do that?"

"Man, I told you, I took a lot of money off them in the Keegan."

Gabriel rolled up the papers, tucked them in the back pocket of his green coveralls and gave them a loving pat.

"They're not out to get you, Tyreal. They're just trying to make sure it takes some above average putting to win your tournament."

"That good, huh?"

"Oh, they'll be better than good. I'm going to cut those cups myself."

Tyreal left Dunn feeling good about the weekend. The Ebon Invitational was finally going to do the Sumter family proud again.

*

Karl took advantage of the lull in business to put things back in order and rearrange his office. He started working on it over the weekend. He got the old record books dusted and back on the shelves, but he soon found himself distracted again by the history that lay around him. Gretchen helped for a while, but after a couple hours she left him on his own. She simply couldn't fathom his infatuation with all of the meaningless minutiae, the yellowed volumes, the bundles of old scorecards, the piles of dog-eared, faded photos of men in high-waisted baggy pants, faces half-hidden under wide-brim hats, proudly posing with their tiny-headed wooden drivers. What did any of this have to do with the world they lived in? What was the sense of keeping all that stuff around?

Karl saw it differently. For him all of those players and all those long-forgotten tournaments were still important as long as the Zebulon Pike survived, maybe even beyond that point. G.K. Chesterton once said tradition was democracy for the dead. Karl may have struggled with the subtlety of the aphorism, but not the underlying sentiment. He, too, believed that the past had a place in the present. He always had, and that belief had only increased since he came to the ZPGC. How could it not? Wasn't this whole place a bit out of synch with the world, a three-dimensional flashback to a time and a temperament that had passed from most people's memory? Perhaps that's why everything about it intrigued Karl.

His parting with Gretchen had not been affectionate. She tersely announced she was going back to school as he puttered through another pile of old papers and walked out. He followed her, apologizing, trying to get her to smile, but to no avail. She stood with the car door handle in her grasp for a moment before turning to him. She swept a wisp of hair away from her face and sighed deeply. He knew it was time to stop talking and listen.

"I like this place, Karl. I practically grew up here. But you're getting a little weird about it," she said, making a sweeping gesture. "Take a good look around, Karl. It will take more than a good cleaning to change things here. This place is rundown and it's going to keep running down; everyone knows the Parks Commission and the City Council have no intention of changing that. It's an old place, Karl. Old places get torn down sooner or later and turned into something different. Old layouts like this aren't where people want to play golf anymore. Everyone likes the latest thing. It just makes no sense for you to be spending your time getting so deep into all this; I mean, is this really where you want to spend your life? *Seriously?*"

The way she said it made Karl feel cold, as if she were implying she would not be part of that life. She gave him a quick kiss on the cheek and got in the car. As it rumbled across the parking lot and down the drive, Karl wanted to call out to her, to ask her to come back so he could tell her she was more important to him than this place. But she was gone.

Karl went back to his office, closed the door, and took a deep breath, hoping the faint fumes of fresh paint that still lingered in the air would anesthetize his sense of foreboding. Maybe she was right. Maybe he was becoming obsessed with the Zebulon Pike.

She had only been guessing, but he knew it for a fact: the ZPGC's days were numbered. So why did he keep delving into the musty files and dusty packets of photographs of long-forgotten faces? He couldn't come up with the answer; they just had a Svengali-like effect on him. No matter how good his intentions, sooner or later he would find himself thumbing through some newly uncovered file, searching for he knew not what.

*

Karl wasn't the only one with an unquiet mind. Milbank, too, brooded; not over love's torturous path but the even more convoluted ways of local politics. His well-laid plans lay on the ash heap and he was at a loss about what he should do next. He conceded Midge had played him for a fool. That left him with two choices: cut his losses and accept defeat magnanimously, or take a more scorched-earth approach and find a way to torpedo Midge's whole project. The latter would gain him nothing but personal satisfaction. Enticing as that was, there was no way to exact that revenge without identifying himself as its author. And torpedoing Midge's project wouldn't dull his family's political clout; Ralph would soon feel the repercussions of crossing the Midges. The trick was to find a way to derail Midge's plan without doing the same to his career and, as of the moment, Ralph could conjure no way of doing that. He decided to get out of the office for a while.

At first, Milbank drove without a destination in mind; then he headed toward the Zebulon Pike. Where better to try to sort through his dilemma? He drove down the long, shaded driveway and into the parking lot. The last time he came here volunteers were sweeping, cleaning, painting, and planting everywhere. Now the new landscaping and the sunlight glinting off the sparkling windows gave the place a charm and character Milbank hadn't noticed before. He wasn't a complete philistine; he had an aesthetic and a sensitive eye for lovely things and a heart that, albeit warped by ambition and intrigues, nonetheless could still appreciate a scene such as this. As he beheld what they had achieved, he wanted to thwart Midge all the more. As a politician, however, he knew better than to waste energy on things that were unlikely to help him.

Ralph Milbank walked into the clubhouse and took in the room. It was far from what it could be, yet still a wonder to behold, brighter, cleaner, and more inviting than he or any other living soul had ever seen it in many years. He couldn't help feeling the tingle Lopes and Bakken had gotten from the freely volunteered collective effort that had done all of this. Milbank's eyes fell on Pike's plaque. He was a student of history and knew the general outline of Pike's career, the accomplishments that never seemed to gain accolades, a life of "what ifs." Ralph sighed. Was that to be his fate, too? He went to Karl's office and tapped his knuckles on the doorframe.

Karl looked up and greeted Ralph, but with none of the deference of earlier meetings; Ralph took it in stride.

"The building looks great, Ketterman. And your office! It's amazing what a little soap and water and paint can accomplish, isn't it?"

"All materials and work were volunteered, Mr. Milbank; not a penny of Parks Commission money was wasted on this place."

Was Ketterman trying to start a fight? Milbank refused to rise to the bait. He took a stack of books off a chair, set them on the floor, and, after inspecting it for a moment, sat down, crossing one leg over the other and folding his hands in his lap. He felt an avuncular tone would be the right approach.

"I've come by, Karl, to see how you were doing and how things were coming together for Mr. Washington's tournament."

"I'm fine, thank you. Everything seems to be going well with the Ebon Invitational, as far as I'm aware; you'd have to ask Mr. Washington or Ms. Clayfield about that."

Milbank changed tact, addressing Karl's hostility head on. "Do we have a problem Karl? I'm getting the feeling you have something you need to get off your chest."

"No, we don't have a problem, Mr. Milbank," Karl said, setting a stack of photos down on his desk with more force than necessary, "but I don't see any reason for this little dance you're doing. I know all about the project you've been working on with Mr. Midge to close the ZPGC. I've signed his nondisclosure agreement so I'm legally prohibited, as I'm sure you know, from speaking about it. But since you're in on the whole thing, I'm sure I'm okay talking about it to you." He went to the door and closed it, again with more energy than required, and went back to his desk. "You are determined to shut this place down. Fine. Just know that I plan on hanging around to the bitter end; I imagine it will take at least a year or two to wrap up all the details before you can tear this place down. Until then, I'll do my job and keep my mouth shut. But don't treat me like an idiot."

Milbank set both feet on the floor and furrowed his brow. "Don't get ahead of yourself, Ketterman, and don't say anything you may regret later. I was clear with you from the beginning that the Zebulon Pike was under scrutiny; I told you its income was falling, had been falling for years, and its expenses were significantly ahead of revenues. Yes, I was aware of Midge's interest in the property and, yes, I asked him to keep his evaluation of the land under wraps; something, it seems, he wasn't able to do very well. But don't for a moment think I'm some sort of a Machiavelli manipulating things behind the scenes. If you spent one minute, just one, with the Parks Commissioners you'd find out every one of them has a pet plan for the Zebulon Pike. Times change, Karl, and things that seemed wonderful once suddenly don't anymore. When this place opened, golf was considered a worthy activity, something everyone in the middle class could afford to enjoy. It's what dads did back when weekends were a real hiatus from the workweek, when businesses closed on Sundays and everyone went to church, when life was slower and people were content with the simpler pleasures; at least that's what we like to believe. Now a lot of people look at this place and what do they see? Elitism, exclusion, and income disparity, it doesn't matter whether that's the truth or not, Karl, that's the *perception*. And perceptions are what politicians feed on. Are the Zebulon Pike's days numbered? You bet! Can you or I do a damn thing about it? I doubt it."

He paused to let his speech sink in. He could see Karl was thinking and that he was winning him over.

"You picked a tough career path, Karl. I don't know much about golf, but I do know play is down at all our courses; the Zebulon Pike isn't the only one with falling revenues, it's just the worst of a bad lot. The private clubs are hurting, too, and daily fee courses in this area are closing down right and left. The same is true across the country, and you know it. So don't act like I've led you down the primrose path. I gave you a great opportunity; your first job out of school and you're the manager of a golf course. How many of the people you graduated with have had an opportunity like this?"

Karl frowned, but he knew Milbank was right. He was lucky to even have a job in this business, and there was no doubt this experience would help him get another.

Milbank, with the adroitness of a skilled yachtsman, tacked his delivery to meet the shift in Karl's mood.

"I understand your frustration, Karl, I do. But Midge is a rogue operative off on a mission that I do not in any way endorse. If you feel used, Karl, find some solace in the fact you're not alone. Believe it or not, at this point we're allies, although I can't offer you much aid right now. Your best strategy, as I see it, is to do your utmost to make sure Mr. Washington's event is a grand success. If anyone could counteract Midge at this point it would be him."

That made sense to Karl. An influential black businessman who'd risen from humble circumstances and made his fortune, who came back to the inner city to revitalize a golf tournament that was once the pride of the black community, might be the very person to lead the counterattack against Midge's grab for the ZPGC. Karl had no idea how he could involve Washington in this battle, or if Washington would even want to be, but Milbank was holding out the only spark of hope. So how could he fan that spark into a flame?

25

Friday's round of the Ebon Invitational was slowed by a steady rain. It fluctuated between a gentle mist and a light downpour, never enough to call off play, but all that was needed to make the golf a little more challenging and bring the play down to a snail's pace. It was just the practice round, though, and the drizzle didn't spoil the fun. The only damper on the day was the notification that there would be no "lift, clean, and replace" on Saturday, meaning if the ball picked up mud when it landed on or off the fairway, it could not be cleaned until it was on the green. That ruling disabused the players of the notion that this was going to be a casual, not-too-serious tournament. The golf would be tested on the same level as any USGA-sanctioned event. Welmont was intent on keeping the tournament's standards to the highest level, even recruiting officials from the state golf association to be on the course during the weekend rounds to resolve any rules questions that might arise. He was determined to do whatever it took to make sure whoever won his Ebon Invitational would have something to brag about.

The day, regardless of the rain, was a great success. All players showed up at the ZPGC in plenty of time, most of them on the range warming up an hour before the official start. There was a pavilion tent on the open turf to the west of the putting green and above the eighteenth green, where Bernadette supervised the volunteers checking in players. Behind the check-in desk was a large board on which the foursomes starting on each hole were posted. As each player signed in they got a gift bag and were directed to the lineup of carts where Tyreal greeted them and assigned a junior golfer to put their bag on their cart. It all went off without a hitch. The rain was no match for Bernadette Clayfield's efficiency.

*

Mo Mittenthal watched it all from the starter's shack, admiring the sheer size and scope of what was taking place and marveling at the organizational skills of the amazing Ms. Clayfield. He'd been on duty during many Ebons over the last few years and had sent off the three or four groups in it with little fanfare. There had been nothing to distinguish those Ebons from the average family get-together or company-sponsored scramble besides a long-winded opening speech from Tyreal. This was a very different affair. The players were nattily attired; they sported the latest equipment, and the vast majority clearly—even to Mo's untrained eye—very serious about the game. Although not a big sports fan, Mo recognized most of the athletes from the local sports teams, along with the broadcasters and the scions of business and commerce. Most of them had barely heard of, much less played, the Zebulon Pike Golf Course, and Mo was flattered when the star of our major league baseball team asked him questions about the condition of the course.

Mo could see many of these newcomers were impressed by both the architecture and setting of the clubhouse. Most were members of local country clubs like the Lochenberry, and used to sprawling clubhouses with spacious locker rooms; sitting on the edge of their trunk to put on their golf shoes wasn't something they normally did, but they seemed genuinely charmed by the now clean-and-shiny clubhouse, especially the large brass escutcheon on the floor. A circle of faces looked down at it, their brows furrowed as they puzzled over the motto's meaning.

"Is that Latin or something?"

"Who's this guy, some kind of soldier?"

"He must be Zebulon Pike, huh?"

"Never heard of him."

"He was a soldier and an explorer of the American West, a contemporary of Lewis and Clark. The motto is Latin. It means, 'the game is life, and life is the game.'"

The players looked at Welmont, surprised a black man would know the language; it was one of the things he carried away from the all-boys Catholic high school his parents had sent him to back when Latin was a standard part of the curriculum at such places. Welmont had shown an immediate aptitude for the language, winning a prize for being the best Latinist in the school his senior year. He still kept a volume of Cicero's letters in his desk. Few were aware he knew Latin, or of his passion for American history.

"I don't get it even in English," one wag replied.

"Think about it: you start every round optimistic and full of confidence. But somewhere along the way, something goes wrong; you get a bad bounce, you lip out a putt or—God forbid—you shank one. The game is really how you handle those things, isn't it? If you let a bad break frustrate you or destroy your focus, the game isn't going to go very well. That's life, too, right?"

When Welmont finished, all eyes were on him. He realized he was waxing too philosophically for his audience so he clapped his hands, rubbed them together vigorously and shouted, "Now, get out there and hit 'em long and straight!"

The crowd cheered. Outside Tyreal blew his air horn. It was time for the players to get in their carts and head to their tee box.

*

Fabio tried to get Bernadette's attention when he was signing in but she was too busy to notice him. Instead of hitting balls, he hung around the practice green, hoping for a chance to talk with her. He watched her move from one station in the pavilion to another, answering questions, clearing up any confusion, and keeping everything moving like clockwork. You didn't have to be a golf professional to see Bernadette didn't know the first thing about the game, yet in the pavilion she handled every detail like she'd been working tournaments for years. Franzen knew what a dismal affair the Ebon Invitational had been and here she was breathing new life into it; actually, she'd done more than that. She'd completely reinvented it, taking it out of the shadows and bringing it to the attention of the whole city. He thought about their lesson and smiled. She hadn't made much progress but at least he'd had her to himself for an hour.

*

The round over and the players gone, Welmont sat down with Bernadette and Tyreal to go over the day. Bernadette, tablet and mobile phone in front of her, was ready to handle any and all questions. Tyreal, tired yet beaming, leaned back in his chair and stretched until it creaked like a wooden frigate in a typhoon. He wished his father could have been here today, to have seen the important people who had come to play in his event, to have felt the energy, heard the laughter and the yelling, and, most of all, to have mingled with all the successful black men and women who'd come to his home course. Even if the skies opened up over the weekend and it rained as in the days of Noah, based on the practice round alone, the Ebon Invitational had regained its status as a premier event for black golfers. Tyreal laid his hand over Bernadette's and gave it a gentle squeeze.

"You are something, girl. You are *really* something."

Welmont seconded that opinion with a nod and a wink. The day had been a great success for him and the Boutiqué Afriqué salons. He had heard nothing but positive things from the players from the moment he'd stepped out of his Bentley. Those who'd never played the ZPGC before were amazed by the condition of the course and the subtleties of the layout, especially the greens. Even though they'd been slowed somewhat by the steady drizzle, their undulations and breaks surprised everyone. The whole experience was far beyond what they expected from a municipal course. Even the coziness of the snug stone clubhouse had won them over and many left determined to play in the Ebon next year, regardless of how they did on the weekend. Welmont was pleased he had seized the opportunity to take over the Ebon. It was turning out better than he expected and it was clearly going to further his reputation around town.

Tyreal grinned as Cybil set an extra large order of fries in the center of the table. Welmont encouraged him to dig in as he kicked off the meeting.

"So far, so good. But we can't let our guard down; we have to make sure the rest of the weekend goes off without a hitch. Bernadette, how did things go on your end?"

She rattled through her report. The numbers didn't lie: the Ebon was going to end up well in the black and they would have the capital to make the event even bigger next year.

*

A few regulars, trying to get in nine holes before dark, were teeing off as Bernadette walked out of the verandah. She took a deep breath and savored the quiet after the maniacal pace of the day. Just then, Mo stepped out of his shack to stretch.

"Ah! The impresario of the big shindig!"

She laughed. "I'm one of them."

The group on the tee mounted their carts and sped off, and Mo invited Bernadette to stroll down the hill with him.

"This is my favorite time of the day. It's so quiet; it's just you, your thoughts, and the breeze moving through the trees."

Bernadette smiled and took his arm.

"You can't see the clubhouse once you get below the tee box. It almost seems like you're a million miles away from the city, doesn't it?"

"It certainly is pretty," she said, and meant it. Then something caught her eye, an odd little mound. "What's that?"

Mo scratched his head, searching for the right words. "Well… it's a grave."

"You're kidding, right?"

"No, I'm afraid not. The first golf professional here, Ambrose Keegan, is buried right there. Not a lot of people even notice it. He was buried a long time ago, during World War Two."

Bernadette walked closer and read Keegan's epitaph. Is this what they normally did when a golf pro died, bury him on the course? She wondered if Franzen would end up here.

"How many other people are buried out here?"

"Just him. I think it was probably because he was decapitated out on…"

"He was *what*? He got his head chopped off?"

"It was an accident, not an execution; a tragedy, really."

Bernadette looked at him wide-eyed. "Well, I assumed it wasn't suicide."

"No, no… the suicide happened over there," Mo said, pointing toward the water near the ninth green. "Mr. McAdoo just walked out into the water with a big bag of golf balls tied around his neck and drowned, poor man."

Bernadette shook her head. "I just took my first lesson. Please tell me not every golf course is like this."

*

While the clubhouse reverberated with activity, Karl Ketterman remained sealed in his office, rummaging through eight decades of clutter, trying to put it all into a coherent sequence on his freshly painted shelves. The contents of the long-locked drawer Gabriel's bolt cutter had opened were scattered across his desk and his attention wandered from one thing to another. He picked up the eight-by-ten photos, untied the string that bound them, studied the first one for a moment, then dropped the pile on his desk. He fanned them out, giving them a desultory glance. It was clear they all had something to do with the opening of the ZPGC, but they weren't in any order, and there was nothing on the backs of any of them to identify the people or exactly what was taking place. He set several aside that he found particularly fascinating. One was of Wilbur Odegaard, Ambrose Keegan, and a smiling, very tanned man in plus fours with slicked-back black hair who stared right into the camera. Odegaard was handing him something. He looked dour and serious, but Keegan, his hand on the man's shoulder, looked quite pleased. Karl felt he might have seen the smiling man's face before, but he couldn't place it. The second photograph showed Odegaard kneeling beside the brass plaque in the center of the clubhouse; he held a trowel in his hand. There was a wall of baggy pant legs behind him.

Odegaard was smiling in this photo. Karl scrutinized the third photo closely. It showed Odegaard and Keegan again, together with two other men Karl couldn't identify. Odegaard was putting what looked like a roll of papers into a metal box. Keegan held a golf ball over the box as if he were about to drop it in. Karl could see the clubhouse was still under construction when the photo was taken; scaffolding and stacks of lumber could be seen behind the men.

Karl found an old magnifying glass and leaned over the photo, but no matter how hard he stared he couldn't quite decipher it. It was an event important enough to commemorate with a photo, but what was it? And where was that metal box now, and what else was in it?

The room was getting dark. Karl stood up and stretched. He listened for a moment and realized he must be the only one left in the clubhouse. He put the three photos in his desk and went home. Even there he couldn't get them off his mind.

*

The sun rose in a cloudless sky. The air was cool and still a little moist from Friday's rain. The forecast called for warm temperatures and moderate winds, a perfect day for golf. Welmont, unable to sleep much, drove to the course early. He could hear the faint hum of the mowers out on the course as he stepped out of his car. The bedewed flowers around the clubhouse sparkled in the sunlight. Inside the clubhouse, he took a seat at the counter and ordered breakfast. He checked his watch. It was eight a.m.; the tournament didn't start until ten. Tyreal had been at the course since seven, pacing back and forth in the clubhouse or out by the first tee rehearsing his remarks. Bernadette, after a fitful night dreaming of a headless Franzen rising out of a pond and chasing her down a fairway, arrived at the ZPGC not long after Welmont, dead tired but determined to soldier through the day. While Welmont and Tyreal fretted, she prepped her crew in the pavilion, going over assignments, checking emails and text messages, and making sure things would go as smoothly as they did on Friday. She was happy to see the improvement in the weather and the bright sunlight helped ward off her sleepiness. Once the players were on the course and the tournament underway, she would turn her attention to getting the volunteers ready for the deluge of scorecards and the mass of golfers who would be hovering around the scoring tent to see if they'd made the cut or not.

*

The temperature was in the mid-sixties as ten a.m. approached, yet Fort Sumter stood behind the starter shack mopping his brow. It was his job to say a few words and signal the start of play and he was terrified. His huge hands crumpled the edges of the short speech he had written. He reread it again. The words sounded awkward, nonsensical. He groaned in despair and stuffed the paper into his pocket. He felt a hand on his arm. It was Scrumpy. The sight of his hangdog face relieved Tyreal's anxiety for a moment.

"Hey, Scrumpy. What you doing?"

Scrumpy just looked up and said, "It's going to be all right, Tyreal. When the time comes you will know exactly what to say."

Tyreal nodded and took a deep breath. He'd been a career soldier and faced adversity before: surprise inspections, inquiries into missing supplies, even a disciplinary hearing for serving minors in the EM club. He had come through it all unscathed. He would get through this as well.

"Where's Tyreal?"

Fort came around the shack. "Right here, Welmont."

"It's time to light this birthday candle, my friend."

Tyreal walked out to meet his fate. He hardly noticed the mass of humanity crowded between the clubhouse and the first tee: players, spectators, the news crews from two local stations were only a blur of colors and shapes to him. All he had to do was make a few remarks and sound his air horn. The players would have five minutes after that first blast to get to their starting hole, then a second blast would tell them to tee off.

Tyreal pushed his way through the throng still clutching his handkerchief, Welmont following in his wake. Once on the tee box, Tyreal took several deep breaths to calm his racing heart. A young guy tapped a cordless microphone and handed it to him. Tyreal took it, looked around him and was seized with panic. A catatonic veil descended over him. If he had been capable of doing a sprint he would have burst into one; the sound of his labored breathing filled his ears. He had a premonition of impending death. He prayed he wouldn't lose control of his bowels.

Welmont watched Tyreal, hoping he could right himself. It was obvious to everyone he was frozen with fear. Welmont felt pity for him, this huge, abrasive man, this bumbling blowhard, incapable of marshalling the forces needed to run a successful tournament, yet still trying his best to honor his father's memory and maintain an event that had once been a symbol of pride and accomplishment for his family.

Welmont put a hand on Tyreal's shoulder and pried the microphone from his hand.

"Mr. Sumter is, as you can see, a little overwhelmed." There were a few scattered laughs. Welmont held up his hand and the crowd fell silent. "I think we all would be in similar circumstances, and I don't mean simply having to speak in public. It has more to do with what I've asked him to speak about, and I feel I owe Tyreal an apology for that." Tyreal, relieved and beginning to regain his poise, looked gratefully at Welmont.

"I asked him," Welmont continued, "to say a few words about his father and the history of the Ebon Invitational. Sounds easy enough, until you realize the scope of Obadiah Sumter's accomplishments and the brief time Tyreal was given; on top of that, I asked a son to speak of a beloved father who is no longer with us, so it's no wonder Tyreal finds it difficult to find the words to do so. Who wouldn't? So let me be the one to say what I believe is in Tyreal's heart right now: Obadiah Sumter stood up for the right of everyone to play on a public golf course. But he didn't stop there. At a time when other tournaments were closed to them, he organized one of the very first for black golfers, not just in this city, but this country. He guided that tournament for thirty years, turning it into one of the most prestigious events for black golfers in the entire country. Legendary players—Sifford, Rhodes, Spiller, even Joe Lewis—battled here. And while PGA and USGA events remained segregated, he welcomed all golfers, regardless of color. We're here today to inaugurate a new era for the Ebon Invitational, to restore its prestige, and most importantly to honor its founder, Obadiah Sumter. And I want to take this opportunity to announce that his son, Tyreal Sumter, co-chair of this year's tournament, has also been named a member of the board of directors and the official community liaison of the newly formed Ebon Invitational Foundation for as long as he wishes to hold those offices."

As Welmont raised his hand again to acknowledge a smattering of applause, Tyreal, shaken from lethargy, put one hand on Welmont's shoulder and took the microphone back with the other. "My father was not an educated man. Neither am I. But we both loved golf. And we loved this golf course because, as Mr. Washington just said, it made black folk welcome long before other courses did. I know my father is busting with pride right now, looking down at this turnout. And we all know who is responsible for it: Mr. Welmont Washington!" A chorus of whoops and cheers and whistles broke out. "But you didn't come here for speeches," Tyreal roared. "You came to play golf!"

He raised the air horn high above his head and an ear-piercing blast sent the crows on the clubhouse into flight and the fleet of golf carts off across the course.

*

The shotgun start guaranteed all eighteen foursomes finished almost simultaneously, which meant the scorers' tent was inundated with scorecards and besieged by players waiting to see if they would be playing Sunday or not. Bernadette may not have known much about golf, but she did know how to organize, and her redundant system of tallying and recording scores went without a hitch. The first table checked the scores entered on each card. Once that was done the card was passed to a second table where the scores were double-checked and the gross score highlighted with a marker. The card then went to a separate station where each player's gross score was entered into the tournament database. When all the scores were in, the field for Sunday was posted. Once that was complete, the scorers reconvened to determine the winners of Saturday's individual prizes. All of this was completed an hour after the last scorecard was submitted.

There was a large flat-screen TV in the pavilion tent and players groaned, shouted, and cheered when all the scores were displayed. Most of the players lingered for some time after Sunday's field was set, having drinks and going over their round shot by shot with friends. Those playing Sunday huddled in groups, discussing which might be the pivotal holes and who they felt had the best chance of winning. The general consensus was the course was better than most had anticipated and the Ebon Invitational was worth every cent they had paid to play in it.

*

The sounds of cocktail-fueled conviviality carried down to the darkening driving range where Charley Lumley sat on his cart and smoked and thought about things. He had watched some of the tournament, positioning his cart at key vantage points to see how the country club hotshots did on his course. He was pleased to see the course and the pin positions gave them all they could handle. They had power and distance, but the old ZPGC counterpunched with cunning and deception. A grin creased his leathery face when he overheard the grudging admiration they gave the Zebulon Pike.

As twilight descended, Charley recalled Ebons long past when he was young and old Obadiah was in charge. It never had a trophy like the Keegan Cap; Obadiah just handed out envelopes of cash to the top six finishers. Money: cold, hard cash, that's what those guys came all the way from Chicago and Saint Louis and Kansas City for. Charley played in it several times when he was young. He'd taken fifth the year Teddy Rhodes won the Ebon. He still remembered the thrill of sitting on the bed in his rented room counting out two-hundred-and-fifty dollars in ten- and five-dollar bills. He won another four hundred dollars in the Calcutta. That was a lot of money back then. He smiled and tossed his cigarette, watching it trace orange loops in the gloaming. It was time to get out on the tracker and pick up balls.

26

Welmont Washington rose and greeted the third day of the
Ebon Invitational, rested and refreshed, bubbling with energy and
a sense of accomplishment. He girded himself in his silk dressing
gown and descended to the kitchen where he serenely glanced
through the paper while breakfasting on coffee and toast. He
paused to bask in a write-up about the Ebon penned by our city's
leading sports journalist, an ancient scribe who could still recall, as
though through a glass darkly, its halcyon days. He heaped praise
on the black professional athletes playing in it and was effusive
in his approbation of those who had labored to bring the noble old
Ebon Invitational back to prominence. Nowhere, even in a second
reading, however, did Welmont come across a single mention of his
name or a reference to Boutiqué Afriqué. He closed the sports page
and, rising, turned the other cheek to the recalcitrant columnist.

*

As Welmont shaved in his marble bathroom, Dunn rumbled
about the ZPGC setting the pins for the final day of competition,
the sheets Tyreal had given him, the ones the Halling brothers and
Crupshaw had labored over so lovingly, in the breast pocket of his
coveralls. Changing pin positions was a normal task for Dunn, but
this time he did something different. He brought along a golf ball.
After referring to the sheets and locating the spot indicated for the
cup, Dunn stuck a tee in the green and rolled the ball at it from

several directions, moving the tee until he felt he had found the most challenging location. Once he did, he slammed his cutter into the green and worked it down into the yielding soil. After setting the cup liner in the hole, he painted the inch or two of exposed earth white, just like the high-end clubs did, then, after setting the flag in place and admiring his work for a moment, he continued on, serenaded by the birds and thinking again of how beautiful Cressida had looked from his vantage point on Ketterman's office floor.

*

With just thirty-six players in the final round there was no need for a shotgun start; all nine groups started on the first tee, the first going off at nine a.m. sharp, the other groups every ten minutes thereafter. This would get them all off by eleven and allow the ZPGC to open to the public by noon.

The atmosphere was much more relaxed than Saturday. The field was smaller and the staff more confident in what they needed to do and how to do it. The competitors were focused and less vocal, more intent on preparing for their round and playing well than socializing. Each of the thirty-six felt he had a chance to win and, indeed, it was mathematically possible, with only ten strokes separating the first- and last-place players. The best score in Saturday's round had been seventy-one—two under par—and with the pin positions Dunn was setting that would be a very difficult score to match.

Tyreal was ebullient; he seemed to glide around the clubhouse. Everyone in the field knew who he was now and stopped to greet him and tell him how much they were enjoying his tournament; *his* tournament, the words sent thrills through him. He felt proud for never giving up on the Ebon Invitational. He was not such a fool, however, that he did not also feel gratitude toward Welmont for all that he had done. Looking about the room filled with celebrities he'd seen on TV or read about in the paper, Tyreal could not help but feel he was finally doing something that would please his father. For the truth was, they had not parted happily when Tyreal joined the Army in 1965. Young Tyreal had been an outstanding high school athlete, a star on both the football and basketball teams, but a poor student with disciplinary issues, a proud boy embarrassed by his father's southern drawl and what Tyreal considered his too deferential behavior around whites. His academic record made an athletic scholarship problematic, and while he loved sports he had no desire for more education so, without consulting his father, he enlisted in the Army before the ink on his diploma was dry. Obadiah said little when Tyreal told him. His parents drove him down to the Federal Building the morning he was to be inducted. They parted by the car, Obadiah shaking his hand and saying, "You've chosen your path, Tyreal, now you've got to walk it. God be with you, son."

A different path and who knows? Tyreal might have been a professional athlete, too; long retired now, and still surrounded, like some in this room, with indulgent, adoring fans. He certainly didn't doubt the possibility, and the myriad trophies his teams had won in base, division, and intra-service basketball tournaments lent it some credence. Now, looking about the clubhouse and contemplating the course his life might have taken, Tyreal felt, if not justified, at least back on the straight and narrow; like the prodigal son he had returned to his father's house, repentant, wiser, and doing his best to make amends for the error of his ways.

Bernadette, too, felt a sense of accomplishment. She had told Washington that morning she was worth hiring and had proved it. There was still work to be done before the Ebon was finished, but the crush was over. As she sat in the pavilion sipping her coffee, she thought about her future. Her senior year at the university was underway and she would graduate with honors after the fall semester. Putting this tournament together had been a great learning experience—and she had to admit it was nice being on speaking terms with so many of the city's powerful and famous, but now her mind reeled with big ideas for the Boutiqué Afriqué. She wanted to take it in new directions, expand its scope, open stores in other cities; there was only one problem: Welmont had yet to speak to her about a full-time job.

"Wish me luck, Bernadette."

"Good luck, Fabio," she said, raising her paper cup.

Franzen turned crimson. It was the first time she had called him that to his face. She wasn't quite sure who Fabio was when she first heard him called that; after it was explained to her, Bernadette thought it apt and kind of funny. Now she could see it hurt him and tried to walk back her remark. "Oops, I guess I struck a nerve. Sorry, Phil. Someone said that's what they call you around here."

"I know they do, but I don't like it."

He was moping, so Bernadette tried to cheer him up a bit. "We all get called things we don't like, Phil. My mother calls me "Dette," I thought it made me sound like I'm a financial burden. And my brothers call me "Bernie." I get it, I don't like it, but if I let them see that, they'd never stop. So I roll with it, and eventually they get tired of it. Maybe you should try the same tactic."

Franzen brightened and Bernadette promised him she'd try to get away later and watch him play a few holes. This guy was smooth, she thought to herself. She was going to have to stay on her toes.

*

The tournament was underway by the time Karl arrived. Cybil, directing her charges from her pass-through, smiled and waved to him as he came in. He sat at the counter and ordered breakfast: scrambled eggs, wheat toast, and bacon, extra crispy. He stirred the cloud of cream in his coffee and enjoyed the hurly-burly about him as players, and those here to watch them, ate and chatted. Karl couldn't remember a time when the place was more vibrant, more alive, more like a clubhouse should be on a beautiful Sunday in September.

But as much as he wanted to just sit there and soak in everything around him, Karl could not ignore the siren call of the three eight-by-ten photos in his desk drawer: the mysterious Dark Man, the metal box, Odegaard kneeling by the plaque. He had been shuffling through them in his mind all night, trying to understand their significance, because they had to be important. Why else would Odegaard or someone else long ago have locked them away like holy relics? Karl went into his office to ponder them some more.

He had been sitting there for an hour or so, holding the photos up to the daylight pouring through the window, trying to solve their mystery, when he saw a face he recognized; a man was standing out by the verandah looking a little lost and out of place. Karl went to the window to make sure it was who he thought it was, then ran out to him.

"Excuse me, Mr. Castle?"

"Yes," Art replied, waiting to find out why this young man had approached him.

"I'm Karl Ketterman. I'm the guy who replaced you."

"Of course, of course! Good to see you again, Karl."

Art had come back for the cleanup day and enjoyed it so much he volunteered to work in the pavilion at the Ebon. Karl, hoping he could help solve the mystery of the three photos, brought Art into the office, sat him behind his old desk, and laid them in front of him.

"Where did you get these?"

Karl pointed to the bottom drawer behind the desk.

"I remembered it as being locked. Did you find the key?"

"No. I cut the lock off."

Art seemed taken aback by the boldness of such a move.

"These photos and a bunch more were in there, along with a lot of papers and stuff. They all look like they were taken while the course and the clubhouse were being built, but I can't figure out what these three are about; I thought you might."

Art looked at all three closely. "This is Mr. Odegaard and that's Mr. Keegan. The other men in these two photos I don't recognize." Art paused. Then an odd look illuminated his face. "Well, I'll be doggoned! Isn't that something? Why I never heard about this." He picked up the photo of Odegaard kneeling by the plaque. "Why, sure! That's exactly what it is!"

"What? What is it?" Karl asked.

"A time capsule. It's a time capsule; don't you see? Look at these two photos. Here are Odegaard and Keegan and two other men putting things in it and here's Odegaard sealing it up. There's a time capsule buried under Zebulon Pike's commemorative plaque."

*

It was an extraordinary feeling, as if both wheels on his side of the cart were slightly off the ground. And he definitely felt the tire rubbing the right rear wheel well. Obviously, golf carts weren't meant to carry a three-hundred-and-seventy-pound passenger, but it was Rambo's job to drive Tyreal around the course today. They were on the back nine in the early afternoon and things seemed to be going swimmingly. They passed the spot where Rambo's bowels had rebelled and Casserly had been so unceremoniously subdued by Dunn. It seemed sort of funny to Rambo now until he remembered Casserly was part of the grand conspiracy that was about to throw him out of his beloved part-time job. He motored on, thanking the gods it hadn't rained hard on Friday or this cart would be sinking up to its axles on the boggy fairway.

"Hey, what's going on over there?"

Rambo looked in the direction Tyreal pointed. There was a group gathered on the periphery of the fourteenth green; a rules official's cart was parked near by. He cranked the wheel toward the scene and raced forward.

There had been a rules infraction; at least that was what one of the players was insisting. The player accused of the infraction was Binky Jones, a once famous defensive back and well-known pain-in-the-ass on the golf course. The issue was this: Binky's second shot landed short of the green. It had come to rest on top of a patch of long grass, a precarious spot where the slightest movement might cause it to move. And that is exactly what happened. Binky, without really assessing the situation, made several practice strokes with his wedge near his ball; after the final one, the ball rolled forward. Everyone saw it. One player pointed it out and told Binky. He denied it, swearing the orientation of the logo on the ball hadn't moved a hair. The other player insisted. Binky was intransigent to the point of being threatening. Another player in the group, fearing an altercation, waved down a rules official.

That official was patiently explaining the rule to Jones as Rambo and Tyreal rolled up. The other players backed up the one who had told Binky his ball had moved, but Binky was having none of it. He blustered and swore and claimed there was a conspiracy to torpedo his round and keep him from winning the tournament—even though he was three over par at this point. Tyreal could see the rules official was intimidated and the resolve of the other players to protect the integrity of the match was wavering. He knew Binky's game, he'd played it himself more than once: get in people's faces until they blinked and backed down. This was different. This was his tournament and Tyreal couldn't allow Binky to get away with it. The Ebon was too important to him.

"'Scuse me, gentlemen. What seems to be the problem here, Binky?"

Binky recapped what had happened for Tyreal, skewing the facts to fit his narrative, and at the same time doing his utmost to cower his accusers and the rules official. Tyreal nodded sagely, seeming to sympathize with him, but as Binky blustered on Tyreal stealthily placed his hand in the middle of his back and walked him away from the others. Binky, realizing what was going on, glowered up at Tyreal, who laughed loudly as if they'd just shared a joke and, grabbing Binky by the arm, hustled him further off. Once he felt he was out of earshot, Tyreal faced Binky, placing both his massive hands on his shoulders.

"Listen to me, man. Listen very carefully." He said, a huge grin camouflaging the menace in his voice. "You're not going to fuck up my tournament with your bullshit, you hear me? You're going to go back there, tell everyone you got caught up in the heat of the moment or however you want to say it. Then you're going to apologize. And then you're going to be sociable and nice to those fellows. You're going to chat it up with them. You're going to laugh. And at the end of the round, you're going to shake hands and tell them you had a great time." Tyreal paused. Binky stared up at Tyreal, watching his chest heave in and out; sensing the barely contained rage, and feeling the massive hands tighten their grip. "Because if you don't, if you cross me on this in even the slightest, I swear to God Almighty, on my father's grave, I will beat the ever-living *life* out of you. Do we have an understanding?"

Binky grew up in a tough neighborhood with tough people. He had played professional football for twelve years. He had a well-earned reputation as a badass. But he was not prepared to stand up to Tyreal Sumter. Standing in his shadow, Binky appreciated why he was called "Fort," and did not doubt the sincerity of what Tyreal had just said. He nodded, and Tyreal led him back to the green.

"Everything is cool, fellas! Binky was a little upset. Hey, we all get that way sometimes, don't we? I just explained the rule again and we're cool, right?" Tyreal laid a hand on his shoulder and Binky sprang to life, making it clear that he accepted the penalty and apologizing to everyone for slowing up the round. "I'll see you again when you boys finish," Tyreal said, eyeing Binky, "so have fun and play well!"

Rambo and Tyreal followed the group to the next tee to make sure Binky remained on his best behavior. They kept watching until the foursome was far down the fairway. The rules official, still a bit shaken by Binky's behavior, came by to thank Tyreal. As he lowered himself onto the golf cart, Tyreal grabbed Rambo's forearm and pointed at his tattoo. "I been looking at that thing all day. Man, what the hell is a 'Divel Dag'?"

Rambo pulled his arm free and hit the gas pedal. "Nothing that wants any trouble with you."

*

The boyish face partially hidden by the high collar, the hair swept down and across his forehead, and the eyes gazing off toward unexplored territory and unlimited opportunities for glory; Karl Ketterman pondered the brass face of Zebulon Pike, thinking of what lay behind it. How, he wondered, could he get at that time capsule? He couldn't force Pike's plaque up with a pry bar without damaging the floor. Besides, he didn't know for an absolute fact that the metal box was under there. Imagine the outrage such an impious act would cause among the ZPGC's regulars if they came in one morning to see he'd destroyed this venerable landmark for no reason. Even assuming the time capsule was there, what possible excuse could he give for unearthing it? Curiosity? All Karl had to go on was a premonition, an unsettled gnawing within him that said that metal box held not just memorabilia of the grand opening of the golf course, but the fate of the ZPGC and all who worked and played here. He needed a collaborator, a co-conspirator, a wiser soul who might see a way out of this conundrum. Unable to think of a better option, he went to see Dunn.

He found Dunn at his desk turning over an unopened envelope in his hands. When he saw Karl he put it away in a drawer.

"What can I do for you, Ketterman?"

Karl pulled up a chair and recounted the tale of the three photographs and the mystery of what lay underneath the floor. Dunn made a droll reference to Poe's *Tell-Tale Heart*; it went over Ketterman's head.

*

The same process of tabulating scores was followed on Sunday. The results were recorded, checked, and rechecked, and posted a half-hour after the last foursome finished. A crowd of players and spectators gathered around the pavilion where the scores of all thirty-six players were being copied onto a huge board by a calligrapher. The course regulars cheered when the results showed that one of ZPGC's own, Phil Franzen, finished fifth. No one could imagine how he had done it, but his playing partners spoke in hushed, reverential tones of his flawless performance on the greens. Such is the game of golf.

The winner was Darnell Johnson, a former professional who'd gotten his amateur status back after failing to make it onto the Tour. He followed an even par round on Saturday with a two under seventy-one on Sunday. The player who shot seventy-one in Saturday's round had ballooned to an eighty-five and finished third. Welmont handed the brand-new Ebon Invitational trophy to Johnson, who spoke highly of both the course and the event. Welmont then called Tyreal up to award the first annual Obadiah Sumter Scholarship. It went to a kid from the youth program Franzen had recommended. He was a good student and black, but rather hopeless as a golfer. The scholarship, however, was to further his education, not lower his handicap. The boy, flanked by his parents, grinned as Tyreal gave him the check and a photographer from the paper snapped away.

When Welmont finally found his way back to the pavilion tent, the volunteers were already packing up and Bernadette was taking the last of her things to her car.

"It looks like your Ebon Invitational was a big, big success," she said.

He smiled, a little uncomfortably. His contribution had been a few phone calls and calling in some old debts. She was the one who'd done all the work. But it did feel good, looking around and seeing what they had achieved.

"I'd like you to come by next week. I think it's time we sat down and discussed your future."

It was Bernadette's turn to smile. "I'll do that."

Bernadette left and Welmont took a seat on a bench by the putting green and watched the slanting afternoon sunlight light up the front of the clubhouse. He liked the look of this place, the way it wore its years, how it made him feel. There was no pretension here, no posturing like at the Lochenberry, just people enjoying the game.

Then he remembered Robert Midge's grand designs for the ZPGC and how he was scheming to change all of this irrevocably, to wipe away every vestige of this grand old muni and smother the very spot where he sat with concrete and steel and glass and shallow opulence. Welmont's brow darkened.

Just then Ketterman scurried around the building in the company of a gaunt figure in oversized green coveralls. Welmont hailed Ketterman and he and his accomplice came over.

"Just wanted to thank you again for all your hard work. Everyone loved the course, and the clubhouse was a real surprise to a lot of them."

"Don't know how much I had to do with it, but thanks. This is Gabriel Dunn, our greenskeeper. He's the one responsible for playing conditions."

Welmont stood and shook his hand. "It's in as good of shape as any private club. You did an outstanding job."

Dunn bowed, solemnly, bending his torso almost parallel to the ground and rising slowly. Then he walked away. Karl shrugged and followed. Welmont watched them go back to the clubhouse: two odd ducks flying off in the same direction.

27

As they rounded the clubhouse, Karl and Gabriel spotted Charley Lumley sitting on the verandah enjoying the cup of coffee Cybil had set out for him. Karl invited Charley into his office to see if he could unravel the mystery of the man getting the check from Odegaard and Keegan. He put Charley in his chair and presented the photo. He watched Charley for some sign the photograph was jogging a memory, but Charley's brown leathery face was as impenetrable as ever.

"Where did you get this?" Charley asked. Karl told him. Charley turned his attention back to the photograph. "I never heard about this."

"Heard *what*, Charley?" Dunn asked.

"That Walter Hagen was at the opening of the ZPGC."

Karl had a vague idea who Hagen was but Dunn hadn't a clue, so Charley told them the story of golf's first professional— and certainly one of its more flamboyant—the man who single-handedly elevated the status of the golf professional to sports hero, the man who achieved worldwide celebrity for his outlandish lifestyle, fashionable attire, swashbuckling play, and uncanny ability to market himself and the game. Charley explained how Hagen, while winning golf tournaments around the world, made most of his money through personal appearances, exhibition matches, and product endorsements.

Charley drifted into one of his monologues, oblivious to Karl and Dunn, and conjured up a vision of Walter Hagen. "He was one of those bigger-than-life characters from the Roaring Twenties, right up there with F. Scott Fitzgerald, Rudolf Valentino, Douglas Fairbanks, and Charles Lindbergh."

"I thought Bobby Jones was the big golfer back then," Karl said.

Charley wrinkled his nose. "To the country club set and the newspapermen and the wealthy, sure. But to the average guy, the working stiff, Hagen was it. He came up from nothing and won seventy-five professional tournaments, including eleven majors. That puts him right up there with Jack Nicklaus and Tiger Woods, but not many people remember Walter Hagen now."

"Sort of like Lloyd Mangrum, huh, Charley?" Karl said.

Charley sniffed and nodded.

"In 1925, Hagen and Jones were both trying to make a buck hustling real estate in Florida. Hagen came up with the idea of them playing a golf match. Now, as an amateur Jones could make all the money he wanted in real estate, but not for playing golf. But Walter Hagen could," Charley said with a wink. "It was promoted as *'The Match of the Century,'* a 72-hole match play event between the two biggest names in the game. Hagen crushed Jones. It wasn't even close." Charley paused for a moment, tapping a finger on the photograph. "By the time the ZPGC opened, Hagen's career was on the decline, but he was still a big draw, and anyone who knew anything about golf would have come to see him hit a golf ball, so this must have been a very well-publicized event, yet somehow it's been totally forgotten. I can't believe they stuck this photo away in a drawer and didn't put it on display."

"Maybe the answer to that is in the metal box."

"What metal box?"

Karl handed the other photos to Charley and told him the whole story, at least as much as he knew. Charley had no idea who the two men by the box with Odegaard and Keegan were. They walked out into the clubhouse. Like any late Sunday afternoon, there were still a few patrons hanging around, some had attended the Ebon, others were more recent arrivals; among them, at their usual table, were Sundbaum, Rankel, Armstead, and Hood. Rankel nudged Sundbaum who alerted Armstead and Hood. They watched as Dunn, Ketterman, and Lumley looked down at the plaque. Then Ketterman knelt down and ran his hand around its edge.

"I tell you, something is going on around here," whispered Rankel.

*

"I say we act now and ask for forgiveness later."

"That sounds great, Charley, but if there's nothing under there, or if it's just an old golf ball and a bundle of papers, I'm going to have some explaining to do; I might even lose my job." The hollowness of that threat struck Karl the moment it came out of his mouth; his job was on life support anyway. Still, the idea of bashing up the clubhouse floor on the chance of discovering something that would...do what, exactly? There was the problem.

Karl, Charley, and Dunn had gone back in his office to mull things over. As they sat lost in thought there was a sharp rap on the door. Bernadette Clayfield opened it and peeked in.

"Karl? Do you have a moment?"

She had been about to leave when she remembered she hadn't thanked him for all his help; she also wanted to make sure she got the Ebon Invitational on next year's calendar. Karl suppressed the urge to say there might not be a next year.

"The Ebon Invitational is automatically on our schedule, Bernadette, until the Parks Commission is notified otherwise. That's been the arrangement since long before my time."

"That's good to know. Mr. Washington is really excited about next year already; he's determined to make it bigger and better. And he said he's going to put some pressure on the Parks Commission to increase the budget for the course so you don't have to depend on volunteer labor to keep the place looking good."

Karl said he appreciated that.

"Okay, I'll get out of your hair. I don't know if I'll be here next year, so I wanted to say thanks to all of you for helping make the Ebon a big success."

Charley, a product of another era, had stood up when she entered the room, a gesture Bernadette couldn't fail to notice. She smiled at him as she turned to leave. This flustered Charley and he dropped the photo on the floor. Bernadette picked it up and smiled again.

"Great shot of Walter Hagen at the grand opening. Where'd you get this?"

Charley looked at Karl; Karl looked at Dunn; all three looked at Bernadette.

"How do *you* know about that?"

"The first assignment I got from Mr. Washington after he hired me to work on the Ebon Invitational was to find out everything I could about it. I went down to the library to look through old newspapers. I asked the librarian for help. Of course, she had never heard of the Ebon Invitational, but when I told her it was played at the Zebulon Pike, she brought out a big file of old newspaper articles. I found a few articles about the Ebon, but most of what was in there was about the grand opening, including that photo."

They pressed her for more and she told them all she knew. The grand opening had been a very big deal. All the city fathers were there and, of course, Walter Hagen was the big draw. "He hit the ceremonial first drive, then played a nine-hole match with this guy," Bernadette said, pointing to Keegan. "A huge crowd followed them around. But afterwards, things went south."

She continued. "Keegan was the one who suggested getting Hagen for the grand opening. The only problem was, he never talked to Hagen's agent about the money. Hagen arrives expecting Keegan and Odegaard to have a check for his standard appearance fee, one thousand dollars. In fairness to Hagen, he probably assumed they had been told that. Odegaard is stunned. He's between a rock and a hard place. He's got a crowd gathering and he's in no position to negotiate. You can see he isn't exactly happy here," she said, pointing to Odegaard passing the check to Hagen. "When the mayor and the head of the Parks Commission found out what Hagen got paid, they went ballistic. This was during the Great Depression; times were tough. The city was out on a limb already for building the course and they knew the newspapers would make a big deal out of Hagen's fee, which they did.

"The mayor was furious. He called in the city comptroller and told him to stop payment on the check. There was a lot of back and forth between Hagen, his lawyers, and the city. Eventually,

Hagen settled for five hundred dollars with the stipulation that his appearance or his name never be associated with the course."

Bernadette finished her tale and left, leaving in her wake three more men smitten with her smarts.

*

Ralph Milbank was among the crowd at the Ebon Invitational. He wandered around the course, attuned to everything about him. What he saw, what he heard, what he absorbed was that this event, which had been going on for decades unnoticed by the city at large, was on the brink of becoming something extraordinary, something a Parks Commissioner with political ambitions might be able to parlay to his advantage. He was swimming in a veritable melting pot, a simmering stew of potential voters in need of advocacy and an attentive ear. To others it might be an ordinary golf event; to Milbank it was beginning to look like his springboard to higher office and greater opportunities to serve his community. Ralph Milbank suddenly saw the Zebulon Pike Golf Course in an entirely new light. Maybe there really was more to be gained from its survival than its demise—if it wasn't too late to prevent it.

*

Dunn and Charley were gone, the photos put away, and Karl was about to leave when Milbank came in. There was nothing to be gained by being belligerent with Milbank so Karl tried to make amends for his attitude at their last meeting.

"Ralph," he said, rolling the "R" a little and rhyming it with safe, "I didn't know you were a golf fan."

"I'm not, Karl. I can't for the life of me see its appeal. I am, however, impressed with what Mr. Washington has achieved here. This could be quite the feather in your cap, too."

"I had nothing to do with it, other than trying to stay out of the way. Washington and Sumter and Bernadette are the ones to congratulate."

"There's no need for modesty, Karl. It's wise to take credit when it comes your way. And the success of this event might just prove to be beneficial for both of us."

Karl had never thought of himself as being in the same boat as Milbank; how could they be? When the ZPGC sank it would take him down, but Milbank would still be afloat. So why was he suddenly talking as if the fate of the ZPGC could impact him?

"This tournament is going to help you, Karl. The local stations covered it last night, they will again tonight, and you can bet it will be in the paper, too. Washington is behind this tournament for his own purposes, don't doubt that for a moment, but what he's doing might actually help keep this place going. There are two Parks Commissioners—make that three—who aren't going to make things easy for Robert Midge. He may succeed eventually, but he's going to find out how long things can be dragged out in this city, even with all his father's pull. Don't send out resumes yet."

Milbank gave Karl an awkward thumbs up and left. A baffled Karl was still pondering their conversation when the phone rang.

"Hello?"

"Karl. Art Castle. I've been thinking about that time capsule. There may be a way for you to get at it without disturbing the plaque. Do you know about the bomb shelter?"

"The *what?*"

Art told Karl the story of his mildly deranged predecessor Adolphus Smythe, the Cold War pessimist with the harebrained plan to build a massive bomb shelter under the clubhouse. He never got the support he needed for his grand design; in the end, it was limited to a small room under the kitchen, now as forgotten as Hagen's personal appearance.

"I've never been down in it so I can't say for certain, but you might be able to access the time capsule from there." Art paused. "I'm not encouraging you to do it, Karl, that's completely up to you. For all we know disturbing the time capsule from down there could cause the plaque to collapse. It's a possibility you have to consider. I know you're very curious about what might be in that time capsule, but before you do anything, ask yourself: is it worth it? Personally, I wouldn't risk it."

Karl assured Art he would think long and hard before he did

anything, thanked him for telling him about the bomb shelter, and hung up. Then he went off to find Dunn and Lumley.

*

They met at the back of the clubhouse after dark. Dunn was armed with a hammer, chisel, and an Army surplus entrenching tool. Lumley brought a flashlight and an extra pack of cigarettes. Karl threw on the lights as he walked in the back door; he knew that a lit-up clubhouse was less likely to attract the attention of a Parks Police patrol car than a flashlight beam dancing around a dark building. Once they were in the kitchen, they had to move a large metal table to find the entry to the shelter. Dunn dug the ring handle from its setting with his chisel. It took several tugs before he could get the trap door up. A rush of dank air, circa 1957, rose up out of the dark maw at their feet.

"Hand me the flashlight," Dunn said.

The flashlight revealed a perpendicular steel ladder affixed to the wall below them. Dunn tested the ladder and went down. At the bottom he found a light switch; a bare, unfrosted, hundred-watt bulb snapped out of its six-decade nap. Lumley and Karl came down. The room was rectangular, the floor concrete, and the walls cinderblock. In one corner was a gray metal locker with a red, white, and blue Civil Defense logo on it. Karl pointed to the wall nearest the plaque and Dunn got to work with his hammer and chisel.

It took an hour for Dunn to open up a hole in the wall. He worked with precision, taking out whole blocks, being very careful not to break them, until he had made a large opening into the crawl space that ran under the rest of the clubhouse. The beam of his flashlight revealed footings for the building, floor joists, and, not more than six feet directly ahead, what looked like a small concrete sarcophagus.

"That's got to be it," Karl said.

You're the only one skinny enough to get in there, Dunn," Lumley said, lighting a cigarette.

"Do you have to do that?" Karl asked, waving the cloud of smoke away.

245

"It's a bomb shelter; you're safe down here."

Dunn frowned, took the hammer Lumley handed him, and wiggled into the crawl space. They could hear the muffled sound of the hammer hitting concrete. Lumley and Karl hovered near the opening and waited. The pounding went on intermittently for what seemed like hours. Karl asked if he wanted to take a break but Dunn was determined to finish or die trying. The anticipation was getting to Karl. He paced back and forth. Lumley stood motionless, listening attentively to the rap of Dunn's hammer. Then it stopped.

"I'm through. A couple more minutes and I'll have it out."

The pounding resumed. Karl lost track of time. Lumley sat on a concrete bench that protruded out of the wall. Neither noticed when the hammering stopped the second time. When they saw Dunn's feet wiggling back out of the hole they rushed to help him. He was covered with dirt and concrete dust and smiling. He reached back into the hole. When he turned around he had in his arms the metal box from the photograph.

*

They were surprised by how light it was. Within minutes they had it out of the shelter and in Karl's office. Before they opened it Lumley insisted they go back and put Cybil's kitchen in order; then Dunn went to the men's locker room to clean up. While he was in there, Karl walked out and boldly stepped on Pike's plaque. It held. Karl bent down and gave Zebulon a pat on the head.

While they waited for Dunn, Karl and Lumley examined the metal box closely. It was well constructed with riveted seams and brass-covered corners. They were a little surprised to see it didn't have a lock. The clasp on the side was held shut with a decorative cord tied in a knot and covered with sealing wax.

Dunn came in and Karl was about to ask him to cut the cord when Lumley shouted out, "Judas Priest!" His leathery face was ashen gray and he was pointing at the window. Dunn and Karl turned to see the faces of Sundbaum, Armstead, Rankel, and Hood staring back at them.

Karl went out and tried to get rid of them. He concocted a

pathetic story about being there with Dunn and Charley to plan a surprise party for Fort Sumter to celebrate the success of the Ebon. They didn't buy it.

"Yeah," scoffed Armstead, "who loves a party more than Lumley?"

"Something's going on here and it's been going on for months and we want to know exactly what it is!" Rankel spit out in a throaty, whispered shout.

Karl had no choice. He brought them in and, after swearing them to silence, gave them an abbreviated version of the state of things.

Now seven faces surrounded the metal box.

"Just think, it's been in that hole for over seventy-five years," Sundbaum said breathlessly.

"Longer than Keegan's been in his," quipped Lumley.

Karl paused and looked into the faces of his fellow conspirators. What odd people. What a strange place. What a bizarre situation. He had the strangest feeling: he actually felt lucky to be here.

Dunn took a menacing-looking bush knife out of his coveralls. "Here goes." He cut the cord. The hinges screeched and groaned as the lid rose. Dunn stepped to the side, deferring to Karl; the others silently seconded his motion; Karl brought its contents out of the past.

Everything in the box indicated the time capsule had been sealed before the controversy over Hagen's fee. There was the golf ball, a Spalding Kro-Flite, with Walter Hagen's signature still as crisp and clear as the day he signed it. There was also a green-and-red tin of Lucky Strike cigarettes. Lumley, a connoisseur of cigarette packages, handled it reverently. The seal was still unbroken but Lumley wouldn't think of violating it. Karl then lifted out a bundle of papers, the bundle Odegaard was putting in the box in the photo. It was a thick cylinder of large sheets tied with a string. The outside sheet was heavy brown butcher paper, the inner sheets white. On it in a bold, cursive hand was written, "Plans for the Zebulon Pike Golf Course," along with our city's name and the date, June 9, 1934. Karl set it aside and brought out everything that remained in the box: copies of the newspapers for that day—the city had four back then; the program for the opening ceremonies; the scorecard of Hagen and Kerrigan's match (Ambrose would, no doubt, have preferred that to remain interred); a poem by a local poetess, nicely printed on heavy parchment, praising the virtues of General Zebulon Pike; a dollar bill; a photo of Odegaard, Keegan, the head of the Parks Commission, and the mayor in front of the clubhouse (taken, judging by the happy expressions, before the grand opening event); a pennant for the local baseball team (a minor league club at the time); a copy of the *Rules of Golf*; a framed photo of Franklin Delano Roosevelt; and a letter composed by the valedictorian of the nearby high school—titled *Hail, O Noble Tomorrow!*—addressed to the people of the more peaceful, progressive, international world of the future, where war would be a memory, hunger unheard of, and justice, social and economic equality, and understanding would prevail. That was it.

The group turned its collective attention to the bundle. Karl untied the string and unrolled the cylinder with all the solemnity of a rabbi opening the Torah on a High Holiday. Rankel and Sundbaum moved to the side to hold the ends down. A letter lay atop the drawings. Seven heads bowed to read it. The only sound in the room was the wheeze of Lumley's lungs.

"This can't be real, can it?" Karl whispered.

28

The letter, though typewritten and well composed, seemed incomprehensible at first to Ketterman and company. For the letter he was holding so reverently, and the drawings that had been buried with it, were about to change the Zebulon Pike Golf Course in ways none of them could anticipate.

To understand, we have to go back to that day in 1934 when the photo was taken of the four men putting the bundle of papers into the time capsule. They were the only human beings at the time who knew what the bundle was and why it was being secreted away. One of two men in the photo who Karl couldn't identify, Cosgrove MacMullen, was the only one who knew the whole story.

MacMullen was a local grandee and philanthropist whose family had made their considerable fortune milling the grain grown across the great northern prairie. The MacMullens had emigrated from Dornoch, Scotland, in the nineteenth century. Standing on the quay bidding them farewell on the day they set sail for America was their kinsman, Tom Morris, the man the world of golf considers its Father Abraham, the legendary professional of St. Andrew's from whose metaphorical loins all golfers spring. Old Tom, as he is affectionately known, mentored many golfers, among them the professional-cum-course-designer Donald Ross, whose career began after he met Old Tom in 1892 in Dornoch. Shortly after that meeting, Ross joined the old master as an apprentice clubmaker and greenskeeper at St. Andrews. What history didn't record is that Angus MacMullen, Cosgrove's grandfather and Old Tom's kinsman, made the introduction. But Cosgrove MacMullen knew it. And after our city fathers had offered Ross the job of designing the Zebulon Pike and been refused, Cosgrove traveled east to meet Ross and play his trump card. Where would he be, Cosgrove chided Ross, without the intercession of Angus MacMullen? Faced with the charge of ingratitude, Ross acquiesced.

Cosgrove's good deed, of course, begs a question: why would he be so dogged in his pursuit of Ross, so intent on having him design a golf course for this little city on the wind-swept prairie? After all, it would be a public golf course, not the sort of place Cosgrove and his friends would frequent.

It wasn't altruism or a sense of civic duty that put Cosgrove MacMullen on an express train heading east. You might say it was an act of contrition, an attempt to exculpate himself from a potentially embarrassing and—certainly if Mrs. MacMullen ever learned about it—very expensive dalliance with a lady. It seems MacMullen had had the poor judgment to involve himself with the mayor's wife, an attractive woman very fond of drink, very often drunk, and very uninhibited when in her cups. Poor Cosgrove was unable to resist her and they carried on a clandestine affair for several years. Unluckily for Cosgrove, His Honor came upon some very indiscreet and lurid correspondence tucked away in the recesses of his wife's bedside table. The mayor confronted MacMullen with his erotic missives. Truth be told, the mayor wasn't particularly upset with his wife's behavior; in fact, he was almost grateful to her for giving him some leverage over the imperious MacMullen. Cosgrove, wriggling like a fish on a hook, racked his brain for a way to get his letters back. Then, one evening as he was enjoying oysters and bourbon in a local brothel, a fellow sybarite, who also happened to be an alderman, mentioned that the great Donald Ross had turned down the job of designing the golf course the mayor was so intent on building on the outskirts of town. Recalling his family's role in setting Ross on his career path, Cosgrove saw a way out of the pickle he was in; he ordered champagne for everyone. The next morning a slightly hungover Cosgrove was on his way to remind Ross of the debt he owed the MacMullens.

Ross was an honorable man and he had no choice. He gave in to Cosgrove, but he added one nonnegotiable codicil to their agreement. He insisted his role in the project be kept secret. It seems he had already signed contracts to design several other courses that would demand his undivided attention for several years. MacMullen agreed only if Ross put in writing that he would design the course, albeit under the cloak of anonymity, so he could prove it to the mayor. The mayor read the letter carefully. It was good news but not exactly what he wanted, so MacMullen got only half his letters back. The other half inspired Cosgrove's endowment of our city's world-renowned MacMullen Art Center.

The entire time the course was under construction, the mayor, feeling unfettered by any agreement with Ross and being a thoroughly disreputable thug, boasted to any and all who would listen that Donald Ross was secretly designing his new golf course; no one believed him; he was, after all, a politician. Eight months after the ZPGC opened the mayor dropped dead and the story died with him.

The fourth man in the photo with Odegaard, MacMullen, and Keegan knew why Ross wanted to keep his work a secret, but not how Cosgrove got him to design the course. He was Lloyd Tifft, a junior employee with Donald J. Ross and Associates. He did the preliminary design and supervised the construction of the Zebulon Pike. Tifft, a quiet, unassuming fellow in his early twenties, was the type of person who, when you see him for the second or even the third time, you don't recall meeting before. He left the golf business a few years after the Zebulon Pike opened to become a Methodist missionary in China, from whence he never returned. The photo buried in the time capsule is the only surviving visual proof he ever lived.

The letter Karl pondered was the very one that outlined MacMullen and Ross' agreement, and the drawings buried with it were irrefutable proof that Donald Ross' hand had helped shape every hole on the course.

A Rembrandt, even a simple study in pen and ink, is still a Rembrandt. It reflects the man's genius as much as his largest oil painting. In the same way, it would be clear to any scholar of

Ross' work that the Zebulon Pike Golf Course was the product of his mind. True, he had never visited the site; true, he only had photographs, topographic maps, and Tifft's sketches to work from, but his notes, his corrections, his signature design elements were all over the drawings, especially the ones for the greens.

What Odegaard, MacMullen, and Keegan were doing—and the photographer unwittingly recording—was burying all evidence of Ross' involvement; Tifft was there as Ross' representative to make sure of it. All were confident, no doubt, that the secret would remain hidden as long as the building stood. And why shouldn't they? It was sealed in a time capsule and only these four men knew exactly what it held.

Having uncovered their secret, Karl put a more romantic interpretation on what they were doing: they were laying aside a great treasure that he, in the fullness of time, would discover at the very moment when the Zebulon Pike faced its darkest hour, a treasure that would save the course from destruction and usher in its greatest days.

*

The metal box went home with Karl that night. Even though it had rested undisturbed under Pike's plaque for decades, he didn't want it out of his sight for a moment. Over the next three days Karl, Dunn, and Lumley spent hours studying the drawings at his apartment after work, absorbing every detail, and rehearsing how they would reveal their incredible find to the world. On the following Monday morning, instead of going to work as usual, Karl drove to the Parks Commission office. Lumley and Dunn met him there. At nine a.m. sharp they stood outside of Ralph Milbank's office.

Milbank believed that as a public servant he was always on the job, so he felt no compunction to arrive promptly at his office. While Ketterman, Dunn, and Lumley waited patiently for his arrival, drinking coffee and chatting with his assistant, Milbank spent a leisurely morning on his laptop at his kitchen table. As they waited, Karl clutched the bundle to his chest like a fanatic his political manifesto.

At 9:45 a.m. Ralph Milbank sauntered into the building, greeting the political hacks in the halls and pausing to share a word or two outside the coffee shop with an ally on the Parks Commission. Seeing Dunn and Karl waiting for him surprised him a bit; Parks Commissioners didn't often have unannounced visitors. He had no idea who Lumley was. He escorted his visitors into his office and told his assistant he was not to be disturbed. Milbank, comfortably situated behind his desk, indicated that Karl had the floor. Karl set his bundle gently on Milbank's desk.

"Ralph, the other day you told me the battle for the ZPGC wasn't lost yet. I'm here to tell you it's won. We have discovered something that is going to make the Zebulon Pike one of the city's most famous landmarks and, what's more important, a very popular and profitable golf course," Karl said, spreading out the drawings before Milbank. Milbank could see they were plans of some sort, but other than that they were Greek to him.

"That's from *Donald Ross*," Lumley growled, landing a tobacco-stained index finger on the letter like a lawn dart.

"Gentlemen, I'm doing my best to muster the same excitement you seem to have, but I have no idea who that *is*," he said, putting his finger on the letter, "or what the rest of this means," he added, waving his hands over the desk.

Dunn took over. He explained to Milbank who Donald Ross was and the significance of the city owning a course he designed. He cited the famous venues across the United States he had created, legendary courses that golfers dreamed of playing someday. Putting his name on the Zebulon Pike would give it a prestige no other course in the vicinity, public or private, could match. Dunn went through the drawings, showing Milbank where Ross had revised preliminary drawings and his meticulous handwritten notes outlining the changes he wanted made. Dunn pointed out features of the Zebulon Pike that were consistent with other Ross designs: the mounding, the slanting fairways, and the diabolically contoured greens.

"There's no doubt about it," Dunn concluded, "The Zebulon Pike is no longer an ordinary, run-of-the-mill municipal golf course. It's a landmark. Now it can be mentioned in the same sentence as

Pinehurst, Aronimink, Seminole, and Oak Hill."

Milbank listened attentively, every so often stealing a look at Ketterman and Lumley. It was beginning to dawn on him that, even though the details were still a little unclear to him, this could possibly be the feather in his cap that catapulted him out of the Parks Commission and into higher office.

"Does anyone else know about this?"

Karl thought about mentioning Sundbaum, Rankel, Armstead, and Hood, then lied. "No."

"Where did you get this?" Ralph asked.

Lumley, Ketterman, and Dunn exchanged looks.

"From Mr. Ross?"

"He's been dead sixty years," snarled Lumley.

"Of course, then *how* did you get possession of this? Did you find it at the Historical Society? City Records, the lost and found? Or did you just dig it up at the golf course?"

Milbank couldn't help noticing them squirm at his question. "My God, you didn't *steal* this, did you?"

"No, no, no!" Ketterman said. "It's nothing like that. Actually," he stopped to rub his head, "we did dig it up."

"Okay, guys. I'm through playing twenty questions."

Karl told of opening the locked drawer, finding the photos, and removing the metal box from its concrete tomb in the dark of night. To keep the story simple he left out Art Castle's role and didn't mention Walter Hagen. Milbank found the idea of exhuming even a metal box of old memorabilia at night more than a little creepy; it gave Karl's story a ghoulish undertone he didn't care for.

"I think it best if we just say you found all this in that drawer in your office. Once you get into digging up time capsules and abandoned bomb shelters it gets a little weird. Besides, I think I heard once that opening a time capsule is bad luck. The basic fact is this: it was happenstance, a fortuitous twist of fate, which is true. And it's a shorter story. Now let's talk about where we go from here."

The four of them remained sequestered in Milbank's office until late in the day.

Robert Midge went to the monthly meeting of the Parks
Commission on Tuesday evening exuding confidence and the faint
aroma of vodka. He felt he had earned the celebratory quaff or two
he'd had earlier at the Lochenberry. All his proverbial ducks were
neatly in a row. Now he was ready to face the commissioners and
pick them off, one after another.

He was scheduled to follow Milbank's report on current revenue
projections for all Parks Commission properties. With Labor Day
past, the Parks Commission already knew the ZPGC was on its
way to another losing year, a point Milbank would emphasize in
his report. He would then introduce Midge, a well-known citizen
with an interesting and relevant proposal. Robert would open by
dropping a little bombshell: the legislature's recent approval of
the Department of Natural Resources' new regulation concerning
lands adjacent to protected wetlands. That would be news to about
every person in the room, especially anyone planning a new use
for the ZPGC. Then he would present his modest proposal; his
civic-minded solution to the conundrum presented by the Zebulon
Pike: an eight-and-a-half million dollar donation to the Parks
Commission to use however they saw fit, and the land, which the
DNR had now sequestered from other uses, taken off the city's
hands and metamorphosed into a course that would bring affluent
golfers into the city where they would spend lots of money on goods
and services.

It began exactly as planned. Milbank painted a dismal financial
picture for the ZPGC and then turned the floor over to Midge.
Supported with drawings of the new clubhouse, estimates of the
economic impact of the project, and construction timelines, Midge
laid out his ideas for the renaissance of the property; his delivery
was sober and reserved, every word weighed carefully. The
commissioners were attentive, their questions pointed and focused on
the details of Midge's proposal; none seemed to be dismissing it out of
hand. Midge finished and took his seat next to Frank Chartreuse.

Then Milbank asked Midge a question, his voice low, almost
inaudible; he was a skilled public speaker and knew this would

capture the attention of everyone in the room more than shouting at the top of his lungs.

"Who is Donald Ross, Mr. Midge?" Milbank folded his hands and looked directly into Midge's eyes.

Midge squirmed and looked over at Chartreuse, as if asking him to make sense of the question. Midge leaned into the microphone in front of him. "Ah, the only Donald Ross I'm familiar with, Mr. Milbank, is the golf course architect."

"Is he a well-known golf course architect?"

"Yes," chuckled Midge, "I'd have to say he's pretty well known."

"Would you say he's one of the *most* well known?"

Midge conceded the point.

"He's designed some very famous golf courses, hasn't he?"

Again, Midge agreed.

"Most of the courses he designed are private aren't they, Mr. Midge?

"I think so, yes."

"Are there any Ross-designed golf courses around here?"

Midge conferred with Chartreuse. "I think the closest would be Interlachen Country Club in Minneapolis, so, no, none right around here."

"Is it fair to say that a golf course with Donald Ross' name attached to it—especially a public one—would be a very special place?"

A little jest popped into Midge's head. "It would indeed, Mr. Milbank, but I don't think Donald Ross had anything to do with the Zebulon Pike."

Ralph Milbank was not a religious man. Still, he paused and gave thanks to whatever force in the great cosmos had shoehorned that snide little remark into Robert Midge's mind at this particular moment.

"As a matter of fact, Mr. Midge, he did has something to do with the Zebulon Pike, and, if my colleagues will indulge me for a few minutes, I'll lay out irrefutable proof that he did, in fact, design it. On Monday morning, it was brought to my attention..."

Thus Milbank began his presentation. While not as slick as Midge's, it had a much greater impact on the commissioners.

Not long after Ralph began his presentation, Frank Chartreuse picked up his legal pad and started making notes about a development idea his brother-in-law had brought him last weekend. A realist who knew when a project was dead in the water, Chartreuse had cut bait and was rowing on.

*

Needless to day, Milbank's revelation left his fellow commissioners stunned. Bakken asked the first question, more followed from the other commissioners. The room was alive; no one could recall a Parks Commission meeting like it. Few at the meeting had ever been near the Zebulon Pike, but after Milbank finished they all made plans to go there the next day. Just like that, the most obscure, overlooked, and undervalued piece of city-owned real estate became a place every politician and opportunist in the room felt obliged to visit.

Midge walked out while Milbank was still fielding questions, waiting to pounce on him in the hallway. Ralph, several moves ahead of him as usual, emerged from the room flanked by the mayor and Commissioners Bakken and Lopes.

"Ralph, could you come by tomorrow morning? I have a few things I'd like to discuss with you privately," said the mayor.

Ralph, of course, was more than willing to oblige her. She squeezed his forearm affectionately and went on her way. Milbank turned to Midge, seemingly taken aback to see him.

"Robert! Say, I really must apologize to you. That whole thing about Donald Ross came out of the blue. I don't know the first thing about golf and had no idea how all this could impact your incredibly generous proposal, but I felt obligated to bring it forward. I mean, it was the only fair thing to do, wasn't it? Imagine the position the city would be in if it came out after the fact that we had allowed a Donald Ross golf course we owned to become a private country club? The mayor, all of us, would be through politically. Hell, we'd probably go to jail! And you, Robert, would be portrayed as some kind of a robber baron who had swindled the city out of a valuable asset. I think we all dodged a bullet here tonight." And Ralph

Milbank smiled the biggest smile it was physically possible for him to smile and walked on.

Midge fumed, but with Bakken and Lopes hovering around he couldn't vent his rage. A hundred thoughts—ninety-nine more than it was capable of processing at any given time—tumbled like acrobats around in his mind. He decided the best tactic was to furl his colors and retreat from the field of battle to lick his wounds and plan his counterattack.

*

On Wednesday afternoon, Welmont Washington came across Frank Chartreuse sitting on a bench in the men's locker room at the Lochenberry Country Club staring blankly ahead.

"Frank, you okay?"

Chartreuse looked up and smiled, "Oh, sure, Welmont, I'm fine. Just lost in thought, contemplating the fickleness of fate, that sort of thing."

Welmont laughed. "Didn't know you were such a deep thinker."

"It's the times; I see signs and portents everywhere. I think the end may be near."

"Do tell."

Frank turned around to face Welmont, now standing by his locker, struggling to get out of his golf shirt. "Well, when you see Midge—and when I say Midge I refer to both father *and* son—being thwarted and their well-laid plans torn to shreds," said Frank, "it causes one to pause. I mean, what's next? The Seven Seals are surely about to be opened."

Welmont sat down next to Chartreuse. "All right, Frank. In English."

Chartreuse told Washington all about the Parks Commission meeting, how Milbank had pulled Donald Ross out of his hat and Midge's grand scheme had gone up in smoke. Just this morning, Chartreuse had learned, both Midges had tried to salvage the situation by making a personal appeal to the mayor. Milbank was right. Once the cat was out of the bag, once the world knew the Zebulon Pike was a Donald Ross design, there was no way the city would surrender the property to the Lochenberry Country Club Board—a.k.a., the Midges—for any amount of money. It was just bad politics.

"Midge didn't notice the mayor was at the meeting until it was over, but I saw her as soon as I walked in the room. She was there for the whole thing, sitting in the back row, listening to Robert's pitch and grinning like the Cheshire Cat after Milbank threw that hand grenade in his lap. He must have tipped her off that he had something up his sleeve; you got to hand it to old Ralph," Frank said, rolling the "r" and rhyming it with "*safe*." "He blew the whole thing up right in our faces. He told Bob to let him handle the politics. He warned him not to go rogue; Bob should have listened." Frank sighed and pulled a sock over his gnarly toes. "It will be all over the news when you get home tonight."

Welmont offered to buy Chartreuse a drink but he said he preferred to drown his sorrows on the driving range and they parted company.

Chartreuse's news was a pleasant surprise to Welmont. He had been wrong. Midge's grand plan hadn't been foolproof after all. The Zebulon Pike would survive and its new status would redound to the benefit of the Ebon Invitational. He didn't have to change venues after all. Who wouldn't want to play in a tournament on a Donald Ross course? He was pleased too that Midge's plans to move the Lochenberry had come to naught. Now that Midge's grand scheme had failed, Welmont pondered as he walked to the grillroom, maybe it would mean he would see less of him around the old place. That thought pleased Welmont even more.

*

Karl was walking on air all day Wednesday. Milbank had called after the Parks Commission meeting and told him everything that happened, but cautioned Karl to keep it under wraps until the mayor's office sent out an official press release. Karl passed that message on to Dunn and Lumley, then called Gretchen. He couldn't wait to share the news with her, to tell her what his rummaging through all that old stuff in his office had accomplished, and the bright future that now lay ahead for him at the Zebulon Pike Golf Course.

Gretchen didn't understand everything he told her because she had no idea who Donald Ross was, or Walter Hagen. She was pleased and happy for Karl, for everyone at the Zebulon Pike, for Cybil and Mo and Rambo and Phil and Charley and even Dunn, although she didn't really know him.

Karl had an odd feeling he couldn't shake the whole time they talked. There was something awkward about their conversation. Something was amiss. She didn't sound like the same old Gretchen; she was distracted, not really following what he was saying. What was worse, she didn't seem genuinely interested in his news. Karl asked her if it was a bad time, if he should call back later. She said no. Karl was perplexed, almost embarrassed, as if he were bothering a total stranger. Gretchen brought the call to an abrupt end by saying she had to study. He held on for a moment after she hung up, listening to the dial tone and suddenly feeling very sad.

29

Frank Chartreuse was right. The Zebulon Pike story led the evening news on Wednesday. And it didn't stop there. The next day ESPN, the Golf Channel, and all the major news outlets were carrying the story. Karl Ketterman became a bit of a media star. He was interviewed on local and national television, filmed reenacting his discovery of the long-forgotten plans in the locked drawer his predecessors had never bothered to open; holding the photo of Odegaard, Keegan, and Walter Hagen, and pointing out telltale Ross features around the course. There were articles about him in *Golf Digest* and *Golf* magazine and on countless online sites. The city of Dornoch, Scotland, even sent a proclamation honoring him. The Donald Ross Society made him an honorary member. There was even scuttlebutt that the Golf Channel was going to hire him as their resident expert on golf course design.

Karl soaked all of this up. It was a fantasy come true: suddenly he was someone. People wanted to know what he thought about anything and everything that had to do with the game of golf. They hung on every word as he recounted how he, through tenacity and old-fashioned detective work, had unraveled a secret hidden for decades, a secret that brought a forlorn, rundown, old Midwestern municipal golf course into the international spotlight.

The edited version of the story of the plans' discovery that Milbank had suggested was now gospel. A locked drawer in the manager's office had been overlooked for decades. Karl Ketterman opened it and brought an unknown Donald Ross-designed golf course to the world's attention. The time capsule was back under the plaque—sans a few items—its sarcophagus patched, and the wall of the bomb shelter no one knew about closed up and Dunn, Lumley, Sundbaum, Rankel, Armstead, and Hood sworn to secrecy.

The Historical Society took possession of the drawings and the letter. There was a little ceremony, covered by all the media, of course, of Karl handing them over to the head of the society's board of trustees, a post fittingly held by Boswell MacMullen, Cosgrove's grandson. There they remain to this day, available—after a written request to see them, of course—to historians, architects, and academics.

Before the capsule was resealed, Karl secretly slipped six typed pages inside it. It was the story of how the capsule had previously been unearthed by Karl and his companions, what they found inside it, and how that information prevented the demise of the Zebulon Pike, along with photos he had taken of Lumley, Dunn, Armstead, Sundbaum, Rankel, and Hood, each clearly identified on the back. He knew the truth would be unimportant to whoever opened the time capsule in the future—even without his notes they would be able to tell it had been opened before—but Karl felt they deserved to know why. He hated ambiguity, like not knowing the name of the fourth man in the photo. Milbank, a bit of a city historian, had identified Cosgrove MacMullen, but the younger man still remained a mystery. Now the old photograph of Odegaard, Keegan, MacMullen and the young man, his dark, melancholy eyes alone looking directly into the camera, was once again buried beneath Pike's plaque.

*

Alas, no man's life is free from disappointment. It is, the wise say, a vale of tears for us all in the end. Karl's great disappointment came, as they often do, when he least expected it, when his career was in ascendancy and everything seemed to be going his way. The Zebulon Pike had been saved. He was a demi-celebrity and his future at the ZPGC couldn't have looked rosier, yet still Karl knew things were not right with Gretchen.

Two weeks after their stilted phone call she came back to town for the weekend. Karl knew she was in town only because she stopped by the clubhouse for a minute to see Cybil. He asked her to dinner. After first trying to get out of it, she agreed. He picked her up at her parents' and she greeted him at the door with a perfunctory kiss. As they drove to the restaurant she peppered him with questions on trivial matters, barely giving him time to answer one before she asked the next. He'd never known her to be so hyperactive, so obviously ill at ease, as if she'd suddenly found herself with a complete stranger. She talked incessantly throughout dinner about the oddest things, anything, it seemed, but what they really needed to talk about. When they were alone in the car again, she was quiet, distant, preoccupied. Her behavior was so unnatural, so unlike the Gretchen he was in love with, it put Karl's stomach in a knot. He knew the worse possible thing to do at this moment was to take her back to his apartment. He drove to the ZPGC, hoping against hope she might return to her old self there. The weather was balmy for fall and the evening shadows stretched low across the golf course as they started down the first fairway. They hadn't gone far when she stopped.

"Karl, I have something to say."

He turned and looked back at her. The full moon, just coming over the treetops, lit her hair. Karl smiled; she didn't. Her face was tense, her manner agitated.

"I don't think we should see so much of each other anymore, Karl." She blurted out. "I...I think maybe we should..." Her voice trailed off and she threw her hands up in frustration. "I don't know how to say this! I'm at school; you're here. Everything has changed."

Karl knew what she was trying to say; he just didn't want to hear her say it. She'd met someone new, maybe a guy on the golf team, maybe someone she'd met in class. It didn't really matter. He knew everything he needed to know without her spelling it out. She was in love. She was sleeping with him now; *sleeping with*, what a disarming euphemism. Karl knew if she said another word it would crush him so badly he wouldn't be able to hide it. Or worse, he would get angry and say things to hurt her, things he wouldn't mean, things that would make her hate him. He could bear her not loving him, but not her hating him. He knew he had to finish this for her; he felt he owed her that much.

"I get it; let's leave it there, Gretchen, I had a feeling this was coming. I wish it wasn't so, but talking isn't going to change anything, is it?" He had to pause for a moment to get his emotions under control because that's what guys do. "I just want to say this. You are the most beautiful woman I have ever known, and I can't begin to tell you how much I love you." That's what he wanted to say; those were the words he rehearsed in his mind. But he didn't say them. That line might work with some simpering, doe-eyed heroine in a sappy movie or romance novel, but not with Gretchen Schumacher.

Gretchen groaned and put her hands over her face. Karl bent down and replaced a divot someone had left unrepaired. It was a reflex, a habit, a gesture he thought might somehow put everything back in place, make it all right again. It was no use. He knew it was over and accepted it. He thought about Ambrose Keegan, lost in the shadows behind her, bearing mute witness to this little drama and he smiled. The knot that had been in his stomach all night went away and a different kind of pain, a numbing sense of sadness, washed over him. Karl looked at Gretchen; her eyes were on the ground. Even now he could sense she was with someone else. He knew all he would accomplish by prolonging this any longer would be to make her uncomfortable.

"Let's get you home. It's getting chilly." He tried to sound carefree and casual, but the shakiness in his voice betrayed him.

Those were the last words either spoke that night. They rode in silence to her parents' home. When she kissed his cheek and said goodbye, he gave her a big smile. It was that or cry.

*

Milbank and the mayor conferred for three hours, discussing how to best leverage the news about the Zebulon Pike to their advantage. The finding of the Donald Ross plans was a public relations talking point sent from heaven. They had to be sure the discovery was seen as part of the mayor's untiring efforts to serve the citizens of this fair city. Next year was an election year and the mayor wanted one more term, a term she would use to prepare for the next rung of public service, and this story might even help catapult her into the governorship. Expanding Milbank's role in city politics was also part of her plans. She knew the score and she knew the Midges. They played hardball. Outfoxing them was no mean feat and anyone who did so was worth keeping close. It was time, she told Ralph, he moved up the food chain. She needed a liaison between the mayor's office and the Parks Commission, especially now. The news about the Zebulon Pike was a bonanza of political capital, and, as she told Ralph, it was only fair to deposit it in a joint account. She had a vision for the parks, especially that precious old Zebulon Pike Golf Course, but she needed an ally she could trust in a position of real power. The Parks Commission chairperson, Dorothy Hodges, would be more than happy to tap Milbank for this very important, high profile assignment; she would, that is, if she ever wanted her deadbeat grandson's resume to get off the mayor's desk. By the end of her next term it wouldn't surprise the mayor at all, she said to Ralph in whispered confidence, if the political machine she led didn't put forward Ralph Milbank as its next mayoral candidate.

"And Ketterman, Charlotte," Milbank (now on a first-name basis with the mayor) said as their meeting was about to come to a close, "what about him?" He felt he owed Karl something; he just wanted to be absolutely sure that it was amenable to the mayor.

"He's doing a wonderful job with all of this, Ralph. He's a nice-looking kid, well spoken, smart. No reason to make any changes yet."

Milbank left the meeting feeling rather ebullient and pleased with how things were turning out; everything was under control and his future looked quite promising. He had kept faith in the system, even in the dark hours when he first learned of Midge's subterfuge. Ralph knew that in a city dominated by one political party, the party he had pledged fealty to while still a callow youth, his unshakable loyalty to its guiding principles would carry him through in the end. And the possibilities Charlotte had laid before him this morning validated that belief. Ralph Milbank's future never looked brighter.

Midge had tried to circumvent him, marginalize him, thinking Ralph Milbank could be jettisoned with impunity. He had learned differently. Now it was time to move forward; Ralph could afford to forgive and forget and bind up old wounds. He would give Robert Midge a call tomorrow and see if he wanted to do lunch.

*

The wave of excitement around the discovery of the Ross plans died down at the ZPGC by the time the Fall Classic rolled around, but there was a change in the atmosphere at the course, an unsettling sense that things were never really going to be the same anymore. The bubble that surrounded the ZPGC had popped, the snow globe had broken; from now on things were going to be different.

The Fall Classic, the last Men's Club event of the year, was still held, as it had been for the last fifty-five years, on a sunny Saturday in late October. The weather was not warm but not particularly cold for this town at this time of year. Dunn's crew had harvested the first crop of fallen leaves; thousands more continued their descent, and the course regulars declared the Leaf Rule in effect during their weekday rounds.

The Halling brothers stared up at the newly installed photograph of Donald Ross above the fireplace, the very spot where Keegan's putter had hung for generations. It was now relegated to a dark wall near the front door. This was the first significant change in the clubhouse's décor that Es and Jay could remember, and they were not warming to it. A large, handsomely framed print of Wilbur Odegaard and Ambrose Keegan handing Walter Hagen his check now hung over the door out to the verandah, but that didn't offend their sense of propriety since it had not displaced anything. They were thinking of confronting Ketterman when they overheard Cybil explaining to another displeased patron that the placement of the Ross photograph was a mayoral dictate. Jay and Es understood being a Ross design was a great thing for the ZPGC, what they couldn't fathom was how that piece of recent news justified displacing an object—a sacred relic, really—that was such a significant part of the course's traditions. They shook their heads and walked away.

"Roll Tide, Dan!" Fort Sumter shouted as he and Scrumpy came through the front door. Dan Doherty sitting at the counter grinned, a chunk of egg salad sandwich escaping his lips, and pumped his fist in the air. "Roll Tide!"

"I hear we're playing together today, boys," Fort said, as he took a seat at the Halling brothers' table.

"Yeah, and your pal Murlofsky *ain't*," replied Jay.

Fort held up his hands in protest. "Hey now, you boys know I had nothing to do with the pairings in the Keegan. You're playing me and old Scrumpy here. Now, he's a seventeen and you know I ain't lying; check the computer. That's his handicap and it's legit. So, let's discuss strokes."

The negotiations were loud and spirited. The Halling brothers were determined to recoup at least a portion of the cash they'd lost at the Keegan. Fort, his position at the course and in the community raised to a level he could never have imagined by the success of this year's Ebon, could afford to be generous. Besides, he liked Es and Jay. They were assholes but they weren't coy about it. No hidden agenda; Fort appreciated that. They settled on three strokes a side and went down to the range to prepare to do battle.

Crupshaw and Clayton Doherty, hitting a few putts before their tee time, waved as Fort's cart, groaning under its load, rolled by the putting green.

"I'm taking you down today, Crupshaw! The Fall Classic is mine!" Fort shouted.

Tom turned to Clayton. "Will this be your first time playing our Donald Ross course, Mr. Doherty?" he said with a wink.

"Since I've been *aware* it's a Donald Ross course? Yes it is. I was out of town for work when all this hoopla started. It's incredible, isn't it? I mean, all these years we've played here and nobody had a *clue*. I always thought this was a great golf course, but a Donald Ross? Never in a million years. I guess we can expect a lot of things to change around here now."

Crupshaw missed a short putt. He didn't want to think about that. There certainly were more golfers here lately, far more than usual for this time of the year. He wanted to believe they were just curious, one-timers who wouldn't come back. But he knew he was deceiving himself. Doherty was right, things were going to be different. How could they not be? Tom Crupshaw looked around. Year after year, things had always stayed pretty much the same here. Change came infrequently and in small doses. He liked that. Why did Donald Ross have to come along and spoil it all?

The Fall Classic was, as usual, a great success. Esau Halling won it, plus he and his brother took thirty-two dollars apiece from Fort and Scrumpy Scroggins. Merril Stokes had an eagle on four, Tom Crupshaw, uncharacteristically, pulled his second shot into McAdoo's pond, and Gretchen, back from college for the weekend, told everyone she served from her beverage cart that this was her final day at the Zebulon Pike. She made over a hundred dollars in tips. Everyone said it was one of the best Fall Classics ever, yet they all went away feeling sad somehow. It's not unusual for golfers to feel a tinge of melancholia as the season winds down. This was different. Change was coming to the Zebulon Pike and its patrons were filled with apprehension about its future.

*

By the end of October, King Borealis had begun to reclaim his realm in earnest. It was unusual, but not unheard of, for the cold weather to settle in so early. There was no snow but the air was bitterly cold and driven by a north wind. Only a few diehards wandered the fairways, and the clubhouse was quiet except at noon when locals and city employees came by for lunch. On a raw day in the final week of the month, Ralph Milbank, his face reddened by the wind, walked into Karl's office once more.

Karl, still grieving over the loss of Gretchen, was lost in thought. She had stopped in on her last day to say goodbye, hanging back in the doorway; afraid, no doubt, he might misinterpret her visit if she came all the way in. It was just a courtesy call. She was just saying goodbye to another one of the people she'd worked with, that was all. Karl stayed behind his desk. That put her at ease, but she still didn't come into the office. It was a short conversation, then she smiled and gave him a little wave and left his life forever.

Karl was looking over the course's revenue for the month—it was more than double last year's, despite the cold weather—but his mind kept wandering off, memories of his time with Gretchen crowded out the numbers. Would he ever see moonlight without being reminded of how her hair had looked in it?

"Hello, Karl."

"Mr. Milbank, how are you!" he said, putting on a mask of affability and holding up the sheet of paper in front of him. "Remember last spring when I said I felt we could turn things around here? Well, with what we've done since the Ross news broke, it looks like total revenue is going to be up slightly over last year. Next year is really going to be something; let's hope for an early spring."

Milbank gave him a nervous smile and Karl knew he had something on his mind, something that was making him feel uncomfortable. Ralph closed the door quietly and took a chair close to Karl.

"There's no way to sugarcoat this Karl, and no reason to dance around it. We're letting you go."

Karl heard everything Ralph said clearly enough, but the syntax came apart in his head; it was just a jumble of incomprehensible sounds, like the language of an alien race. Karl's face had a puzzled, stunned look.

"I know this is a terrible blow, Karl. For what it's worth, I fought for you," Milbank said in a soft and sympathetic voice.

There was an element of truth in this. When the mayor told him to fire Ketterman, Ralph asked if it was really necessary. That was all he said; to him that seemed a spirited defense on Karl's behalf. When the mayor knitted her brow ever so slightly he knew the battle was over. She explained to Milbank that the Zebulon Pike was now an upper-echelon golf course, and while the city would always be grateful to Karl Ketterman for the innate curiosity that drove him to discover the true heritage of the course, it was time for a more seasoned captain to take the helm.

Karl blinked and took a deep breath. Milbank could see he was beginning to recover his equilibrium and coming to grips with the unpleasant news he'd just been handed. "Karl, I'm genuinely sorry about this but it was the mayor's call. It was completely out of my hands." Milbank had tossed off that little phrase a thousand times before; it being true made it sound especially feeble to him now.

Karl looked around, trying to orient himself, struggling to find words. The faces of Wilbur Odegaard, Adolphus Smythe, Clarence McAdoo, Mike St. Mane, and Art Castle looked down at him; his peers seemed to be judging him from the great beyond; Karl felt their opprobrium descending on him. After all, none of them, no matter how incompetent, had gotten fired. McAdoo's eyes seemed to penetrate his soul. You know how this feels, Karl said to himself, you had a job you loved taken from you, too. He gave a great sigh and sat back in his chair.

"So, I'm fired." It was a statement with a hint of a question in it, a subtle plea for mercy.

"I'm afraid so, Karl. But I've gotten you an exceptionally good severance package. The mayor agrees we owe you that. Along with six months' salary, you're also getting a bonus of sorts: this check for fifteen-thousand dollars." Milbank put an envelope on the desk. "There are also letters of recommendation in there from both the mayor and the chair of the Parks Commission. The mayor also said you're to list her as a reference on your resume and include her direct line; of course, you can depend on me for one too."

Karl rubbed his forehead. It was sinking in now. He picked up the envelope with the check in it.

"You want me to leave now?"

"It's completely up to you, Karl. If you want to make today your last day, no problem; if you want to stay until the course closes down, that's perfectly fine, too."

That could be today too, Karl mused, since the day the ZPGC closes for the season is completely up to the greenskeeper. Or was Dunn done too?

"Is Dunn getting fired?" Karl asked.

Milbank studied the floor for a moment. "No. He's staying. I don't know if you know it, Karl, but Gabriel Dunn has a very impressive background; apparently, he's a very well educated man. His file shows he has a graduate degree in plant biology, or something like it. There's even a letter of recommendation in it from Roberto De Vicenzo, who, apparently, is a very famous golfer from somewhere in South America. Imagine that? And a couple weeks ago the president of a big golf course design firm in Florida sent the mayor a letter saying great things about him; Dunn is unquestionably qualified to be the course superintendent—that's his job title as of today—at any golf course in the country. I think we're lucky to have him."

"You are," Karl said.

Milbank lingered a little longer until Karl assured him he was fine, that he was reconciled to the mayor's decision and appreciated the generous severance package.

"I do have one request, Ralph."

Milbank squirmed slightly in his chair and pursed his lips nervously.

"I would like to know that once I'm gone my photo will be up there," Karl said, pointing to the rogue's gallery of past course managers.

Milbank, relieved at the banality of the request, smiled paternally at Karl. "Of course! Absolutely! Have your picture taken; expense it, of course; tell the photographer to frame it and send it to my office and I will personally see it goes up there."

Milbank shook Karl's hand and left. Karl sat for some time, fingering the envelope and pondering where life would take him next.

The next morning, very early, he went down to the maintenance building. With the dawn had come a new perspective. Karl Ketterman was not the same inexperienced kid who had arrived at the ZPGC the previous spring. He had taken on a challenging job and proven himself, and, what was more important, just about everyone in the golf business knew who he was now. True, he'd failed to win the woman he loved; that was definitely a very big check in the "lose" column, but it wouldn't take him long to bounce back, to find a new job and, yes, a new love too; he had no doubt of it. So it was a happier, more upbeat Karl Ketterman who walked into Dunn's dark, dank demesne. Gabriel was standing at a worktable performing a postmortem on a lawn-mower engine.

"Looking for more lost artifacts?" said Dunn, reaching for his coffee.

"No, Gabriel. I've just come to say goodbye."

Dunn gestured him to his office where Karl recounted his visit from Milbank.

"You're safe, though," Karl concluded.

"I know. The mayor called me last week. She dug up a lot about me and felt I was capable of 'preserving Ross' vision for the Zebulon Pike,' if I remember her words correctly. I told her the way I took care of this course wouldn't change an iota, whether that met with her approbation or not. I'm sure she had to look that up after I left." A grin flashed across Dunn's face.

Karl asked him not to tell anyone that he was leaving. Dunn assured him his lips were sealed, and they parted ways.

As Karl left, Dunn shouted out, "Via con Dios."

Karl stayed around until the end of the week. He had long conversations with Cybil and Mo; he stopped to kibitz with Sundbaum, Rankel, Armstead, and Hood at their table; he made a point of telling Fort Sumter he was looking trim and he chatted with Tom Crupshaw and Merril Stokes as they were about to play a final blustery nine. The last person he spoke to before leaving the Zebulon Pike was Charley Lumley.

He was, as always, down at the range. The day was the warmest in weeks and Charley was taking the opportunity to work with an old student, a regular at the ZPGC who had been under Lumley's tutelage since he was a boy. Karl watched and listened for the better part of an hour, soaking in Lumley's weather-beaten, smoke-stained wisdom. When the man left Lumley turned to Karl.

"Trying to get a free lesson?" he said, followed by a throaty cough and a violent spit.

"Just trying to imagine how busy you're going to be next year."

Charley gave him a stare. "I'm as busy as ever I want to be, kid." He watched the low gray clouds gathering on the horizon. "Season is just about over. Time to call it quits."

"Where do you go in the winter, Charley?"

Karl got another piercing look. "I go home."

Home for Lumley was a studio apartment within walking distance of the Zebulon Pike. Until a few years ago, he had gotten away for a week or two to visit his brother in Texas, but not anymore.

Karl couldn't think of anything else to say so he turned to go.

"You did a good job here this year, Karl. I heard things didn't work out with the girl; Cybil told me. I know how tough that can be, but you're a good kid. You'll be okay."

Karl hugged Charley. He did it suddenly and unconsciously, succeeding because he caught Lumley completely by surprise. When he realized what he had done he expected Lumley to push him away. He didn't; he just tapped Karl on the back and Karl knew it was time to let go. He walked away quickly; the only sound was the snap of Lumley's Zippo.

Karl stayed in his office until everyone went home. When he knew he was alone he put the few personal effects he'd brought to work into a cardboard box. Going through his desk for the last time, he found the old watercolor of the clubhouse, the way the architect had envisioned it would look: the dream the Zebulon Pike was based on. Karl took it out and looked closely at it. "Well, I'll be damned," he said. In the lower right-hand corner, written in black over a dark green hedge, he could see, in beautiful cursive barely legible after all these years, *Lloyd Tifft*. Karl smiled and held the painting out at arm's length. A final discovery and another mystery solved; now he knew the artist's name. The landscape outside his window, monochromatic and bleak, was in stark contrast to the watercolor. Karl leaned back and laughed. He thought he'd found a home at the Zebulon Pike. He thought he'd found love here, too. Both turned out to be dreams. He put the watercolor into his box.

"You guys don't mind?" he asked.

The faces on the wall took no notice.

30

The really bad weather held off for several weeks after Karl left. The day before Dunn closed the Zebulon Pike Golf Course for the season was one of those rare November days, almost spring-like, chimerical. The trees, denuded by fall winds, stretched their limbs sunward as if pleading for the warmth to stay. In the afternoon Phil Franzen came through the clubhouse door; he was quiet and moved purposefully about the room. He went to the counter where Cybil stood smiling down at Dan Doherty eating his sandwich.

"Lumley needs you," he said.

She didn't hesitate for a second. She got her coat and followed him out to his golf cart. She got in and they drove down to the range. Riding in the cold air made their eyes water. Phil stopped the cart. Cybil gasped and put her hand to her mouth.

"I didn't know how to tell you. I couldn't tell you." Phil sobbed and put his face in his hands.

Cybil sat in the cart for a moment. Then she rubbed Phil's back to both comfort and rouse him and told him to go back to the clubhouse and call whoever had to be called. He left and she walked over to Lumley. He was leaning over, his face almost touching the steering wheel. She took his shoulders and pushed him back. His face was gray, his eyes and mouth open. She felt his cheek. It still felt warm. Cybil found herself trying to imagine exactly what she had been doing when he died. Probably making Dan's sandwich. She took Charley's hand. As she patted it she felt something wet hit hers. She wiped the tear away quickly, as if it were a bad thing.

Charley's cigarettes and lighter were sitting on the seat. Cybil took his Zippo and put it in her pocket. She wanted something to remember him by, something that had meant something to him. She stayed with him until the ambulance arrived.

*

Life in La Quinta was good. The California sun was warm, the golf courses pristine, and several local resorts Karl had sent resumes to had already called to schedule interviews. At the very least they wanted to meet the guy they'd seen on TV and read about in all the golf publications. The local newspaper was even doing an article about him in next Sunday's edition.

At times, Karl's thoughts still returned to those voluptuous hours he had spent in the arms of the golden-haired, bronzed-skin Goddess of Sport and Earthly Pleasures, but he was slowly getting over Gretchen Schumacher. Yes, she had forsaken him as easily as she had taken him up, yet he bore her and those who had sacked him so unceremoniously no animosity. Besides, the thought of surveying the fairways of the ZPGC next summer and not seeing her majestic form bouncing down the fairway in her motorized chariot was too bitter to contemplate. He understood now that it was all for the best. His time at the Zebulon Pike Golf Course had been, all things considered, happy and professionally fulfilling. Ralph Milbank was right. What other up-and-comer, barely out of college, had been vouchsafed such an experience? Which of his contemporaries could say their name had passed the lips of golfers in every corner of the globe? His days at the helm of the ZPGC, brief as they had been, had catapulted him to a position he could never have predicted or even imagined. His future was bright, so much so that he could afford to take the winter off, lounge his days away at his parents' home, and enjoy the fruits of his severance package. Karl Ketterman had no beef with the Fates.

As Karl dozed by the pool, luxuriating in desert warmth, his younger brother dropped an envelope in his lap. It was a large manila one with a familiar return address. He tore it open and a photo slid out. There was Cybil Stumpher, standing in his old office pointing to the wall where his photograph now hung in its proper place, right next to Art Castle's. There was no letter. Karl smiled. Ralph had come through. And Cybil hadn't forgotten him. They may have dismissed him, and he may have lost Gretchen, but this photograph proved he would always be a little part of the Zebulon Pike. Who knows? Maybe someday the story of Karl Ketterman would be recounted in hushed and reverential tones in front of the old fireplace. Karl lowered his sunglasses and dozed off.

*

It was several months before Karl learned of Charley Lumley's death. He ran into a regular from Zebulon Pike wintering in the desert who told him how Fabio had found him, all alone on the range, his last cigarette still smoldering on the floor of his cart. The news spoiled an otherwise idyllic day.

*

Gabriel Dunn spent the day tidying up the maintenance building. His crew was gone and he was finishing up closing the course on his own. After making sure everything in the building was properly stored away, he sat in his office and stared down at the letter that had been delivered to the clubhouse and brought down to him several days ago. He looked at the upper left-hand corner; the return address said it was from Dan Casserly. Why was Casserly writing him; was he suffering from double vision and contemplating a lawsuit? Wasn't the nondisclosure agreement he signed supposed to protect him from that sort of thing? Or had it been voided when Midge's deal fell through? Dunn frowned and opened the envelope. He recognized the handwriting. The letter wasn't from Casserly. It was the same handwriting on the two unopened envelopes in his desk, but it's hard not to read an opened letter, and Gabriel read on. The letter ran for five pages. Dunn read it three times before putting it back in the envelope. He had never read anything like it: smart, cogent, direct, unsentimental. No one else could have written it. She even quoted

Shakespeare: "...love is not love, which alters when it alteration finds." Sonnet One-Hundred-Sixteen. His favorite.

Later, as he was locking the gate of the driveway, an idea crossed his mind: maybe he would drive to Florida this winter. Just to get out of the cold for a while.

EPILOGUE

The following spring, the Zebulon Pike opened with pomp and fanfare. The newspaper devoted a two-page insert to it in the Sunday sports section, recapping the happy discovery of the Ross plans and laying out the city's plans for improving the Zebulon Pike Golf Course "experience" and making it a true golfing destination. There was also a photograph of the mayor, the new chairman of the Parks Commission, and the new manager, a very distinguished-looking gentleman in his late fifties who had previously been in charge of one of Chicago's most elite private clubs. They were standing by the ZPGC's new sign. It's quite a bit larger than the old one and much closer to the street; it is impossible to miss the entrance now. The sign's large, hand-painted serif type proclaims the course's new status: *The Zebulon Pike Golf Course, a Donald Ross design.*

The renovation of the clubhouse the mayor ordered is still underway. The whole building is being repainted and refurbished inside and out. The interior work is mostly finished: the small, dingy locker rooms have been gutted and are being turned into larger, spacious and modern bathrooms; the old counter where Dan Doherty loved to sit is torn out and the kitchen has been completely refitted. The whole space has been opened up and brightened; the terrazzo floor refinished and polished and the fireplace sandblasted. The clubhouse now has the feel of a very trendy restaurant or coffee bar. The Keegan Cap was somehow misplaced when the place was emptied out. Most of the old furniture and fixtures went to a Parks Commission facility to be sold off at auction; it'll probably turn up eventually, a little worse for wear, but safe.

When Cybil was notified about the big plans for the clubhouse, she retired. She still comes around once in awhile but never goes in the clubhouse. She stuck her head in the door once but didn't go in. She stays at home most of the time now. She does some volunteer work and Franzen checks in on her every so often; he doesn't seem to mind when she calls him Fabio.

They say construction on a new building to the north of the clubhouse will begin soon. It'll be just beyond the parking lot. That's where the new manager's office will be, along with a catering kitchen and a room large enough to accommodate weddings and other events. A group of local architects sent the mayor a petition asking the new building be "architecturally compatible with and reflect the aesthetic of" the existing clubhouse. Considering the financial state of the city, that's unlikely.

Dunn's budget has more than tripled. As course superintendent, he now commands an elite company of green-coveralled and white-pith-helmeted minions who swarm over the golf course every day, keeping it in immaculate condition. Everyone who plays the Zebulon Pike agrees it is a true tribute to the genius of Donald Ross, a hidden gem every serious golfer should play at least once in his life.

Rambo Burchell had to be let go. Merril Stokes, after a very pleasant interview with the new manager, was hired as a part-time ranger and now roams the fairways, keeping play moving with a kind word and pleasant smile. Mo Mittenthal, ensconced in a new, roomier starter's shack and dressed in the new staff uniform, still works the early shift.

Tee times are only available online and the tee sheet is full most days; you have to know someone to get out early on the weekend. There are not as many of the old faces around. Tom Crupshaw and a few others still play on weekdays. With greens fees around fifty dollars, the Zebulon Pike is a bit rich for most of them now, but they still come by to sit on the verandah and marvel at the changes.

The biggest of those changes is the absence of Ambrose Keegan. The mayor was greatly distressed when she learned he was lying at rest at the ZPGC; she ordered the body exhumed and the site cleared, leveled, and sodded over. It was done quietly and discreetly, very early on a Monday morning in April. Ambrose

Keegan was reburied in the national cemetery with the full military honors due a veteran of the Spanish-American War. Mo was the person in attendance.

Robert Midge, Sr., the head of the board of trustees at the Lochenberry Country Club, recently announced it would be closed all next season for a complete renovation. The job has been awarded to a Florida firm. The president of that firm has asked the city to allow Gabriel Dunn to consult on the project. The press release didn't say if the Lochenberry's grand old clubhouse would also be renovated, or replaced.

There is one last thing to mention, although it's just a rumor at this point. There is some talk going around that the city wants to change the name of the course. I suppose it makes sense. Zebulon Pike is a long-forgotten, quixotic figure with not the slightest connection to this town or the game of golf—but the politics involved in choosing a new name would be very complicated. And then, what would they do with Pike's plaque?

ACKNOWLEDGEMENTS

Whether this novel was worth the effort to print, the reader will judge. The writer knows, however, it would never have happened without the care and guidance of bright young minds more familiar than he with the ins and outs of graphic design, electronic publishing, public relations, and digital media: sons-in-law Jeremy Wilker and Aaron Purmort, daughters Meghan Wilker and Nora Purmort, and niece Mary Clare Jensen. Without their efforts, along with the editorial help of sons Austin and Patrick, and the constant guidance of my Muse and mentor, Margaret, this little entertainment would have remained just a collection of ones and zeroes in the recesses of my laptop. I thank them all, sincerely. SJM

Also available as an ebook.

ABOUT THE AUTHOR

Stephen J. McInerny is a third generation municipal golfer with a handicap that hovers between 12 and 15. He lives with his wife Margaret and way too many golf clubs in Minneapolis, Minnesota.

www.pikesplaque.com
www.silverbaypress.com